INFORMAL INSTITUTIONS

INFORMAL
<u>INSTITUTIONS</u>

Alternative Networks in the Corporate State

edited by
Stuart Henry

ST. MARTIN'S PRESS   NEW YORK

© 1981 individual authors

All rights reserved. For information write:
St. Martin's Press, Inc., 175 Fifth Avenue, New York, NY 10010
Printed in Great Britain

First published in the United States of America in 1981

ISBN 0-312-41664-4

Library of Congress Cataloging in Publication Data
Main entry under title:

Informal institutions.

  Bibliography: p.
  Includes index.
    1. Social institutions—United States—Addresses,
essays, lectures. 2. United States—Social conditions—
1945-   —Addresses, essays, lectures. I. Henry,
Stuart.
HN57.I64   1981   973.92   80-28529
ISBN 0-312-41664-4

Printed in Great Britain by Mackays of Chatham

CONTENTS

ACKNOWLEDGEMENTS

In preparing a book of this kind one incurs many debts. Jenny Towndrow and Godfrey Golzen of the Architectural Press deserve a special mention for having the vision to take on an unpredictable project. The Social Science Research Council provided the funding for research on which the chapters by myself, Gerald Mars and Michael Nicod and Christopher Whelan are based. Middlesex Polytechnic have supported studies of the whole area through its Centre for Occupational and Community Research; a special debt is owed to the Centre's head, Gerald Mars, for his stimulus, encouragement and enlightenment in promoting a programme of research in this major new area of social science. James Cornford, director of the Outer Circle Policy Unit not only contributed his concluding chapter but helped in formulating the framework of interpretation I adopt in the introduction and provided valuable editorial comments on the early draft chapters. Any clarity in the presentation of the introduction owes much to Ruby Bendall to whom I am more than grateful.

The following contributors would like to extend special thanks to people and agencies associated with their chapters: Louis Ferman and Louise Berndt wish to thank the Centre for Studies on Metropolitan Problems of the National Institute of Mental Health and the Bureau of Employment and Training of the Michigan Department of Labour for sponsoring their investigation of the irregular economy. Gerald Mars and Michael Nicod thank Peter Mitchell and other members of the Centre for Occupational and Community Research Seminar. Tony Lake wishes to thank Ann Hills for her help in the research on which his chapter was based.

Chapter five by J. I. Gershuny and R. E. Pahl appears here, with minor editorial alterations, by kind permission of the *New*

Universities Quarterley where it first appeared as 'Work Outside Employment: Some Preliminary Speculations' *N.U.Q.*, vol. 34, Winter 1979/80.

Finally Ann Lea deserves our gratitude for doing a first class job in converting a variety of different scripts into a clean and presentable manuscript.
Stuart Henry

Note on references

References to other works are given in the text in abbreviated form. The reference is given in full in the bibliography on page 198.

NOTES ON CONTRIBUTORS

JEREMY ALDEN, B.Sc., M.Litt, Ph.D., is senior lecturer in urban economics and regional planning in the Department of Town Planning at the University of Wales, Institute of Science and Technology. He has carried out research on regional planning, community development and industrial relations and has published articles in a wide range of journals. He is author of *Regional Planning* (Leonard Hill, 1974).

LOUISE E. BERNDT, A.B., A.M., is research associate and co-director of the Irregular Economy Project at the Institute of Labor and Industrial Relations, University of Michigan, Wayne State University, USA. She has conducted research into women's status, helping networks and the irregular economy.

JAMES CORNFORD, M.A., F.R.Hist.S, was formerly professor of politics at the University of Edinburgh and is currently director of the Outer Circle Policy Unit. He is the literary editor of the *Political Quarterly* and as well as writing numerous articles on party politics and devolution of political power has edited *The Failure of the State* (Croom Helm, 1975) and William Stubbs *The Constitutional History of England* (University of Chicago Press, 1979).

LOUIS A. FERMAN, A.B., M.A., Ph.D. is professor of social work at the University of Michigan and research director of the Institute of Labor and Industrial Relations, University of Michigan, Wayne State University, USA. His research career has focussed largely on studies of unemployment and manpower development. He is editor of *Poverty and Human Resources Abstracts* and *Policy Papers in Human Resources and Industrial Relations* and has co-authored numerous books including *Poverty in America* (University of Michigan Press, 1965), *Economic Failure and Alienation* (University of Michigan Press, 1968); he is the author of *The Negro and Employment Opportunities* (Praeger Books, 1968).

J. I. GERSHUNY, B.Sc., M.Sc., D.Phil, is research fellow at the Science Policy Research Unit of the University of Sussex. He has carried out research on public policy making and patterns of change in economic and social organisation. He is author of numerous articles on planning and policy making, is co-author of *World Futures: The Great Debate* (Martin Robertson, 1979) and author of *Towards a Social Assessment of Technology* (HMSO, 1976) and *After Industrial Society?* (Macmillan, 1978).

STEPHEN HATCH, B.A., P.PE., is head of the Voluntary Organisations Research Unit of the Policy Studies Institute. He has conducted research on higher education, community development, voluntary organisations and mutual aid. He is co-author of *Graduate Study and After* (Weidenfield, 1968) and *Residence and Student Life* (Tavistock, 1971) and author of *Outside the State* (Croom Helm, 1980).

STUART HENRY, B.A., Ph.D., is honorary research fellow at the Centre for Occupational and Community Research, Middlesex Polytechnic, and senior lecturer in sociology at Trent Polytechnic. He has done research on amateur crime, informal trading networks, self-help groups, private disciplinary procedures and community justice. He is co-author of *Self-help and Health* (Martin Robertson, 1977) and author of *The Hidden Economy* (Martin Robertson, 1978).

TONY LAKE, Cert.Ed., B.A., Ph.D., is self-employed consultant psychologist and author. He co-authored *Affairs* (Open Books, 1979) and authored *Loneliness* (Sheldon Press, 1980) and *Relationships* (Roxby Press, forthcoming).

MARTIN LOWENTHAL, A.B., M.A., Ph.D., is director of the Social Welfare Regional Research Institute and assistant professor in the Department of Sociology, Boston College, USA. His research has focussed on studies of work among poor, employment planning, informal mutual aid networks and community and welfare development among low income workers. He is author of many journal articles on poverty and community welfare development and is co-author of the special issue of *Journal of Sociology and Social Welfare* on social policy.

PETRINE MACDONALD, B.A., is a research assistant at the centre for Occupational and Community Research, Middlesex Polytechnic, where she is conducting research on informal marriage for her Ph.D. She is co-author of the bibliography on *The Relationship between Education and Technological Change* (UNESCO, forthcoming).

GERALD MARS, M.A., Ph.D., is reader in sociology at Middlesex Polytechnic and of the Centre for Occupational and Community Research. He has carried out research on dock labour in Newfoundland and a wide range of studies on occupational pilferage and fiddling and their implications for industrial relations. He is co-author of *Room for Reform* (Open University Press, 1976) and *Manpower Problems in the Hotel and Catering Industry* (Saxon House, 1979). He is author of *Dockland* (LSE Monographs in Social Anthropology, forthcoming) and *The Black Economy at Work* (Allen and Unwin, forthcoming).

MICHAEL NICOD, B.Sc., M.Phil., is senior research officer for the Training Services Division of the Manpower Services Commission. He has conducted research on food as a system of communication and is currently completing his Ph.D. on a study of hotel workers which was researched while he was a research assistant at the Centre of Occupational and Community Research, Middlesex Polytechnic. He is co-author of *Worlds of Waiters* (forthcoming).

R. E. PAHL, M.A., Ph.D., is professor of sociology at the University of Kent. He has carried out research on a wide range of urban issues and on different sections of industry including directors, managers, workers and the unemployed. His books include *Patterns of Urban Life* (Longman, 1970), *Managers and their Wives* (Allen Lane, 1971) and *Whose City?* (Penguin, 1975).

STEPHEN PLATT, B.Sc., is research officer and co-ordinator of the Self-Help Housing Resource Library at North London Polytechnic. He is currently completing his Ph.D. at the London School of Economics on self-help housing and public policy. He is author of numerous SHHRL pamphlets and is co-author of *Self-help Housing* (*Architects' Journal*/Calouste Gulbenkien Foundation, forthcoming).

COLIN WARD was formerly education officer for the Town and Country Planning Association and is currently a self-employed research fellow at Middlesex Polytechnic. He has done considerable research on housing and community education and is currently working on a study of 'plotlands'. He is editor of the *Bulletin of Environmental Education* and *Vandalism* (Architectural Press, 1973), co-author of *Streetwork* (Routledge, 1973) and author of *Tenants Take Over* (Architectural Press, 1974), *Anarchy in Action* (Allen and Unwin, 1973), *Housing – An Anarchist Approach* (Freedom Press, 1976), and *The Child in the City* (Architectural Press, 1978).

CHRISTOPHER J. WHELAN, LL.B., is research officer in law at the Centre for Socio-Legal Studies, Wolfson College, Oxford. He has carried out research on alternative methods of dispute resolution in civil law including conciliation, mediation, arbitration and tribunal procedure. He is currently completing a Ph.D. on national emergency industrial disputes and is co-editor of *Sociological Theories and the Study of Law* (1980, forthcoming).

INTRODUCTION

We argue in this book for a new perspective on social institutions. Until now those who have not theorised about the state or macro-social structure have concentrated almost exclusively upon the formal institutions of society: marriage and the family, industry and employment, education, medicine, social services and the institutions of law. This attention is justified because most of our time and energy is spent within these institutions and it is through them that economic and political power flows. But what is missing from previous accounts is the implicit and hidden contribution of informal institutions. How can we look at marriage and the family, for example, and ignore extra-marital affairs which may maintain the very existence of many families? How can we estimate the real economic activity of a country when as much as one fifth of its workforce may have unregistered second jobs or be involved in informal trading networks? How can we judge the effectiveness of our health care services when the bulk of health care takes place in the family and local community? We need to know how these informal institutions operate, and also how they relate to their formal counterparts.

Although informal institutions and practices are, and have always been, shared and expected by people who are involved in formal institutions, they rarely feature in sociological, economic or political accounts and theorising. One reason why informal institutions have been overlooked is not difficult to understand. Quite simply they are not easy to study. There are no records kept, nor figures published, on the number of people having intimate relationships outside of marriage. Few people will admit to having unregistered second jobs. Most people would deny taking part in fiddles at work, and, while it is not difficult to examine economic exchanges taking place in the supermarket or corner shop, where does one go in order to locate amateur trading networks? Unlike conventional areas of social life, informal institutions do not readily lend themselves to research. There are no registered addresses to which letters can be sent, no information officers, secretaries or treasurers who are available to sit down and explain the ins and outs of what goes on. For obvious reasons, informal institutions are everywhere and nowhere, all about us but nowhere to be seen.

A second reason why there is an absence of material on this area is that sociologists and other social scientists are grounded in the same common-sense assumptions and share the same taken-for-granted understanding as everyone else, concerning what constitutes our social institutions. When a man is asked what he does for a living he will most probably describe his formal occupation. He might be a 'manager', 'dentist', 'plumber', 'lecturer', 'waiter' or 'factory worker', and such job descriptions have specific ideal-type characteristics which invoke similar pictures in our minds. What we do not picture are the informal but related practices of being in any one of these jobs. Waiters are seen as rushing between the kitchen and customer serving wine and food; they are rarely envisaged as fiddling bills, pilfering food and having second jobs in neighbouring hotels. How often does one think of a dentist being paid in fresh fruit and vegetables or a surgeon receiving a case of whisky for removing a patient's appendix? In short, a person's primary job and formal job description are augmented by a wide range of secondary activities which to the uninitiated might seem irrelevant. Outside their formal jobs people participate in other ways of earning a living such as doing 'odd jobs', 'part-time work', 'do-it-yourself' work and 'favours for friends'. None of these things would be apparent from a person's description of him or herself as a 'dentist' or a 'waiter'.

So, in order to appreciate more fully the functioning of social institutions, the implicit informal roles that people carry out must be given as much emphasis as the explicit formal ones. We need to know how the formal roles are modulated by informal customs and practices and how far they feature in the meaning structure of peoples' everyday lives. Social science has an obligation to reintegrate a study of the everyday practice of social life with the commonly expressed theory of it; to see the informal and formal institutions as complementary parts of a whole; and to acknowledge that official accounts given by conventional approaches exclude informal institutions. As James Cornford rightly points out in the conclusion to this book, such institutions have *always* existed and have always been depended upon. In the context of a discussion on industry Graeme Shankland expressed the view that both informal and formal institutions are necessary and that:

In a healthy society these two sectors sustain each other and their relationship should be a symbiotic one of mutual support. The formal sector effectively controls the commanding heights of the economy and the political system, but the informal sector is essential not parasitic or residual . . . it operates rather in the interstices of the formal institutions of modern urban society; it cannot offer an alternative society but a complementary economic activity to the formal with a different, informal and more personal life style. Many industries thought of as formal are in fact deeply dependent on the informal sector . . . this has been a feature of the urban industrial landscape since the first industrial revolution.
Shankland, 1977

The implications of adopting this new direction in our approach to the study of society will lead us to question the way in which levels of activity are measured. At present these are based upon people's contribution to formal institutions; but a large amount of informal activity is unrecorded. Therefore if official rates of say, unemployment, divorce or criminal offences go down, it might simply reflect *increasing* unofficial, informal activity such as more people taking part in unregistered work or 'moonlighting', more 'affairs' and more hidden crime. If governments are to make realistic planning and policy discussions they need to know about informal institutions, the way these institutions operate and their relationship to the process of change. In order to understand change in society it is necessary first to understand how formal institutions co-opt the parts of informal institutions that they see as useful (see Platt, chapter 6) and how those co-opted aspects then become part of the established institutions of society. For example, the health care industry has begun to offer services that informal self-help groups have shown to be of value. In America now that the Childbirth Education Association has developed and demonstrated a market for prepared childbirth, all the under-utilized obstetrical units are busily engaged in developing educational programmes, hiring nurse-midwives and letting fathers into delivery rooms. As Jack Geiger cynically described it, 'when the counter-culture develops something of value, the establishment rips it off and sells it back' (Geiger, 1976, p.95).

The contributors have been brought together from different disciplines within the social sciences to write about the informal institutions into which they have been researching. Drawing on their material gathered in Britain and the United States, the contributors demonstrate the important characteristics, functions and implications that informal institutions have in our industrial society. Although there are many different ways of interpreting these institutions, as can be seen in this collection of papers, and an endless variety of ways of classifying them, I shall adopt a typology which will attempt to draw out some basic distinctions. It is in the context of this typology that I will discuss the individual contributions to the volume.

A typology of informal institutions

The idea that the whole of the activity of a society is not locked up in a total economic or social system, nor that any one mode of transaction or relationship dominates is not new. Polanyi (1957) for example, argues that rather than having one economy, *most* societies have several systems of exchange and operate 'multi-centric' economies with separate economies for different classes of goods. He argues that the system of market exchange which appears to be of overriding importance in money-based industrial societies is only one of many systems of exchange. Most non-industrial societies possess at least one and sometimes two non-market systems, such as the 'redistributive' and the 'reciprocal' spheres of exchange. Each of these has its own rules, its own reality and its own language consisting of words that are appropriate only to exchange in that specific economy.

A good example of this is shown in a study by R. Salisbury (1962) of the New Guinea Siane Society which has three distinct economies, one for each of three different classes of goods: *valuables,* which are essentially pigs; *luxuries* such as palm oil and pandanus nuts; and *'things of no account',* comprising mainly vegetable food. The goods which circulate in each of these economies cannot be equated with goods in another and therefore cannot be exchanged: pigs, which are valuables, cannot be exchanged for vegetables ('goods of no account') because the two kinds of goods are in separate economies. When the Siane came into contact with the western market economy and the labour market, they acquired cash in the form of pound notes, shillings and coppers. Rather than treat these as money, the Siane identified pound notes as valuables, shillings as luxuries and coppers as 'of no account'. Because of the separation between economies, a pound note could not be changed into shillings and coppers, neither could a shilling be changed for coppers (Salisbury, 1962, p.130). Similar studies by Bohannon (1955) of the Tiv of Northern Nigeria and by Firth (1965) in Polynesia have also demonstrated the presence of multi-centric economies.

Applying this kind of analysis to our own society, Davis (1972) says that the United Kingdom has at least four sub-economies each distinguishable by the rules which govern transactions within it. The *market economy,* he says, is governed by laws of commercial trading, employment and labour relations. It includes all legal transactions in services and commodities. The *redistributive economy* is governed by laws of taxation, welfare and state expenditure. The *domestic economy* is governed by customs and expectations concerning the relationship between family members. It also includes all productive activities which are not mediated by a market such as making, mending and food processing. Fourthly, says Davis, there is a *gift economy* which is governed by rules of reciprocity and includes all those transactions which we call giving a present, making a gift and so on. He says that rather than talking of one mode of transaction predominating over the others we should be examining the relationship between the different sub-economies.

For our purposes Davis's typology has certain inadequacies. While it includes the domestic economy or household economy, it does not accommodate other informal economies such as the hidden economy or the black economy. Where in the typology would we place unofficial work done outside formal employment but not in the family context? Where would we put amateur trading networks that occur inside a community but not as part of the official economy? Where do we locate care which is independent of the state redistributive system? Neither does Davis's framework allow a distinction to be made between economies which are legal and those which are illegal or proscribed by the economic regulations governing a society. The insight in Davis's scheme is that it sees *our* society, and not just non-industrial society, as composed of different sub-economies rather than simply being dominated by the market economy, and he directs us to look at the relationships between those different economies. In order to accommodate the full range of informal economies and their social institutions it is necessary to develop Davis's typology further.

Rather than differentiate between informal institutions on the basis of the kinds of rules which govern the transactions and relationships within them, we can distinguish between them according to the degree to which they are integral to, or an alternative to, official institutions and also according to their legal status. Taking official institutions to be all those activities which are a recognised, regular feature in society's systems of accounting, we can identify two kinds of official economy. There is an official legal economy which we can term the *regular economy* which includes: all market economic activity, formal production, consumption and employment; all official redistribution through state benefits; formal marriage, education, housing, health and social welfare; as well as the administration of justice and government. The regular economy is characterised by being capital intensive, having a high technical content, being highly complex and being organised on a hierarchial, command basis. Participation in the regular economy's formal institutions confers nominal status upon individuals. This regular economy is paralleled by an officially recognised illegal economy or *criminal economy* that includes all those illegal activities which are measured by the official criminal statistics as 'offences known to the police' such as theft, robbery, burglary, handling stolen goods, and so on. The criminal economy is the mirror-image of the regular economy in so far as there would be no market for criminal enterprise unless there were a public restriction or ban. Without such illegal classification these activities would be little different from those of legitimate business (see McIntosh, 1975).

Separate from the regular and criminal economies are four more economies, two of which make up a continuum of unofficial institutions – which are integral to the official economy – and two of which constitute an alternative set of institutions to the official ones. The unofficial legal economy which we can call the *informal economy* would encompass all those activities and institutions which occur within official institutional settings but which are not officially recognised as part of these formal institutions. Where unofficial activities and institutionalised practices were illegal or extra-legal these would constitute a separate economy which we might term the *hidden economy*.

The third pair of economies are distinguishable from their official counterparts on the grounds of being alternative ways of doing things. They comprise self-generated informal institutions in which people control things for themselves on a do-it-yourself or self-help basis. Unlike unofficial economies, alternative economies operate independently of, and outside the contexts of the regular economy's institutions, although as contributors to this volume point out, they are in many ways dependent upon the regular economy's existence (see Ferman and Berndt, chapter 1; Platt, chapter 6). Where such institutions are legal we can refer to them as constituting a *social economy*. Where the activities are extra-legal or illegal, we might describe them as a *black economy*.

Overall, as can be seen from table 1.1 this gives a six-fold typology of economies and their institutions.

We can see how this typology applies if we take work as an illustration. A man might obtain official employment in a factory

TABLE 1.1 A TYPOLOGY OF INFORMAL ECONOMIES AND THEIR INSTITUTIONS

	OFFICIAL	UNOFFICIAL	ALTERNATIVE
	REGULAR ECONOMY	INFORMAL ECONOMY	SOCIAL ECONOMY
Legal	marriage, employment, health and social services etc.	perks-payment, voluntary organisations, tribunals etc.	cohabitation, domestic production, barter and exchange, self-help groups etc.
	CRIMINAL ECONOMY	HIDDEN ECONOMY	BLACK ECONOMY
Extra-legal or illegal	prostitution, professional theft, drug trafficking etc.	extra-marital affairs, pilfering and fiddling, amateur trading etc.	irregular work, 'moonlighting', some fringe medicine etc.

where he will be given a formal written job description detailing his functions and duties for his role in the *regular economy*. His work might comprise assembling pressed steel parts. Before long he may discover that following the officially laid down techniques it is not possible to align the holes in those parts that have been slightly distorted during pressing. More experienced workers in the plant might show him that his job *is* possible if he resorts to a special unofficial technique for retapping the holes. Thus he soon learns that it is only possible to do his job with a degree of additional, unofficial, *informal* knowledge and practice which has become institutionalised as part of the job. In another example, Ditton (1977a) found that bread salesmen were expected to avoid any mistakes made when collecting their sales money and were penalised by having deductions made from their wages should mistakes occur. In practice shortages were impossible to avoid by legitimate means. During his sales training the novice bread salesman learns that shortages can be preempted by overcharging customers for their bread, thus fiddling the customer on behalf of the company and on behalf of himself. He therefore takes part in an *illegal hidden economy* in order to carry out his formal job.

The same process operates in nearly all occupations. Behind the official rule and theory exists the unofficial and hidden practice. In order to carry out the official job functions an employee must rely to a considerable degree on informal relationships and institutions, and he knows that many of his tasks could not be completed without these 'tricks of the trade'.

At another level informal institutions operate outside of the official system as an *alternative* way of providing income, goods and services, which might otherwise be unobtainable. When the official system fails to provide work or to deliver the basic commodities or services, or does so at too high a price or in too inhuman a way, people may resort to 'irregular' economic activity (Ferman and Ferman, 1973). Our factory worker in the example above, might prefer to employ a friend to do some plumbing and decorating rather than to take this work to an established firm in the regular economy. Should his car break down he might take it to the man on the corner who is known to fix them for cash. In so far as none of these skilled workers have registered their 'business' with the relevant authorities then they will be part of the *black economy*. Our factory worker might prefer to pay the black economy car repairman, plumber or decorator by supplying him with some specialist tools obtained 'cheap' from the factory where he works. Doing so would make him part of the *hidden economy* and he might find his assembly job meaningful largely in terms of its usefulness in enabling him to participate in a network of such informal activity. Finally, he might instead prefer to do his decorating or car repair work himself at the week-end. In this case his activity would become part of the *social economy,* but would not show up in the official regular economic measurements as work done.

But informal institutions are not restricted to production and consumption. As we shall see during the course of this book they feature prominently in education, welfare, housing and law, and are as common to marriage as they are to medicine. In what follows I will describe in more detail the characteristic features of the *informal, hidden, black* and *social* economies, and look briefly at some of the explanations that have been offered for their emergence. In this context I will locate the specific contributions to this volume.

The informal economy

Although this label has been applied to all activity outside the official economy, I would like to restrict its use here to those legal institutions which take place in the context of the official regular economy but which are not formally acknowledged as part of that economy. Informal institutions in this category lie 'outside the state' (Hatch, 1980) but not so far outside that they represent alternatives to it. Rather, they tend to be institutions relied upon by the formal institutions of the regular economy to enable people to 'make out', 'bring off' or otherwise accomplish formal roles and functions. Thus in addition to institutions like the payment of 'perks' and other unofficial 'kind-payments' at work, the informal economy includes those like voluntary organisations upon which the state health and welfare services rely for support (see Hatch, chapter 8). Likewise we might include the activities of housing co-operatives and housing associations as well as family or peer group education, and private disciplinary hearings (chapter 12), tribunals and conciliation and arbitration procedures (see Whelan, chapter 11).

A good illustration of the characteristics and role of institutions within the informal economy is given by looking at voluntary organisations. In his chapter Stephen Hatch concentrates on those institutions providing care that are outside the family and the state but for which care giver is not paid. He shows that the extent of such activity is substantial: around 10 per cent of adults in England take part in voluntary work at least once a month and, importantly, that the rate of participation is rising at about 2-3 per cent per year. Hatch explains this in a variety of ways saying that increasing participation might be a substitute for more informal kinds of caring which have declined, or that it might result from the pressure of rising expectations for social services beyond that which the state can afford or can deliver. He also suggests that changing patterns of caring requirements might be a factor in the growth of informal care as might increase in leisure time and the need to make more constructive use of this leisure.

Chris Whelan (chapter 11) accounts for the growth in informal judicial-procedures in terms not only of a failure of the formal procedures to cope with increasing demands but also as a result of a move toward making justice more widely accessible to the public. His chapter outlines the various ways in which legal services have been extended and describes the informal way in which techniques of conciliation and arbitration have come into use in dispute settlements and how growing legislation in particular areas like consumer protection and employment protection has seen a growth in the use of tribunals.

Some more sceptical commentators, however, suggest that the growth of informal institutions is not so much a result of collective populist reaction to changes in social needs, as to a change in government policy towards less expensive public spending programmes. It is no surprise, for example, that as central funding faces the harsh economic realities of our time, world governments are beginning to recognise the 'limits' to medical and social services and to reassert the value of 'self-medication', 'individual and personal responsibility', 'family and community care', 'voluntary help' and any other *Way Forward* (DHSS, 1977) which cuts costs. There are dangers in not being aware of this possibility.

The existence of a legal but unrecognised informal economy provides ground for governments and authorities in the official regular economy to off-load their more difficult functions, to dodge their responsibilities and to have a ready-made excuse to avoid social change. Being able to refer all the less interesting insolvable problems such as alcoholism, depression, or schizophrenia to self-help groups or voluntary agencies, or leaving custodial after-care to ex-prisoner groups, allows more time for the professionals to solve the more interesting cases and shifts the onus for solving the problem on to the victim. As Taylor has pointed out, at a time of economic crisis in public expenditure, when governments are recognising the economic value of natural helping networks and shifting policy towards 'care in the community', volunteers, family, friendship networks and neighbourhood schemes, it is important not to lose sight of who is doing what. 'It is important to consider how far the "community" can care and how far unpaid, privatised and invisible care does meet the need of individuals' (Taylor, 1979, p.131). The point is well put by Lapping: 'When we talk of community care we are employing a linguistic sleight of hand. What it often means is care by an individual family for a sick member for whom at one time the whole community through a hospital might have taken responsibility' (Lapping, 1970, p.589). The crucial distinction to be maintained is between the desirability of the informal economy as an organisational form and the degree of redistribution of resources within the official system. The 'sleight of hand' is that if governments push public services into the informal economy they are preventing the redistribution of money since lower taxes mean more to the rich. The private provision of health and education is possible for the rich but the poor are not able to afford these services and since self-help alone is inadequate, they have to rely on public services.

The hidden economy

This refers to the illegal or extra-legal forms of unofficial institutions that exist within the shadow of official society. A striking example of a hidden social institution is the extra-marital affair (see Lake, chapter 10). Although this is not seen as part of the way formal marriage operates, Lake draws on statistics which show that in eight per cent of marriages one of the partners admits to 'full affairs' and that more than one in five marriages experience some form of extra-marital sexual activity. Lake takes the extra marital affair to be a sexual relationship between two people in which either partner or both is actively married to someone else and in which deceit is used to conceal the relationship from the spouse so as to produce or preserve the appearance of stability in marriage. He explains the phenomenon in a way which has general applicability for informal institutions. He argues that the informal institution occurs when the participants to the formal institution perceive it as failing to live up to the ideal of that institution as it is featured in their childhood and adolescent socialisation. At the point where marriage partners enter a stable affair they are able to pick up those aspects of their 'adolescent agenda' which were left incompleted at the time of marriage because of their incompatibility with formal marriage's ideals of total mutuality. While marriage is a series of compromises, the extra marital affair is seen by Lake as the way 'people cheat in order to grow'.

Cheating is also one theme of the more typically described hidden economy activity of pilfering, fiddling and amateur trading (see Mars and Nicod, chapter 3) that takes place in the context of the regular economy. These activities make up a functional set of covert institutionalised practices that enable employers to enter into individual contractual arrangements with employees to overcome government rules and restrictions on income and equality legislation. More specific labels are used such as 'covert reward system' (Mars and Mitchell, 1976) or 'invisible wage system' (Ditton, 1977b). As Mars and Nicod show in their discussion of pilfering and fiddling in the hotel and catering industry, any understanding of the way regular hotel work takes place and any explanation of its non-unionisation is meaningless without a detailed discussion of the structure of hidden-economy activity; who gets what kinds of informal reward for what purpose and how far managements exploit the informal system. Also, like extra-marital affairs, pilfering and fiddling breaks certain rules and restrictions and therefore requires systematic concealment from others as well as from oneself if one is to maintain both self-identity and a sense of moral rectitude.

Although it is extremely difficult to estimate the numbers of people taking part in pilfering and fiddling at work, some indication might be obtained by scanning the few self-report studies available. These suggest that between 75 per cent and 92 per cent of employees admit pilfering and stealing from their employers (Zeitlin, 1971; Cort, 1959; Laird, 1950; Horning, 1970). Another perspective on the size of the hidden economy might be gained from looking at estimates of losses and stock shrinkage attributable to pilfering and fiddling which some observers put at around 1.8 per cent of a country's GNP (Ditton, 1977a; OCPU, 1978).

In part, explanations for hidden economy activity depend upon what is seen as the motivation of those who take part. The disillusionment with an ideal and the desire for personal growth, by which Lake explains the extra-marital affair is just as applicable to pilfering and fiddling. Employees may see that these activities provide them with status, self-control, excitement, freedom of expression and creative enterprise – things that many discover are denied in their formal jobs (Henry, 1978).

Not incompatible with this interpretation is the view of commentators which accounts for the prevalence of hidden economy activity in terms of the increasing intervention of the state in people's lives. Thus the Outer Circle Policy Unit argue that we have moved towards an administered economy in which government plays a larger role in the distribution of rewards through its policies in the fields of wages, taxation, welfare and prices. This has brought the system of rewards into the centre of the political arena and made it much more visible, without generating any underlying concensus about the fairness of the system. Secondly, they argue that rapid inflation has disturbed relationships and differentials in unintended and unanticipated ways. These changes have been difficult to accept because of government intervention, complex tax and welfare arrangements and an uncertain economic future in which there is little comforting reward from government and only a policy of equality of sacrifice. 'In these circumstances', says the OCPU, 'the emphasis on informal, unofficial, illicit and illegal sources of reward may increase as a means of avoiding inflexibilities in the official system of providing incentives and of assuaging grievances' (OCPU, 1978, p.3).

However, more structuralist explanations for the growth of the hidden economy locate the cause in capitalist society itself, arguing that pilfering and fiddling are no more than a wry reflection of the regular economy. Ditton (1977a) for example, suggests that fiddling is just a subculture of the state and cannot be understood without reference to it. He argues that fiddling is not in opposition to society's values and that fiddlers 'do not believe that fiddling will eventually overthrow the capitalist economy' (Ditton, 1977a, p.173). Ultimately the very same norms which support conventional business also support fiddling: 'Fiddling, like selling, epitomises the capitalist 'spirit'. The subculture of fiddling reflects the sort of dutiful anti-hedonism which provides the normative bedrock of capitalism'(Ditton, 1977a, p.174).

Similarly in work on amateur trading networks (Henry, 1978) I showed how the very same behaviour that makes a person an able 'consumer' in a free-market capitalist economy, i.e. seeking out bargains and special offers, buying things cheaper in bulk, direct from wholesalers or at a discount if damaged or of poor quality, also motivates him to purchase goods and services from the informal economy. For example, when stolen goods appeared ambiguously presented ordinary people would not interpret their purchase as an attempt to undermine the legitimate economy. They would simple draw on their stock of everyday purchasing knowledge and resolve any moral ambiguity in a way which unwittingly masked the illegality of the purchase; the goods became 'bargains' and 'everyone wants a bargain'.

Clearly, however, some hidden economy activities are a product of direct changes in the way society has redefined its boundaries of legality and illegality. What were once unofficial but legal institutions such as payment-in-kind or perks have been transformed into hidden economy activities because of new laws passed for the convenience of administering a formal economy. An extremely good example of this is given by Ditton (1977b) who shows how kind-payments have been allowed to continue as perks for white-collar workers in the form of company cars, private health insurance schemes and other fringe benefits, but that they have been progressively criminalised for manual employees, becoming known as pilfering and fiddling. He argues that, 'The extended package of common rights ... made a significant material contribution to the domestic household budgets of tenants' but that the Acts of Enclosure of the eighteenth century effectively took away those rights and made them into crimes. Woodgathering, game rights and grazing rights, for example, became wood theft, poaching and trespassing' (Ditton, 1977b, p.41). Later, taking home part of the products of one's daily labour from the factory was redefined as employee theft and rather than being seen as a psychological 'cost' of production was interpreted as an economic 'loss'. Indeed, a similar explanation is also given for the black economy.

The black economy
Of all the informal institutions that have received popular

coverage, those comprising the black economy have perhaps received most attention. As well as the 'black economy' (Dale, 1979; Freud, 1979; Junor, 1979) these institutions have been described as an 'irregular economy' (Ferman and Ferman, 1973), an 'underground economy' (*Business Week* 1978, Ross 1978, *The Economist,* 1979), a 'subterranean economy' (Gutmann, 1977) and a 'submerged economy' (Clutterbuck, 1979). In spite of the proliferation of labels it is generally agreed that the black economy comprises the unregistered employment of people outside their primary job, sometimes in order to get round government restrictions on employment, taxation and trading. Moreover, since tax is simplest to evade if the activity is unregistered, and insofar as all transactions that go through a written invoice-cheque-receipt system can be monitored by the authorities, black economic activity is best transacted in cash.

Those who supplement their primary incomes with a second job, not usually declared to the tax authorities, are called 'moonlighters' (see Alden, chapter 2), and as Ferman and Berndt (chapter 1) show their 'irregular economic activity' can occur in a variety of ways. Factory workers might run market stalls at the week-end or discotheques in the evening. Other workers might form cottage industries which are manned by workers who take sick leave from their primary jobs on a rota basis. In Britain, teachers give extra lessons for cash, doctors, lawyers and architects 'free-lance' their skills for cash, and professionals of all kinds seek to work for foreigners on a cash basis.

However, the significance of the black economy is not in its illegality. As with some aspects of the hidden economy, illegality might result from changes in legislation designed to govern the regular economy. Insofar as the participants to the black economy are not registered and do not meet the kinds of laws that have been established to regulate economic behaviour such as taxation and fair trading laws, then they are illegal but are not, as Dow (1977) points out, on the whole criminal. Attempts by the state to organise, tax and control have shifted various activities from the formal economy into the informal. 'Yesterdays "enterprise" thus becomes part of today's black economy'. (Gershuny and Pahl, 1979); 'What were once perfectly innocent private transactions can be transformed into criminal activities and the increase of official surveillance and interference increases the temptation for individuals to conceal what they have previously done openly, or to switch into illegal activities, which are less visible' (OCPU, 1978, p.2). The point is succinctly put by Gutmann: 'The subterranean economy, like black markets throughout the world was created by government rules and restrictions. It is a creature of income tax, of other taxes and limitations on the legal employment of certain groups and of the prohibitions on certain activities' (Gutmann, 1977, p.20).

What is important about the black economy is that it is an alternative and an additional source of employment and income for many people and in this sense parallels the 'informal sector' of the third world (Elken, 1978) where we find:

... the roadside and empty-lot mechanics who will weld on a Bournville Cocoa tin to mend an exhaust pipe of the Civil Servant's Mercedes, the leather workers making hand-made bags for the tourist trade, the furniture makers, the men who collect empty Essolube cans from garages twice a day and have them processed into serviceable oil-lamps by sunset.
Dore, 1976, p.74

As such the black economy is the way in which large numbers of people in under-developed countries make a living and a critical component in urban employment, providing half of all jobs in Lima, more than half in Bombay and Djakarta and over two-thirds in Belo Horizonte (Shankland, 1977). It is in this context that Stephen Platt (chapter 6) discusses how the majority of the world's population house themselves. In a brilliant examination of squatting in the developed world, he points out the crucial connection between the failure of state-run formal institutions and the increasing tendency of people to want control over their own lives.

Some indications of the amount of black economic activity at any one time could be found from direct measurement of how many people take part: what proportion of the population have two or more jobs? As Jeremy Alden shows (chapter 2) some of this information can be obtained from official government household surveys and expenditure material. He shows, for example, that based on such sources from the UK and USA, up to 8 per cent of a country's population can be said to hold two jobs, and that these figures remain relatively constant. From US data he also shows that workers most likely to hold second jobs are those whose primary job ends between 7 a.m. and 1 p.m.

Another way of measuring the size of the black economy is that used by Peter Gutmann (1977) who bases his analyses on the assumption that if we have a large cash-based black economy, then this will show up in an increased amount of cash in circulation. His figure for the size of the black or 'subterranean' economy at 10 per cent of the GNP of the USA is achieved by taking the 1937-41 period as the norm for legal economic activity and declaring the difference between this and recent levels of cash to be a measure of the amount of currency held for illegal purposes. A refinement of the 'excess cash' argument has been the use of econometric models to measure the increase in circulation of large denomination currency. The assumption here is that large notes are used by participants in the underground economy to evade tax because of the need to avoid written evidence of transactions. 'People tend to pay for their "Black" plumbing bills for, say £100, in £10 or £20 notes rather than in £1 or £5 notes' we are told in *A Guide to Underground Economics* (Freud, 1979, p.16). According to calculations in the USA and the United Kingdom, the circulation of large denomination notes has increased disproportionately at three or four times the rate of increase for all notes and this is taken as an indication of the increase in the underground economy.

Both the 'excess cash' and the 'excess notes' methods of measurement have been criticised for assuming that the 'excess' is due to black economic activity. Large amounts of currency held by countries overseas would seriously affect the calculation as would changes in the rate at which a typical unit of demand deposit moves through the economy. According to some estimates both these rates have been going in opposite directions which would tend to detract from the significance of the excess cash thesis (*Business Week*, 1978, p.73-74). In addition, Gutmann's argument fails to consider whether or not the increased ratio of cash to demand deposits has occurred because of a shift from demand deposits into time deposits (Ross, 1978, p.92). It also underestimates the amount of cash hoarding that occurs as does the 'excess of large notes' technique which in addition fails to consider the turnover rate of the currency used for informal black economy transactions.

Nevertheless Gutmann and others who are convinced of an increase in black economic activity suggest that the cause is to be found in a combination of factors: inflation providing the incentive to maximise income by evading taxes; the growth of the welfare state which means a person does not need a permanent, regular full-time job to ensure a basic income; and the growth of employment protection and equality legislation which mean there are clear economic advantages for an employer taking someone on 'off the books'. But the suggestion that government intervention is the sole cause of black economic activity is shortsighted. As Ferman and Berndt (chapter 1) point out, there is a wide variety of social, as well as economic, reasons why individuals take part and, indeed, there is a range of structural explanations which go beyond the simplistic government intervention argument toward a critique of the modern state. In earlier work Ferman (Ferman and Ferman, 1973) outlined these 'structural underpinnings' and this is developed in the chapter by Ferman and Berndt. They argued that 'its very origins lie in structural conditions and processes in the larger society and cannot be divorced from them' (Ferman and Ferman, 1973, p.5) and identified certain key features of modern society which encourage the growth of the irregular economy. It creates low income categories and ethnic and cultural segregation which means that many people have relatively low or non-existent incomes. It fails to provide goods and services for these groups at price levels they can afford because it is overburdened with costly and alienating bureaucratic machinery for regulating and monitoring standards of production and distribution. Economic specialisation resulting from the demands of the complex technological system requiring high degrees of technical expertise, together with the growth of protection of trades unions and professional associations, coalesce so that some goods and services are not widely available or are too expensive for large sectors of the population. Finally, specialists, professionalisation and protection exclude many people from jobs in the more rewarding areas of employment. Thus a *market* for cheap goods and services is created outside the formal economy at the same time as there exists a pressure towards less fulfilling jobs and even unemployment. In these circumstances we have a 'fertile field' for the development of the black economy and 'once irregular patterns are established they provide training and opportunity for those members of the community who choose to earn their livelihood in this way and are supported by a population that has few viable alternatives for the purchase of goods and services' (Ferman and Ferman, 1973, p.17).

The social economy

This includes the range of informal institutions that operate legally and which provide direct and independent alternatives to the official institutions. Examples in this category are more numerous than the others because, in some ways, the social economy is the embodiment of the counter culture. Its institutions range from cohabitation or informal marriage in which people live together without getting married (see Macdonald and Mars, chapter 9), some legal forms of self-help housing as outlined by Platt (chapter 6), community education (Ward, chapter 7), community courts (chapter 12) and the whole range of domestic production, barter and similar irregular economic exchange (Ferman and Berndt, chapter 1 and Lowenthal, chapter 5).

Unlike the black economy which *could* be explained by economic gain, no such explanation is appropriate for the social economy which is directly attributable to need. It is, as Lowenthal, (chapter 5) points out, none other than the support system of the working classes who use it as a survival mechanism to get by in an isolated community or urban ghetto (Dow, 1977) where economics are governed more by 'the etiquette of valued exchange' than by the 'calculus of exchange value' (Faberman and Weinstein, 1970, p.450).

This is not to say that the middle classes are any less aware of the benefits of the social economy. Indeed, it could be argued that they are more conversant with the alternatives available, 'know their rights' and are better able to articulate their philosophical and political position. The social economy is perhaps better described aside from any class reference. More generally, it is the way in which people come together to satisfy needs that have not been met by the formal system of the regular economy. Thus it is any pattern of activity that results in the production of goods and services that are hard to obtain or expensive, given the price mechanisms of the regular economy, and which is not registered by the economic measurements of society (Ferman and Ferman, 1973). It often comprises voluntary small group structures formed by people 'who have come together for mutual assistance in satisfying a common need or overcoming a common handicap or life-disrupting problem, and bringing about desired social and personal change' (Katz and Bender, 1976, p.9). Thus it might include activities such as food-making or mending that form part of domestic production and make up the household economy

(Burns, 1977) or exchanges of produce through barter, and even local self-help groups which provide alternative sources of community care and support (Robinson and Henry, 1977).

Like the other types of informal activity it is impossible to make any estimate of the social economy at present. However, Ferman and Berndt (chapter 1) do reveal the results of their research in the USA which found that 60 per cent of the services households reported using were secured through the social economy. These services were produced within the household or provided by friends, relatives and neighbours or co-workers without monetary payment. A further 10 per cent of the services were purchased with monetary payment from the 'irregular economy' and the remaining 30 per cent were purchased from the regular economy. When attempting to estimate the size of the social economy it is as well to bear in mind the point stressed by Platt (chapter 6) that alternative informal institutions in some sectors, such as housing, far from being exceptional are in fact the normal way most of the world's population satisfy their basic needs.

In the context of a discussion of self-help Katz and Bender have given a highly comprehensive summary of the reasons for the apparent recent rise in informal social institutions:

Industrialization, a money economy, the growth of vast structures of business, industry, government – all these have led to familiar spectres: the de-personalization and de-humanization of institutions and social life; feelings of alienation; powerlessness; the sense for many people that they are unable to control the events that shape their lives; the loss of choices; feelings of being trapped by impersonal forces; the decline of the sense of community, of identity. These problems are compounded for many by the loss of belief in the church, the state, progress, politics and political parties, many established institutions and values. These same conditions give rise to many of the important social movements of the day ... all of which countertrend against the dehumanization and depersonalization, the discrimination and lack of nurturance in social institutions.
Katz and Bender, 1976, p3-4

Others however see the emergence or growth of the informal institutions of the social economy less as a reaction to the failure of existing institutions to meet our needs and more as a response to the inevitable social changes which accompany continued industrial change. Rather than saying we have an inefficient set of institutions, it is argued that we require new forms of social organisation to keep pace with our changing patterns of industrial production.

Gershuny (1977a; 1977b; 1978) starts from a critique of Bell's (1974) view of the change in industrial society towards a service society, by demonstrating that on the contrary, the trend is away from expenditure on services and towards expenditure on goods. However he points out that at the same time (Gershuny and Pahl, chapter 4; Gershuny, 1979) we are entering a period of industrial decline as the society shifts into a post-industrial phase. Manufacturing will continue to decline and shift its patterns of production towards new technology and high wages. As a result of these changes there will be increasing numbers unemployed, perhaps as much as 15 per cent, reduced levels of overtime, earlier retirement, longer holidays, shorter working hours, and work-sharing.

In addition to these changes, governments are shifting to a policy of decreasing public spending as a result of world economic conditions, energy crises and inflation. There is also an accompanying political/ideological shift away from collective provision and towards individual provision. While this latter change is a political choice, its occurrence in the context of the technological changes and world recession confuses the situation. As Gershuny points out, the combined outcome of these changes is that we are entering a 'self-service' society which, rather than purchase services from the formal economy, individuals are increasingly providing such services for themselves.

But there is a difference between how people choose to use increased free time and being forced to work outside the regular economy because they have not got a job. A further difference is between using leisure time to help provide informal services and being forced to use and rely on self-help services because there has been a political decision to change the way in which wealth is redistributed.

Moreover, while some sections of the social economy might have increased for these reasons, it would be a mistake to infer that all aspects of the social economy have similarly changed. A valuable reminder of this emerges from Macdonald and Mars' (chapter 9) discussion of informal marriage in which the apparent change that has occurred has been argued to be in the openness with which this informal institution is now viewed. While informal marriage has been a commonplace state of affairs of the working class for years, it is now emerging as a conscious choice among the educated middle class. As a result it has gained acceptability and relative respectability. The same can be said for self-help as a whole. What we are seeing is not, as Cornford (in the conclusion to these studies) forcibly reminds us, a growth in self-help as a phenomenon, since self-help and mutual aid have always been with us. Rather, we are seeing a growth in self-conscious awareness that self-help is relevant.

Finally, it is worth pointing out that there is a tendency to romanticise informal institutions as some kind of 'better life' of the past. While it is the case that in many respects informal institutions have certain major advantages over formal institutions, this should not lead us to overlook their limitations. We have already stressed the dangers of confusing a trend toward a more autonomous personalised and less alienating organisational form with a political decision to change the pattern of redistribution of resources within society. In reading the following chapters it is as well to remember four key issues. The first is that not only can informal institutions act as an integral part of the official economy, as the cement which keeps it together, but they can also mask its failures. While such institutions might provide their members with otherwise unobtainable income, goods, services and socially nutritional environments, in doing so they effectively palliate those with immediate needs and pacify the most vociferous of society's critics who are deluded into thinking their problems are solvable through local action. Energies are then diverted from any more fundamental criticisms of the social structure because of the demands of everyday localised problem solving. Second, informal institutions provide the grounds for governments and authorities and companies in the formal economy to off-load their more difficult functions, to dodge their responsibilities and to have a ready-made excuse to avoid social change. Third, it is important to realise (as shown in chapter 12) that in spite of their romantic appeal informal institutions are themselves subject to some of the worst problems of formal institutions; to inequalities, injustices and abuses which can stem from their own internal undemocratic constitution or from manipulation of the institution behind the veil of 'democracy' and 'collective' decision making. Fourth, and this is perhaps one of the most disturbing aspects of informal institutions, they are not availabe to everyone in society. What happens to all those who for whatever reason are not able to plug into an informal network of exchange or local self-help scheme but who are also unable to gain satisfaction from the formal economy? It is arguable that in so far as informal institutions are self-serving and do not have broader political aims, then their participants benefit at the expense of similarly suffering non-participants. The danger is of a future society comprised not so much of self-interested individuals but of competing bands. In some areas, such as housing, this is already happening, for example when some so-called 'co-operatives' build up a relationship with local authorities whereby the co-op members get cheap housing and the council has its unlet properties occupied. Having struggled to establish a good working relationship the co-operative might be fearful of new co-ops setting up in the same area as they will compete for its 'resources'. There is little more merit in the spirit of 'ours for us' than in that of 'mine for me', when the 'ours' does not include 'all of us'.

PART ONE

INFORMAL ECONOMIC ACTIVITY

1
THE IRREGULAR ECONOMY

Louis A. Ferman and Louise E. Berndt

Although estimates of employment, unemployment and Gross National Product form the basis for policy development and administration by a society, these estimates do not encompass all the economic activity within that society. They are based on information that is recorded by the economic measurement techniques available, and a certain amount of economic activity goes on that is not monitored or recorded. Part of this activity is based on money as a medium of exchange and comprises the irregular economy.

The production and distribution of goods and services can be conceptualised as belonging to one of three classes on the basis of whether it is accounted for by the economic measurement techniques of the society, and whether it uses money (either currency, coin, bank draft, credit card or other credit as a stated value of reckoning) as a medium of exchange. Exchanges can be categorised as social, irregular or regular according to the presence or absence of these features.For expedience we shall refer to each type of economic activity as a distinct economy (see table 2.1).

The social economy is that sector of economic activity which is not registered by the economic measurement techniques of the society and which does not use money as a medium of exchange. The *irregular economy* is that sector of economic activity that is not registered by the economic measurement techniques of the society but which uses money as a medium of exchange. *The regular economy* is that sector of economic activity that is registered by the economic measurement techniques of the society

26

TABLE 2.1 CLASSIFICATION OF ECONOMIC ACTIVITY

Types of economic activity	Enumeration by economic measurement techniques	Money as a medium of exchange
Social	−	−
Irregular	−	+
Regular	+	+

and uses money as a medium of exchange.

Regular. irregular and social economic activities combine forces in provisioning a society. While most of the services and goods that are crucial to the maintenance of the economic performance of the society, as measured by the Gross National Product, are produced and distributed to a mass market through the regular economy, the day-to-day process of distribution operates through social or irregular channels in the form of exchanges of goods and services among relatives, neighbours, friends and acquaintances. While any one exchange may be small and of little consequence, taken as a whole they may become important both in the provision of goods and services that are unavailable or difficult to obtain through the regular economy and in the distribution of products produced in the regular economy for local or marginal markets.

The Detroit household study

In 1977 we surveyed 284 households in Detroit, Michigan, focussing on the households' use of irregular and social sources as an alternative to the regular economy in obtaining common home-related and personal services (Ferman, Berndt and Selo, 1978). Using a combined survey and ethnographic approach we found that 60 per cent of the services households reported using were secured through the social economy. They were produced within the household itself or provided by friends, relatives, neighbours or co-workers without monetary payment. 10 per cent of the services were purchased through the irregular economy and 30 per cent through regular suppliers. Of all the services we asked about, fully 25 per cent of those for which payment was made were purchased through the irregular economy. Over half of the households surveyed (51 per cent) had purchased at least one service through irregular sources. For our sample there was no significant variation in the use of the irregular economy based on income level, and participation in the irregular economy seems to be widespread throughout all levels of society. This chapter is based largely on our findings from the Detroit study.

Range and characteristics of irregular economic activity

The range of services and goods represented in the irregular economy is very broad, extending from a child's lemonade stand to the empires of organised crime. We have isolated seven types of activities that characterise the irregular economy. These are sale and/or production of goods; home related services provided to consumers; personal services provided to consumers; 'off the books' employment by a regular establishment; rental of property; provision of entertainment; and criminal activities.

Each encompasses a wide range of variation in terms of the size and scale of the activity, the levels of investment in time or money, the relationships between providers and users, the levels of return for work done, the frequency of the activity in terms of provision or use, and the relative availability of the service or goods through regular sources. Clearly also there is some overlap between types, such as when the 'sale of goods' is based on an illicit or semi-illicit source.

The sale and/or production of goods includes such diverse enterprises as church sponsored bake sales, garage sales, lemonade stands run by neighbourhood children, production of arts and crafts, door-to-door peddling, resale of automobiles, sewing, and furniture making. All can be termed irregular if they involve an exchange of money and are unrecorded. Yet, even within one activity type, enterprises can differ radically. The housewife who decorates and sells five ash trays a year to her friends for two dollars and the potter who earns over $10,000 annually at art fairs and through galleries without reporting her income are both engaged in the irregular economy.

Similarly, diversity extends through each of the remaining categories. Home related services range from a child mowing an elderly neighbour's lawn for fifty cents to a crew of unlicensed builders constructing a new house or garage. Personal services include such items as running an errand for a nickel, weekly housecleaning or long-term nursing care. "Off the books' employment by a regular establishment covers a teenager sweeping the floor once a week for five dollars, a waitress working for cash at a bar while receiving aid for dependent children and a dispatcher working for a trucking firm and depositing his cash income in an out-of-state bank while receiving total disability payments. Rental of property might be the occasional rental of one's automobile to a local funeral home or the rental of a room or apartment in one's home. Provision of entertainment runs from an unrecorded two-dollar bet on a baseball game, to a band working regularly for cash payments which they do not report to the tax authorities. Criminal activities also extend from the relatively minor and insignificant, such as a teenager selling marijuana cigarettes to his buddy, to large-scale, high-profit enterprises such as wholesale importing and distributing of heroin.

Almost every type of economic activity that is found in the regular economy is probably found in the irregular economy; goods are manufactured and distributed, services are provided; people are employed by others, and income is earned from capital investments. While the range of different types of activities in the irregular economy reflects the same types of activities as in the regular economy, the *nature* of these activities is somewhat different.

The size and scale of activities in the irregular economy may be generally much smaller than in the regular economy in terms of both the numbers involved and the levels of investment, in time and money. With the notable exception of organised crime and similar overtly illegal activities, irregular enterprises are generally small, frequently involving only one person acting as an entrepreneur and seldom involving more than three or four people working together. The scale of irregular enterprises is likewise small. Producers and consumers of goods and services generally meet face to face and arrange the terms of their own transactions (usually within a limited geographical setting). Importantly, irregular exchanges are characterised by direct distribution of product and little or no specialised division of labour within the producing unit.

Levels of investment in most irregular activities are low in terms of operating capital, equipment and supplies. Frequently the irregular entrepreneur utilises his or her regular employment for access to necessary tools. A clerical worker who types manuscripts 'on the side' may depend on a regular employer to supply not only the typewriter but also the paper, ribbon and office space and in some cases the time. Most irregular enterprises are intermittent. The general low level of capitalisation does not allow for on-going activity when there is no demand for products. Few irregular activities allow full-time, all-year-round employment and production. More often they are engaged in as part-time pursuits, either intensively for short duration, such as a garage or yard sale or roofing job over the weekend, or as a 'side line', involving one or two hours on a more regular schedule.

The levels of return for work may vary more widely than in the regular economy. Certainly the irregular economy is more integrated than the regular, with fewer intermediate transactions between production and final consumption and substantially less overhead costs. However, these factors do not necessarily translate into lower costs for the consumer *or* higher rates of return for the producer. Although, as a whole, our respondents did pay less for the services which they obtained through the irregular economy than for services obtained through the regular economy, there is no evidence that specific services are cheaper in the irregular economy since the range of prices there is greater. However, the specific services most often purchased from irregular producers may be, in general, less costly than those purchased from firms or businesses. Pricing in the irregular economy is idiosyncratic and often particularistic, depending in part on the nature of the relationship between the parties involved in the exchange.

The relations between providers and users of irregular goods and services are frequently grounded in personal ties, which in some cases override the economic content of the exchanges. Many exchanges that are irregular involve an unrecorded exchange of money and are virtually indistinguishable from similar transactions that do not involve overt payment. Money is a general purpose commodity – the mere fact of its changing hands does not of its itself define a market relationship. Gifts can be in cash or in kind; international business can be conducted by barter as well as bills of exchange. In the irregular economy the price is as often dependent on the nature of the relations between the parties involved as it is on the 'market' value of the service or goods exchanged. An irregular auto mechanic might rebuild his mate's engine for 'free'. He might do the same for his in-laws at the cost of parts and a discount; but his neighbour may have to pay the going hourly rate. Certainly factors other than capital, supply, and demand, mediate the cost of the product.

Technological constraints on manufacture, division of labour, overhead, distribution, capitalisation, licensing laws and other regulations act in concert to limit the irregular manufacture of durable goods in highly industrialised economies. Although letting out piece-work to unregistered shops or employees has not been entirely eradicated, we suspect that the manufacture of consumable or specialty goods and the production of services are more characteristic of irregular activities in North America. While we do not have systematic survey data to support the argument our research strongly suggests that the provision of services is more prevalent in the irregular economy than is the manufacture or distribution of goods.

The services most frequently obtained through the irregular economy generally demand a higher level of technical expertise and more capital investment in equipment than similar services provided by the social economy. In turn they are usually less complex and capital intensive than services produced in the regular economy. In our sample, a remarkably high rate of services was produced without monetary payment, either by the respondents themselves or through their social networks. But as the skill level necessary for a service, the amount of money required to produce it, or the degree of complexity involved in the task increased, there was greater likelihood of a monetary transaction. For example, three types of kitchen cabinet work were reported: new cabinets were built and installed; pre-built cabinets were installed; and existing cabinets were repaired. Installing pre-built cabinets accounts for 64 per cent of irregular work; 35 per cent of social and only 18 per cent of regular work; while building new cabinets accounts for 56 per cent of regular work, 40 per cent of social and 36 per cent of irregular work. No cabinets were reparied by irregular workers, repair work being generally a 'do-it-yourself' activity, or else done 'free' on the social economy. The skill level involved in irregular work is intermediate. People who do not install cabinets for free through their social channels, tend to pay irregular workers to install pre-built cabinets, but to go to regular sources to *build* and install cabinets.

The services for which the irregular producers were used most frequently were lawn care, exterior painting, interior painting, panelling, carpentry, babysitting and child care. These services were secured for free through the social economy by the majority of the respondents. If purchased, they were more often secured from irregular sources than from established firms or businesses. The irregular economy was generally utilised for services that most people would otherwise secure without monetary payment through their social channels, and which are usually not provided by regular firms and businesses. The irregular sector seems to function as an alternative service provider in instances where the household is unable to perform the service or unable to have it done without payment. In this sense it fills an intermediate position between the regular market economy and 'do-it-yourself' activities.

Interdependence of the irregular and regular economies

The irregular economy is highly dependent on the regular economy for its source of goods, since the regular economy provides the source for manufacture and initial distribution of most new goods for the society. Even those goods most likely to be produced in the irregular economy are dependent, for the most part, on materials procured through the regular economy. An artist may paint a picture and sell it irregularly, but the materials used – the canvas, brushes, oils and turpentine – will probably be purchased through regular sources. The raw materials used to produce goods in the irregular economy, whether furniture, baked goods, clothing or art, are almost invariably purchased from regular outlets and manufactured or processed by regular firms. Irregular producers of goods are *steady* consumers of *regular* products. In this sense the irregular economy is part of the market of the regular economy. Persons who produce goods in the irregular economy are *consumers* of goods produced in the regular economy.

The irregular economy serves as a means of *distribution* of regular products in a number of ways: through their transformation into new goods that are sold irregularly; through resale of used goods originally produced and sold in the regular economy; through irregular sale of goods purchased from regular sources; and through products purchased from regular sources and used in providing services irregularly. The role of the regular economy in providing raw materials for irregular manufacture or processing has been described above. The regular economy is also the source for used and new goods *resold* through the irregular economy.

The merchandise sold at garage sales and through 'want ads' was usually purchased from regular sources. Its subsequent sale in the irregular economy is a continuing means of redistributing regular goods. Door-to-door and street peddlers who do not report their income usually purchase their wares from suppliers whose profits are monitored and recorded. Services provided through the irregular economy frequently include the installation of new goods manufactured by and purchased from regular sources. An irregular plumber who installs a new faucet acts as a distributor for regularly produced goods.

Many products produced in the regular economy may be dependent on the irregular economy for repair and maintenance. For example, chimneys are built from bricks manufactured in the regular economy and are constructed by regular workers – there are, however, very few regular chimney sweeps working in this country. Small appliance repair is another area in which maintenance services are often obtained through the irregular economy. It is unlikely that one can find a repairman attached to an established business who will fix a broken toaster for a cost that is less than the replacement price of the appliance.

The irregular economy also acts conversely as a producer of goods and services that are distributed through the regular economy. A worker who is employed 'off-the-books' produces profit for the regular employer. A painting that is produced and sold irregularly by an artist may be distributed quite regularly by a gallery. A seamstress who sells her product to a store may not report her income, but the store will record their purchase and sale of the 'irregular' clothing as a regular transaction.

In summary, the irregular economy serves four basic functions with respect to the regular economy. It is a *consumer,* a *distributor* and a *maintainer* of products produced in the regular economy. And, it is a *producer* of products sold in the regular economy.

Structural underpinnings of the irregular economy

There a number of structural elements in our society which act as underpinnings for irregular economic activities: the structure of the economy may create a demand for and supply of irregular products; political factors define irregularity through licensing regulations and tax laws; aspects of social structure provide the networks of access between producers and consumers and instil norms and values that condition participation in the irregular economy.

The economic underpinnings of the irregular economy condition both the demand for services and goods from irregular sources and the supply of irregular workers to provide these products. In this sense the irregular economy cannot be viewed separately from the general economy. The demand for the irregular economy may be a function of a number of factors such as: the imperfect distribution of goods and services; the lack of supply of goods and services from regular sources; the general state of affluence in the economy; or some combination of these.

If customers are unable to secure desired goods or services from regular sources they may turn to irregular providers. Some products are simply unavailable in the regular economy for a number of reasons. Insufficient demand may make regular production of certain goods or services unprofitable. For example, certain 'ethnic goods' such as special foods for festive occasions may not have a market large enough to ensure regular production and may be available only through irregular channels. Inadequate rewards for services such as babysitting might lead to very few workers being willing to supply such services, particularly if their incomes are also subject to government withholdings or overheads. Other items, such as marijuana or heroin cannot legally be provided by the regular economy. Occupational specialisation and new product development may act to create situations where there simply is no supply of regular producers for such services as repairing or patching plaster walls.

Some services or goods that are usually obtained through regular channels may not be available to specfic populations: home repair companies will not work on structures in certain neighbourhoods, clothing is not manufactured in a particular size. Some people may be unaware of certain regular sources for some products. Customers who are unable to afford goods or services from regular sources may be able to purchase irregular products at a price they can afford. A mother who does not have the resources to purchase a toy for her child at a large store might be able to buy one at a garage sale. Even if it is not the case, some people may *think* that irregular sources are cheaper and choose not to contact a regular firm for services such as plumbing. People who assume that using a regular source for home repair necessitates a building permit, inspection and subsequently, higher property taxes, may employ irregular workers to avoid further payments to other recipients, even if the irregular source itself represents no savings.

It may be that an expansion in the general economy increases demand for both regular and irregular products. Alternatively, more people might turn to the irregular economy during periods of economic contractions or high inflation in efforts to stretch their income. Different groups make use of the irregular economy for different products; the wealthy for custom-made or other luxury items, the middle class for savings on home repair services, and the poor for the necessities of day-to-day survival.

Similarly, several economic factors affect the supply of workers in the irregular economy. More people may seek irregular work during periods of economic recession when options for regular employment are limited. There is certainly a clear tendency for the numbers of small businesses to increase during periods of high unemployment (Newcomber, 1961, p.492-493). Self-employment in the irregular economy is another alternative to no work at all. If demand for irregular products contracts as does demand for regular products, these individuals would be competing for a limited market. If the demand for irregular products is higher during periods of economic expansion, workers might be drawn into the irregular economy. However, other workers who have been seeking employment in the irregular economy may move into regular employment or drop irregular supplementary employment in favour of regular overtime or a new, better-paying position.

People may choose irregular employment for a number of economic reasons; because no other work is available to them, because irregular employment is perceived to be more lucrative than regular employment, in order to make ends meet on transfer payments, in order to supplement regularly derived income or in order to avoid overhead costs of regular enterprises such as book-keeping requirements, social security payments, or in order to withhold taxes. There are a variety of reasons for working in the irregular economy, and in most cases there is more than one factor involved. The economic benefits of participation are very important, but coupled with this may be the fact that opportunities for participation in the irregular economy surpass those available in the regular sector. Certain characteristics of irregular activities other than their economic benefits, such as the relative freedom and autonomy and flexibility they offer, are also important.

Political organisations, laws, local ordinances, tax regulations, monitoring systems and criminal statutes define the irregular economy. Without the political framework governing the economy, exchanges would be neither 'regular' nor 'irregular'. The regular economy, like the formal sector, is 'officially recognised, fostered, nurtured and regulated by the State' (Weeks; 1975, p.3). Policies formulated to encourage economic development and stability, to protect workers and consumers and to produce tax revenues may inadvertantly tend to encourage participation in irregular activities. Criminal statutes that outlaw certain goods and services for social or moral reasons do not eliminate the demand for these services, rather they ensure that this demand will be met irregularly. While irregular activities are frequently illegal, the bulk of the irregular economy 'might more correctly be termed *extra-legal* rather than *criminal* in that its illegality stems from the fact that people who engage in such work ignore administrative codes both by failing to report taxable income and by failing to obtain the licensing necessary to legitimise the work' (Dow, 1977, p.111). Other irregular activities are entirely legal and in violation of no criminal or civil ordinances. Most irregular activities are not illegal in nature. Similar economic activities are conducted through regular and social channels quite 'legally'. Without tax regulations, monitoring systems and licensing restrictions these activities would not be irregular.

Government regulations may tend to foster participation in the irregular economy. Prepayment of tax estimates may be impossible for the marginally self-employed or new business begun on a shoestring. The savings on overhead rates entailed in not keeping records or preparing paperwork required from regular enterprises might make the difference between a profitable and unprofitable undertaking, particularly for small-scale businesses. Individuals might work irregularly for additional income which, if reported, would alter their official situation and negate the economic benefits of their work. If an irregular worker were otherwise regularly employed and reported irregular income, the increase in tax rate might wipe out any additional earnings. A worker collecting unemployment insurance would jeopardise the regularity of these payments by taking regular employment of a limited duration. This could result in a net loss of income.

Restrictive licensing regulations, implemented so as to limit the number of workers in an occupation, might effectively bar otherwise qualified individuals from regular employment in that field. Moreover people may be unaware that their activities are in violation of regulations; they may have no idea that they are engaged in the irregular economy at all.

The irregular economy operates outside the protective web of legislation and regulation characteristic of the regular economy. It is regulated informally through morals and custom. While no economic relations are maintained in a social vacuum the irregular economy is particularly dependent on social sanctions for its operation. At one extreme irregular exchanges are virtually indistinguishable from social relations. When a woman accompanies an elderly neighbour to the market and receives a token payment for transportation costs her motivation more likely stems from a social obligation to a community member than from expectation of monetary reward. At the other extreme irregular activities operate as if they were part of the regular market, impersonally aiming to maximise profits but relying on informal controls to secure the safety of their enterprise. Organized crime relies on social relations frequently based on ethnic lines, for recruiting labour and ensuring secrecy. Threats and sanctions are communicated through informal networks and are well understood by the community of participants.

Although it is unregulated, the irregular economy is not an open market. Much irregular activity operates within a nexus of prior association and personal ties. In our survey more than three quarters of the services obtained irregularly were purchased from suppliers with whom the respondents had a prior relationship and who had been recommended to them by someone they knew and trusted (see also Henry, 1978). Membership in a social network is necessary for participation in much of the irregular economy, for making contacts, recruiting and job opportunities and in ensuring the quality of the products. Concern for maintaining friendship, reputation and status in the community are often better guarantees of performance than written warranties.

The workforce of the irregular economy

The workforce of the irregular economy is composed of people from all walks of life. The irregular labour force includes workers employed full-time and part-time in the regular economy; persons currently unemployed in the regular economy; new entrants into the labour market; and people not officially in the labour force; such as children, students, homemakers, and retired individuals. There is no *one* type of irregular worker. Some irregular workers depend on transfer payments for basic income; others are financially secure. Irregular work is not dominated by any racial, ethnic, social or occupational group. Anyone who derives any unreported income from any source is a member of the irregular economy. This includes earned income from professional consulting, sideline construction work, artistic endeavours, babysitting or prostitution as well as unearned income from dividends, rentals, sale of capital goods, or bribes and 'kickbacks'.

Obviously individuals do not have equal access to potential sources of irregular income. The irregular economy, like the regular, is characterised by diversity in job opportunities, in work situations and in its labour force. Irregular work possibilities, like regular career choices, are conditioned by one's personal aptitudes, skills and training and by one's general environment, social status, and personal connections. The single female head of a household receiving government assistance does not have the same opportunity to pocket unreported earnings from speaking engagements as does the university professor.

Almost everyone has had the opportunity to join the irregular labour force in one manner or another, but not everyone has done so. Motivation to participate stems from a variety of sources. People may be drawn into irregular activities through their normal process of acculturation, through recruitment by friends or neighbours who need a particular service, from the outgrowth of a hobby or leisure-time pursuit, as an outlet for skills not utilised in regular employment, and as a way of avoiding or evading taxes. Irregular work may be an economic cushion during slow periods in regular work or it may be a means of supplementing insufficient income, of earning extra money for specific purchases, or an attempt to increase general standard of living. It may be a way to keep going between regular jobs or the only alternative available for earning an income. For some, irregular work is a way of surviving without submitting to the routine of a regular job, a way to develop new skills leading to a change in occupation; or an informal market testing ground for a fledgling business venture. These and other considerations often combine to set the incentive for participation.

People with different employment statuses, incomes and other characteristics may work in the irregular economy for similar reasons. Persons in similar circumstances may engage in irregular activities for a variety of different reasons. The nature, intensity and duration of the irregular work experiences of any individual are conditioned by the possibilities available at any particular time. The choice to engage in irregular activities stems from interaction between situational variables – opportunities and constraints – and personal aspirations, norms and values. A belief in self-sufficiency and the virtue of work can be as strong a motivation as a desire to beat the system.

We do not know what groups or categories of people comprise the bulk of the labour force of the irregular economy or what type of participant reaps the greatest gain from irregular pursuits. Arguments that the irregular economy is the particular domain of any category based on distinctions of occupation, income level, employment status, social class, sex, age or race are at present no more than unfounded speculation. In our study we found that some fully employed persons needed their irregular income to make ends meet; others utilised it for extras and to raise their standard of living. Some worked irregularly for personal satisfaction in the work. Others combined part-time regular employment with irregular activities.

Irregular workers who were receiving unemployment insurance payments used irregular income to supplement these benefits and to maintain their households until they were called back to their previous jobs or were able to secure new regular employment. Aside from the obvious financial benefit, these pursuits allowed them to occupy their time while out of work, and for some it provided the opportunity to experiment with new career options. For most, the irregular income earned was not enough to live on without the base income provided by unemployment insurance. All wanted to return to regular employment and viewed their irregular work as supplemental and temporary only.

Income derived from irregular work is usually supplemental to a base income stemming from regular sources – whether wage or salary employment, transfer payments such as public assistance, aid for dependent children, social security, pension plans or private investments and savings. Most of the irregular workers we interviewed valued the security of a predictable source and level of income. Those few individuals we met whose entire livelihood depended on their irregular activities valued the freedom to set their own time and working conditions. None of these 'full-time' irregular workers had heavy financial or family obligations. They were working only to support themselves in their day-to-day lives. Most of these workers had previously worked in the regular economy and most expressed a desire to return to regular work if the job and pay met certain standards.

While the economic incentives for irregular work are most evident for people who are unemployed or receiving subsistence level support from public assistance programmes, increased income is not the sole motivation. In situations where people had little work experience and low confidence in their abilities, irregular work provided a way of testing options without endangering the security of their major source of income. For many it is a way to keep in touch with the community by providing needed services which yield more in involvement and self-esteem than monetary reward. For some it may provide a transition into regular employment through the development of skills and work behaviours that will then be transferred into conventional jobs.

Individuals whose opportunities for regular employment are blocked or limited due to their own personal characteristics and situations or the constraints of the labour market often face the same problems in the irregular economy as in the regular. In our research we found little evidence to support popular contentions that the poor, the unemployed, the unskilled, and the disadvantaged are actually gainfully employed in the irregular economy. Usually their irregular employment is in low-skill, low-wage, insecure activities that offer no real alternative to public assistance as a main source of support.

Significance of the irregular economy

As Eric Wolf has said, complex societies are 'not as well organised or tightly knit as their spokesmen would on occasion like to make people believe' (1966, p.1). Official economic statistics are generally assumed to measure accurately the real production of the society and the current deployment of its labour force. Our immediate response to news briefs announcing the government's latest estimates of Gross National Product, employment or unemployment betrays our acceptance of the official models as true reflections of economic activity. Our research has shown that there is a widespread irregular economy that is ignored in official estimates of economic activity. The magnitude of the economic activity that escapes enumeration in the national accounts is unknown, but recent estimates based on slippages in macroeconomic statistics for 1976 vary from 176 billion dollars (Gutmann, 1977) to 369 billion dollars (Feige, 1979). That is, the size of the irregular economy in the United States in 1976 may have equalled up to 19 per cent of the regular, enumerated Gross National Product. Furthermore, both Gutmann and Feige assert that the irregular economy is continuing to grow, and that its expansion is at the expense of the regular economy. If this is so, the success of monetary and employment policies and programmes based on official statistics may be doomed from the onset.

Our study of the irregular economy underlines the fact that there are alternative informal activities that generate *paid work*. Quite apart from the large blocks of unpaid work – the social economy, and the block of recorded paid work – the regular economy, there are mechanisms in the economy where flexible work arrangements for pay are available. The importance of these arrangements is that they offer to some workers an opportunity to cope with life situations that require new sources of income; for example, layoffs, inadequate transfer payments, inflation and any pressures on prices. What should be recognised here is that this form of income support is controlled by relationships between buyers and sellers in the irregular economy and not by public agencies. In this sense, it may be a more flexible tool to produce income than institutionalised aid programmes where eligibility . rules play a prominent role.

Conventional constructs of labour force analysis must be revised to account for unconventional patterns of work. Conventional categorisations of 'employed workers', 'unemployed workers', and 'persons not in the labour force' have to be recognised as analytical distinctions not wholly in step with *real* labour force behaviour. Some employed workers in our study did far more work than was officially recognised or recorded. Some officially unemployed workers actually worked during their period of unemployment, and some workers who were officially 'out of the labour force' actually did some work and were actively seeking work in the regular labour market. Conventional constructs obscure the actual operations of the labour force and the economy.

We need new models to represent work careers more adequately. Most careers are described in terms of job changes from one regular job to another; or in shifts from a regular job to a period of unemployment; or in shifts from a work or unemployment status to a 'left the labour force' status. Certainly we must now add to career analyses some concern with periods of irregular employment and the function that it plays in the total organisation of the career. Adding this information may be made more difficult by the fact that irregular activities can co-exist with other labour force statuses. This means that some theories of the neat stages of labour market behaviour may have to be revised to include an overlay of various kinds of irregular activity.

Finally, we speculate that the rules and regulations, the entire bureaucratic apparatus that has been built up to protect and nurture the regular economy, have created an environment where informal mechanisms of production and distribution are actually necessary. The regular economy is increasingly dominated by large concerns whose products are geared toward mass markets and mass profits. Regulations designed to protect workers and consumers and the bureaucratic red tape they involve have tended to create an atmosphere antithetical to regular production for a localised or specialised market unless there is some guarantee of profit margin. The irregular economy is not merely a stepchild of recession and high unemployment. Nor is it simply the bastard of excessively high tax rates and general inflation. The *irregular economy* is the legitimate child of the marriage of business and the state, an elegant economic and social welfare structure which *sets the context* that makes the *irregular economy* necessary and is dependent on informal processes for its continued operation.

2
HOLDING TWO JOBS:
An Examination of
'Moonlighting'

Jeremy Alden

Increased interest has been shown in recent years in the extent to which some economic activity is not recorded in estimates of employment, unemployment or Gross National Product. In April 1979, the Chairman of the Board of Inland Revenue in Britain estimated that this 'black economy' accounted for some $7\frac{1}{2}$ per cent of Gross Domestic Product (i.e., for Britain, some £11,000 million for the 1978-79 financial year). Any likely growth in such activity has substantial implications for economic management. In the current debate on the 'black economy' considerable reference is made to 'moonlighting', the colloquial expression for holding two paid jobs, though it is usually used when one of these jobs is unofficial. Particular attention has focussed upon the nature and extent of second jobs, the link between moonlighting and tax evasion, and the likelihood of more people holding two jobs in the future.

The primary purpose of this chapter is to examine the main features of moonlighting, in Britain and other countries, and to assess the extent to which this phenomenon may be regarded as a significant element of economic activity.

The extent of people holding two paid jobs depends on the definition used. Table 3.1 shows the rate of double job holding in Britain during the period 1971-76, based on the two main sources of data available. While the Family Expenditure Survey (FES) indentified 7.3 per cent of the labour force holding two jobs in 1976, the General Household Survey (GHS) put the figure at 3 per cent. The FES figure represents just under two million people having recorded their second jobs, and the GHS around three-quarters of a million. The main reason for the difference between the GHS and FES estimates concerns the time reference involved with the double job holding definition. While the GHS measures double job holding according to whether a second job had been held in the previous week, the FES relates to whether a person holds a second job at all. The notion of holding a 'second job last week' is more precise and restrictive a concept than 'do you have a second job' and because people may regard themselves as 'having' second jobs even though they are not currently involved actively in them, the FES catches more occasional jobs than does the GHS.

TABLE 3.1 RATES OF DOUBLE JOB HOLDING IN BRITAIN 1971-1976

	FES (%)	GHS (%)
1971	6.9	3.1
1972	7.5	3.1
1973	7.5	3.5
1974	8.3	4.0
1975	7.6	3.0
1976	7.3	3.0

Source: Department of Employment unpublished FES data, and annual reports of GHS

While there is no internationally accepted definition of double job holding, government studies in the USA, Canada and Australia adopt the GHS type definition, and this has also been used by member countries of the European Economic Community in the new EEC Labour Force Surveys undertaken in 1973 and 1975. A 1976 government survey in the USA, for example, showed that 4.5 per cent of all employed workers had more than one job, compared to 3 per cent in Britain.

A major feature of the British FES data is not only the much higher rate of double job holding than that shown by the GHS but also a marked differential between male and female rates. The FES data for 1976 identified female rates of 9.3 per cent, substantially above the male rate of 5.9 per cent. The reason for the high female FES is explained largely by the FES picking up occasional jobs which are done mainly women. Such secondary jobs for women can be accounted for by activities such as baby sitting or from work such as Tupperware selling parties or running mail-order catalogues. FES data for 1975 has shown that only about half the males and one quarter of the females regarded as double job holders actually have two jobs of employee status. Corresponding figures for the GHS, based on the more restrictive 'de facto' definition, show much smaller proportions in the self-employed category. The divergence between the results of the FES and GHS is largely due to definitional differences particularly regarding female work.

There is no reliable statistical data available on unrecorded second jobs. However, with high levels of marginal taxation there is inevitably a strong incentive for evasion. In these circumstances holding a second job becomes a sensitive issue, and this suggests that official figures may significantly under-estimate the size of this activity. There are other good reasons why people do not put their second job on record. One such reason is fear of adverse comments by their employers, who consider that extra hours of work (but not extra hours of leisure) may be detrimental to their performance on the main job. During my research I have found that both tax evasion and attitudes of employers are given as reasons why people are reluctant to identify themselves as moonlighters.

The EEC Labour Force Sample Survey is now becoming a major source of labour force data and EEC manpower policies for member countries are increasingly being placed on a more uniform basis. As I have illustrated elsewhere, (Alden and Saha, 1978) comparable labour force data for EEC countries has recently become available from the EEC labour force sample surveys which began in 1973. A number of problems have arisen over countries adopting different definitions and concepts of labour force variables. By the time of the 1975 survey these early difficulties had largely been eliminated. The 1975 EEC labour force sample survey data was published in the Eurostat series (by the Statistical Office of the European Communities) in 1976, and the EEC definition of second job holding followed the British GHS and American CPS (Current Population Survey) concept of using a 'de facto' basis. It is worth pointing out however that while the 1975 British GHS recorded a second job holding rate of 3.0 per cent, the 1975 EEC Labour Force Survey recorded a British figure of only 1.6 per cent, which is the lowest of the EEC countries, as shown in Table 3.2.

However, the difference between the EEC and British based data on second jobs can be explained by the different methods of

TABLE 3.2 RATES OF DOUBLE JOB HOLDING IN THE EEC 1975.

	Total (%)	Male (%)	Female (%)
Germany	1.9	2.8	0.4
Italy	2.7	3.3	1.1
Netherlands	2.1	2.4	1.3
Belgium	2.7	3.5	1.0
Luxembourg	3.7	4.7	1.3
UK	1.6	1.8	1.4
Ireland	3.6	4.3	1.5
EEC*	2.1	2.7	1.0

Source: Compiled from Eurostat EEC Labour Force Survey, HMSO, 1976

* France and Denmark failed to submit data on second jobs to the survey

approach. First, fieldwork on the Labour Force Survey takes place over a limited period of time in May and June whereas the GHS is spread evenly throughout the year and stands a better chance of picking up seasonal activity in second jobs. Secondly, a standard feature of the EEC Labour Force Survey is that respondents may often not be aware of other family members' second jobs. Such proxy interviews are rare with the GHS in Britain.

The American studies of second jobs have provided information on both economic and social characteristics of double job holders. In the USA the typical moonlighter has been found to be a family man between 25 and 45 years old, working part-time on his second job in an industry or occupation different from that of his first job. His motives have been identified as being primarily financial. From the articles published in the *Monthly Labour Review* issued by the United States Department of Labour, it has been found that double job holders make up about 5 per cent of all employed workers in the USA.

The first comprehensive studies undertaken on double job holding in the USA were made in 1946 by the Bureau of the Census, and since 1959 by the Bureau of Labour Statistics. The development of our information base on double job holding has evolved, therefore, over a thirty year period in the USA, and extra questions have been included over time in interviewing schedules in the Current Population Survey which represent an extension of work. In Britain however, except for one article by the Department of Employment (1972) and data contained in the annual reports of the General Household Survey, there has been no comparable development of an information base on this aspect of the labour force.

The official rate of double job holding in the USA, like that in Britain, has remained remarkably stable over time, as shown in Table 3.3. Between 1962 - 1978 the overall rate has ranged between 4.6 per cent and 5.7 per cent. However, the number of persons who hold second jobs, as again illustrated in Table 3.3, is now higher than in the mid-1960s and early 1970s. Because the number of employed persons rose faster than the number of second job holders, the rate of double job holding − that is the percentage of the employed population with two jobs − has fallen.

No significant relationship has been found between unemployment rates and double job holding rates either in the USA or in Britain. Moonlighting appears to be a pheonomenon unrelated to any wide cyclical swings in the overall economy. The GHS and FES data in Table 3.1 illustrate the stable nature of second job rates in Britain, and Table 3.3 illustrates the same stability for the USA. While unemployment in Britain rose from $2\frac{1}{2}$ per cent in 1970 to $5\frac{1}{2}$ per cent in 1976 the rate of moonlighting remained the same, Hayghe and Michelotti (1971) found no significant relationship between these two variables for the period 1956/7 to 1970/1 in the USA. More recently, while unemployment increased from 4.9 per cent in 1973 to 8.5 per cent in 1975 in the USA, the rate of second job holding remained stable.

The incidence of second jobs among American workers varies widely by demographic and employment characteristics. Double job holding rates tend to be highest among workers in the middle age groups and lowest among those in the youngest and oldest age groups. The rates are also higher for men than for women, and for whites than for blacks. But this might tell us more about the incidence of disclosures than of real comparisons between different populations.

However, a major feature of double job holding in the USA has been the sharp rise between 1970 -78 in the number of women holding two jobs, whereas the number of double job holding men has dropped slightly. This increase in the number of female double job holders reflects the large increases both in the number of women who work and in the proportion who hold a second job. While in 1970 only 16 per cent of all double job holders were women, this has increased to 29 per cent by 1978. This figure is now very similar to the pattern for Britain. The 1976 General

TABLE 3.3 Moonlighting rates in the USA 1962-1978

	Number of moonlighters (thousands)	Moonlighting rate		
		Total (%)	Male (%)	Female (%)
1962	3,342	4.9	6.4	2.0
1966	3,636	4.9	6.4	2.2
1970	4,048	5.2	7.0	2.2
1974	3,889	5.5	5.8	2.6
1976	3,948	4.5	5.8	2.6
1978	4,493	4.8	5.8	3.3

Source: US Monthly Labor Review, Table 1, February, 1979

Household Survey has shown that in Britain 33 per cent of all double job holders were women.

Interpretations of double job holding

A fundamental argument in support of people holding a second job is that doing so provides an opportunity for the individual and his (or her) family to raise their living standards. This is especially important when inflation is forcing prices up and government income polices are holding wages down. Not only does income increase with a second job but it represents freedom of choice as to how people earn their money. Indeed, Paul Samuelson, the well known American economist, in the introduction to Riva Poor's book on the future of changing patterns of working time, has emphasised that while people have long had the right to determine (largely) how they *spend* their money this freedom has not been extended to how they earn their income (Poor, 1970).

A further consideration is that without this particular informal institution, many jobs would not be done, except by part-time workers (Alden, 1977). These include jobs held on a self-employed basis such as decorating, plumbing, electrical work, hairdressing, window cleaning and taxi driving, and also those jobs done on an employee basis, such as barmen, barmaids, telephonists, and cleaners. Moreover, in spite of the view that moonlighters deprive the Inland Revenue of income, people holding two jobs boost national output.

In terms of individual motivation the American CPS data has shown that the economic motive is the strongest reason why people hold two jobs, and by spending the extra income earned, the moonlighter helps create first jobs for the unemployed via the well known multiplier effect of increased spending; one man's expenditure is another man's income.

However, both the American data and my local survey work in Cardiff, Wales, have illustrated that the social motive behind moonlighting is significant, an issue discussed in greater detail later in this chapter (see also chapter 1). Whereas in the USA in 1969 some 40 per cent of double job holders said that meeting regular expenses was their main motive for holding a second job, in 1974 this reason accounted for only 32 per cent of respondents, and fell further to 30 per cent in 1976. Following the purely economic motive, the second largest proportion of double job holders said that they worked at their second jobs because they enjoyed the work; some 20 per cent for both men and women in 1976.

On the whole, those in favour of double job holding are criticised by opponents. For example, governments in many countries attempt to discourage moonlighting because revenue is lost through tax evasion. However, if the extra hours of work do become a necessary input to economic growth, then a reversal of this position may be seen with governments perhaps even giving extra tax relief on second jobs to encourage this activity.

Secondly, trade unions fear that moonlighters may be unqualified to tackle certain jobs (e.g. car maintenance), and that moonlighting encourages people to work excessively long hours, representing a risk to themselves and others (e.g. taxi drivers), or encourages firms to take on part-time workers at lower rates of pay. Following trade union pressure in Belgium a new law was passed in 1976 aimed at making 'travail noir', including some moonlighting, illegal. This was also linked to the government's effort to reduce unemployment by work-sharing and removing possibilities of people holding two jobs. The Trade Union Congress in Britain may have to give greater thought to this subject in relation to their recent demands for work-sharing and a shorter working week.

Thirdly, many companies find that they cannot meet sudden increased demand in the traditional way by asking for extra overtime work because workers have left to work on their second jobs. This has become increasingly the case as new patterns of working time have emerged, and particularly with the rapid spread of 'flexi-time'. On the other hand, the hotel and catering trades in particular have found moonlighters a useful source of labour for the types of job they need to fill (see chapter 3).

In some countries workers such as police and firemen are prohibited by law from working at two jobs, although doubling as window cleaners or mini-cab drivers is a well known occurrence in Britain. A recent study of moonlighting amongst firemen and police in Wichita, Kansas, (Miller, 1972) has also illustrated the high incidence of second jobs held by people in these professions in the USA, with a rate of 76 per cent for the firemen and 39 per cent for the police.

Contrary to popular belief there are a number of reasons to suggest that holding a second job does not deprive the unemployed of first jobs. First, the American and British studies have all shown that over 30 per cent of second jobs are held in a self-employed capacity providing few opportunities for the unemployed whose skills and financial resources preclude them from taking on even a small business. Secondly, the location of jobs and job seekers needs matching by employment sector. While the greater proportion of second jobs are in the service sector (80-90 per cent based upon both FES data and the author's own survey work in Cardiff), this sector has been shedding labour in recent years in an area where new first jobs are needed. Thirdly, while most second jobs are held for only a small number of hours and therefore result in a low level of pay, the unemployed are seeking mainly full-time work. Data from the May 1978 Current Population Survey analysed by Bednarzik (1978) has shown that in the USA over 80 per cent of the unemployed were seeking full-time jobs, i.e. 35 hours.

An important characteristic of both the American and British labour force development has been the increase in the number of persons looking for part-time work. In Britain part-time employment as a proportion of the total labour force has increased from 10 per cent in 1961 to 19.2 per cent in 1975. In the USA, between 1950-1966 the number of unemployed persons seeking part-time jobs as a percentage of total unemployment rose from 5 per cent to 20 per cent, with the number of women growing at a faster pace than men. However, since 1966 the proportion of the unemployed seeking part-time work has dropped slightly, averaging some 17 per cent per year (1975-1978 inclusive).

While moonlighters may not be depriving the male unemployed of their first job, this may not be the case with unemployed women, who to a significant extent are seeking part-time work. One of the features of the labour force in Britain in recent years has been not only the increase in part-time jobs, held largely by women, but also the marked rise in females who register as unemployed. In Great Britain in 1974, 16.9 per cent of the unemployed were women; by 1978 this had increased to 31.3 per cent. Thus, one in three of the unemployed are now women, compared to one in six in 1974. A number of reasons may be cited for this increase in female registration for unemployment in recent years. Withdrawal of the married woman's freedom to 'opt out' of paying higher national insurance since 1976 enables women to qualify for unemployment benefit. Many part-time jobs which are largely held by women are lost in a recession such as Britain has been experiencing since 1974. Pay policies of recent years have placed limits on the incomes of many male employees and encouraged women to supplement family income. Finally, the movement for equal pay and opportunities for women has encouraged more women to seek work. However, there is not sufficient evidence currently available to assess the net balance of costs and benefits of moonlighting for the unemployed, i.e. job creation via increased spending versus job substitution of first jobs by second job holders (see chapter 4).

While a number of arguments can be cited both for and against people holding two jobs, it is important to recognise that it is more than just an issue of tax evasion. There are two other key aspects upon which interest in the practice of double job holding has focussed in both Britain and the USA. First, the interest in moonlighting has arisen largely as a reaction both to the relatively high levels of unemployment in recent years in western economies and the suggested solution that a reduction in the standard 40 hour week would ease this problem. The British trade unions have recently been examining work-sharing and cuts in standard work weeks to combat unemployment. Secondly, increasing interest is being shown in the phenomenon of moonlighting because of the future choice of a shorter working week and increased leisure rather than increased net output as a benefit of increased productivity. The Department of Employment (1975a) in Britain has estimated that in spite of an overall growth in the labour force, the total annual hours worked by 1991 may be lower than in 1971, owing to shorter hours, longer holidays and more part-time working. If the work rates of economically inactive persons prove difficult to raise, further increased emphasis may have to be given to the work rates of the more active in the workforce who take up second jobs. Targets of economic growth may increasingly have to depend on part-time workers such as the moonlighter.

Socio-economic characteristics of moonlighting and the motivation for holding two jobs

The Family Expenditure Survey has shown that the main feature of an industrial analysis of double job holding in Britain is the high proportion of second jobs held in the service industry. Although manufacturing industry covers 28 per cent of all jobs, it accounts for only 5 per cent of second jobs held in the service industry.

The highest rates of double job holding for both the GHS and FES are held by persons in the 20-45 year age group, and these rates show that a relatively high proportion of women hold two jobs. It has already been noted that in 1970 only 16 per cent of all American moonlighters were women compared to some 34 per cent of their British counterparts. By 1978 the American figure was similar to that for Britain, having doubled in eight years.

All the data on earnings from moonlighting confirms that double job holding in Britain is an activity pursued irrespective of the job status and earnings range, although, interestingly, it is higher at the upper and lower ends of the range. The American studies have also shown that double job holding is an activity spread across the whole earnings range, although again weighted most heavily at either ends of the earnings scale (see chapter 1).

Using the results of my 1973 survey of 4000 households in Cardiff, it has been possible to describe the economic and social characteristics of the double job holder, the motivation behind the activity, and the likelihood of non-double job holders' taking on a second job (Alden, 1977). According to the national data on primary jobs, double job holders in the Cardiff study were distributed throughout the earnings range. The study also found that 80 per cent of double job holders' main jobs were in service industry and 17 per cent in the manufacturing sector. The data on hours worked on the main job illustrated the energetic nature of many double job holders, often referred to as 'workaholics'. Indeed, 28 per cent of double job holders also worked overtime on their main job, giving an average of eight hours a week on overtime and an average of ten hours a week on the second job.

In the Cardiff study four groups of occupations accounted for 70 per cent of second jobs, these being sales workers, service occupations, professional and technical workers and teachers. The high incidence of second jobs held by teachers is a feature of moonlighting common to both Britain and the USA. The study found 90 per cent of second jobs held in the service industry sector and only 10 per cent in manufacturing. I found that half of the double job holders held a second job because they could not obtain paid overtime from their main job. Any attempt therefore to reduce the availability of overtime as an attempt to increase work-sharing may be expected to lead to increased moonlighting by those seeking to work extra hours.

One long-standing myth of the double job holder as 'moonlighter' may have been exploded by the Cardiff study in so far as it shows that second jobs are not only held at night. In the Cardiff study, 20 per cent of second jobs were held during weekdays, as compared to the 43 per cent done during week-evenings/nights. Given the changing patterns of working time, the term 'moonlighter' for the double jobholder may become an increasingly less accurate description of those who hold a second job.

With a standard working week of some $37\frac{1}{2}$ - 40 hours, some workers will be forced to work more hours per week than they would if they were free to adjust their work time according to their own personal level of satisfaction — with income relative to leisure. Such workers may be considered 'over-employed'. On the other hand, there are other workers who find that the standard working week prevents them from working enough hours in their main job to achieve the desired trade-off between income and leisure. These workers, including the moonlighter, may be considered therefore 'under-employed'. With standardisation of working hours in the formal economy, there is an inherent inefficiency as a result of this lack of flexibility. There are, however, a number of ways in which under-employed workers can reach their optimum position, one of which is by doing overtime and another by taking a second job.

This raises the question of why people hold a second job. Apart from my own study, little work has been undertaken in Britain on the moonlighter's motivation for holding two paid jobs. I found that over 65 per cent of double job holders gave 'economic' reasons as the primary motive for taking on a second job. The remaining 35 per cent of respondents gave some interesting responses. 17 per cent held a second job for social/interest reasons rather than for the money, and 10 per cent held a second job, initially at least, at a friend's request or to help somebody out, for example, to decorate a house or do carpentry work (see chapter 1). In both these cases, while the extra income was welcomed, the respondents were clear that the economic drive was not the primary factor involved. Interestingly, the younger age groups gave economic motives most frequently, with the highest figure of 75 per cent in the 21-25 year age group. Perhaps not surprisingly, double job holders with relatively low primary job earnings stated economic motives more frequently than those who derived high earnings from their main job.

The Cardiff study also asked those without two jobs if they would consider taking a second job and their reasons for why they had not got a second job at that time. Of all single job holders, 14 per cent replied that if a second job had been available at that time they would have taken one. This proportion rose to 20 per cent when figures were included for those who answered 'yes' to the question of whether they would hold a second job if one became available within the next twelve months or if they had a shorter working week or more flexible working hours. The analysis of single job holders showed that the three main reasons given for not taking on a second job were: a specified preference for leisure, sufficient hours already worked, and the needs of the family.

Holding a second job for purely economic motives is inversely related to both age and earnings on the main job in both the American and Cardiff studies. In the American research the numbers holding a second job for non-economic reasons increases markedly with both age and earnings, for both men and women, and this pattern was also confirmed by the findings of the Cardiff study.

Some brief reference may also be made to the extent to which people undertake unpaid work, i.e. voluntary work. The Cardiff study showed that 13 per cent of the single job holders did some form of unpaid work which was more than double the rate of employed people holding paid second jobs. Although the difference in the pay motive is an important one, so too is the allocation of time to work rather than non-work. In this context, therefore, voluntary work clearly has an important role to play in the overall allocation of time.

Second jobs and changing patterns of working hours

Over the past fifty years a marked change has taken place with regard to work and leisure. In the nineteenth century, reductions in long hours of work were opposed not only because of their possible cost and economic consequences but also on the grounds that leisure for workers was dangerous, leading to drinking and other undesirable pursuits. Today such attitudes are seldom expressed. The history of hours of work is primarily one of the introduction and spreading almost throughout the world of the notion of an eight-hour day or forty hour week. The eight-hour day was advocated by Robert Owen in 1817, and referred to by trade unionists and social reformers in a slogan 'Eight hours' work, eight hours' leisure, eight hours' sleep'. In recent years, owing largely to policies of full employment, workers have been able to choose, to some extent, between shorter hours and higher earnings, or a measure of both.

The Department of Employment (1975b) in Britain has recently illustrated the extent of innovations in patterns of working hours. These focussed upon more flexible working hours, the compressed work-week (popularly known in the USA as the 'four-day week') and staggered hours. Their report emphasised the diversity in patterns of working hours in Britain. Variations on the fixed 9-5 working day such as overtime, shift-work and part-time work, if not already firmly established, were expected to become more widespread in the future and to lead to greater double job holding. With more shift-work, variable work-weeks and rising economic aspirations, moonlighting may be expected to increase in importance in the future.

Riva Poor (1970) found that people in the USA working the four-day week schedule had a double job holding rate of 14 per cent compared to 4 per cent for those on normal five-day weeks. John Deiter's (1966) work on the Akron rubber industry in Ohio, which had operated a short work-week for many years, also found significant variations in moonlighting between those working normal and short work-weeks. In addition, the May 1974 American Current Population Survey showed that workers on four-day weeks were almost twice as likely as all full-time workers to hold a second job (8.6 per cent and 4.7 per cent respectively). Miller (1972) in his study of moonlighting in Wichita, Kansas, showed that while policemen had an overall moonlighting rate of 39 per cent, firemen had a corresponding rate of 76 per cent, the difference being accounted for by different work schedules. The high rates for both groups were due to shift-working, with firemen working 24 hours on duty and 48 hours off, compared to a five day/40 hours shift for policemen.

In May 1974, American CPS also collected data on the rates of double job holding for full-time male workers depending on the time of day they finished working at their primary jobs. Table 3.4 illustrates how finishing a primary job before 5.00 p.m. can provide increased opportunities to take up a second job. American studies, such as those by Janice Hedges (1975), have shown the importance of both the shorter working week and the flexible working week for double job holding.

TABLE 3.4 HOURS FOR WORK ENDING ON MAIN JOB AND RATES OF DOUBLE JOB HOLDING FOR MALES, MAY 1974, USA

Hour work ended	Double job holding rate
10.00 am – 1.00 pm	7.8%
2.00 am – 6.00 pm	4.5
7.00 am – 1.00 pm	11.3
2.00 pm – 3.00 pm	8.3
4.00 pm – 5.00 pm	5.8
6.00 pm – 9.00 pm	4.7

Source: May 1974 CPS, American Department of Labour

There have been suggestions that now flexi-time has won acceptance in the industrial world, several countries (e.g. Sweden, France and Germany) are examining 'flexi-year' schedules. Teriet (1977) has suggested that this is the next step in the process of breaking up conventional working-time structures. In West Germany, Haller (1976) has advocated a fixed amount of working hours per year per worker.

There are important economic and social implications of this new approach to working time, especially for increased female labour activity rates. Working-time flexibility is often a prerequisite for women to participate in the labour force. The notion of the 'working year contract' may help to overcome the segregation that arises from rigid working-time schedules, particularly between the labour markets for full-time and part-time jobs. In addition, the working-year contract may increase compatibility between work and non-work activities, and also between individual careers and family life. The major problems to be overcome in implementing any such scheme are firstly whether trade unions, employers and governments will encourage such arrangements and, secondly, whether work rules and regulations such as social security payments and benefits can be adapted to fit the new arrangements.

Conclusion

In conclusion, while most of the interest in double job holding, or moonlighting, has been developed in relation to economic factors, attention must be drawn to the social, physical and psychological aspects of double job holding, which may be considerable. To some people in both Britain and the USA, holding more than one job for reward represents a retrogressive practice which undermines efforts to obtain shorter hours and higher pay. Others contend that shortening the work-week will only lead to higher moonlighting rates. Others go further to say that people will be tempted to evade tax, that on-the-job accidents will increase because of fatigue caused by excessive hours of work, or that double job holding will lead to lower efficiency on main jobs. Many view double job holding as a threat to job security or rates of pay, arguing that if employers take on moonlighters at lower wages then regular workers are threatened with job loss, lower regular pay, or loss of overtime pay.

However, on the other hand, holding a second job may be seen as representing a freedom of choice, and an opportunity to raise living standards, restricted only by the marketability of one's skills and availability of one's time. Clearly, moonlighting has implications for central government manpower policy, for fiscal policy, in terms of government tax revenue, for companies, trade unions and all members of the workforce. There seems little doubt that we will hear more about the moonlighter in the future.

3
HIDDEN REWARDS AT WORK:
The Implications from a Study of British Hotels

Gerald Mars and Michael Nicod

Research currently being carried out at the Centre for Occupational and Community Research at Middlesex Polytechnic, England, suggests that there is a wide divergence between the informal benefits and the recognised rewards from work in many different industries. And all the evidence suggests that nowhere is there quite such a marked divergence as in hotels and catering – an industry noted for its long tradition of payment by the 'fiddle'. Yet as our research has progressed we have found that an initial interest in fiddled benefits has been superseded. It has led to an increased understanding of a whole range of variables affecting behaviour in this and in other service industries.

Information about the low wages in hotels and catering is continually being pressed upon us by the media and by trade unions, pressure groups, legislation, official reports and academic literature. Although concern about low pay in this industry is well meant, and is certainly valid for some workers, our research suggests that the formal aspects of pay represent only one part of the total income which other workers actually expect to earn. This is because whilst some workers benefit substantially from informal and sometimes illegal rewards others certainly do not. In our experience those who do benefit however, do so with the full collusion of management, and this kind of reward can be considered to be institutionalised.

The popular press and TV news editors have been as guilty as anyone of misleading us on this matter – in particular in their coverage of disputes in the industry concerning union recognition and unfair dismissals. Our research shows that these are often to do with perceived injustices in the allocation of *informal* rewards rather than with what they are projected as being about.

In spite of its notoriously low basic pay, the efforts made over the past thirty years by the major trade unions to organise this industry have been largely unsuccessful. According to a government report no more than thirteen per cent of those working in hotels and catering are unionised (NEDO, 1975). There have been various explanations for this surprisingly low unionism and, as Mars and Mitchell (1977) have argued elsewhere, the single most important reason is that union activists have been primarily concerned to appeal to the more permanent members of the workforce and do so by aiming to raise their basic pay. In doing this the unions have failed to take into account the nature and the extent of informal rewards which mainly benefit these key workers and which would be at risk if rewards were to be collectively set.

Like the unions, pressure groups such as the Low Pay Unit (1975), established to highlight the plight of low paid workers in general, only emphasize the formal aspects of people's income in industries like hotels and catering. And whilst there may be several reasons why the Wages Council has failed to determine minimum wage levels in this industry and has failed to achieve effective collective bargaining (Bayliss, 1962; Mitchell and Ashton, 1974), it seems fair to say that its failure is one of understanding. As with the trade unions and the Low Pay Unit, this too can be attributed to its being all too often insensitive to local labour and product markets, and, again, unaware of the levels of hidden reward paid to catering workers. Ironically, by stressing the general low level of wages in the industry each of these bodies does a singular disservice to those who are really at the bottom of the heap, who genuinely lack the opportunity to gain informal rewards, but whose fate is obscured by a misdirected emphasis on formal pay.

Government reports have consistently stressed both the high labour turnover rates in hotels (NEDO, 1969; 1975) and the low wages which the industry pays its labour (NEDO, 1975) without paying much attention to the value of hidden fringe benefits which underlie and obscure an understanding of both. NEDO has estimated for instance that of hotel and catering workers, 49 per cent of full-time adult men and 88 per cent of full-time adult women are paid below the level which can reasonably be said to constitute low pay (NEDO, 1975, p.13). But these figures are bound to be distorted because they ignore such things as free or subsidised food, accommodation, tips, fiddles and, most particularly, other perks which unofficially accrue to the hotel worker. When it comes to analysing and interpreting the amount of rewards which people actually take home, official statistics hardly tell us anything.

Nor do we find those who have done research in the industry a great source of enlightenment. For example, although William Foote Whyte's classic study of the restaurant industry in Chicago during the forties did not entirely overlook the importance of 'tips', 'service charge', 'bonuses' and other remunerations including pilferage, he seems to have concentrated largely upon the psychological satisfactions these practises offer, without considering their influence on patterns of workplace behaviour. For instance, he quotes a waitress as saying: 'You think of all the work you've done and how you've tried to please people. It hurts when they don't leave anything for you. You think, "so that's what they really think of me" . . . It's like an insult' (Whyte, 1948, p.98). He makes no reference at all, however, to the system of competitive privileges whereby one waitress is permitted more substantial benefits from tipping than another.

Bowey (1976), on the other hand, in her study of the British restaurant industry, took the analysis further by trying to show the relationship between the seasonal variation in tips and the level of labour turnover. She found that the fall in tips arising from seasonal fluctuations often resulted in staff moving from one restaurant to another in which they had friends who were able to find jobs for them. The most useful analysis of tipping to date is to be found in Philip Nailon's (1978) review of the practice of tipping, which he sees in terms of its value as a motivator, both for the recipient and the customer.

What both Bowey and Nailon have written about tips needs to be taken still further if the analysis is to include those informal aspects of hotel workers' income which do not appear to be quite legitimate. In spite of the important implications they have for the pattern of workplace relations, almost all published comment on the hotel industry has coyly neglected giving data on pilferage and theft, the numbers who benefit by its practice, the range and different types of fiddled benefits, and the values and attitudes which tend to be associated with its practice. Even in the kind of study involving in-depth participant-observation, where knowledge of its practice could hardly be ignored, no mention is made of the subject at all (e.g. Spradley and Mann, 1975; Bowey, 1976); or if mentioned, it is discussed in the most condemnatory way as something which 'with sufficient supervision ... will be detected in the long run' (Whyte, 1948, p.89).

This neglect is now giving way to a growth of interest in this branch of occupational studies though this has yet to be pulled together in any really systematic manner. One of our first accounts of the practice of colluding in occupational theft was based on ethnographic experience as a hotel waiter in Blackpool, an English seaside resort (Mars, 1973). Other occupations which have also received attention in this connection include bread salesmen (Ditton, 1977a); milkmen (Bigus, 1972); dockworkers (Mars, 1974); shopworkers (Robin, 1965; Franklin, 1975; England, 1973; 1976); and factory workers (Horning, 1970). But despite this recent interest, the area still remains largely un-developed. There are, for instance, no general principles which have emerged for identifying different kinds of pilferage or to show how they might be related to any ordered classification of occupations. One of our tasks has indeed been to find a way of classifying fiddles through study of the hotel industry, the research for which was carried out between 1976-79 with a grant from the UK Social Science Research Council. If the hypotheses which we have developed are correct, they should have important implications for occupational studies and industrial relations — not only in this industry, but in other service occupations too.

The basis of the study

The data to be discussed concerns a study of six British hotels varying in size, type and location and which is to be more fully reported elsewhere (Nicod, 1981; Mars and Nicod, 1981). Whilst we are aware of the dangers in generalising from such a limited sample, we eschewed the use of traditional survey methodology because the sensitive nature of the research precluded such techniques. Instead we felt it necessary to carry out the research primarily through participant-observation – a research method central to social anthropology, which in this case meant Nicod's absorption into the industry as a full-time working waiter for a little over one year. We did, however, consider some of the key survey variables in the selection of hotels: small/large; conglomerate/owner-managed; low/high prestige; urban/coastal/metropolitan, and we have discussed our findings with lecturers and students involved in this industry as well as with workers and managers outside the six hotels.

After a crash course from an experienced waitress and by posing as an ex-student with some experience as a waiter, Nicod succeeded in gaining entry as a *bona fide* waiter into each hotel for varying periods (the shortest was one month; the longest was three). Whilst at work he watched out for fiddles, participating whenever necessary but not asking too many questions and avoiding emotionally loaded topics until he had been there long enough. A kitchen porter, questioned too closely shortly after Nicod began work in the second hotel became suspicious, asking whether the researcher was 'one of those blokes working for the government'. In the first hotel a waitress who had found him deeply engrossed in Sutherland's *The Professional Thief* while off-duty knowingly remarked: 'Now I can see why you asked me all those questions about fiddling yesterday!' As the research developed, it became apparent that after about two weeks of a discreet and incurious presence a sufficient degree of acceptance could be achieved to enable relevant information to be gathered.

For the collection of data and its analysis we found it useful to use concepts previously developed on work in the hotel and catering industry; 'ad hoc management', 'individual contract making' and 'total rewards system' (Mars and Mitchell, 1976; 1977). 'Ad hoc management' refers to the approach in which a manager copes with the erratic demand on a hotel's services by short-term tactical responses – rather than by the strategic, controlled and regular managerial responses more typically found in manufacturing. In responding to such crises he makes individual deals with his workers. 'Individual contract making' is a term, therefore, referring to collusive arrangements between management and staff whereby the hotel's range of resources is *informally* distributed according to the individual bargaining power of each worker. Included under the term 'total rewards system' are *all* the elements of reward, both legitimately and illegitimately acquired and dispensed, as well as the notions and values underlying the way in which they are distributed in a particular hotel.

As our research progressed it became clear that there were two classes of hotel workers distinguishable by their individual bargaining powers. The first, 'core workers', tend to be relatively stable in their employment, and have full-time contracts. Their labour is considered vital for the smooth running of a hotel or restaurant. This would usually be achieved through acquiring professional expertise, reliability, length of service or alertness against errors during critical periods. The second category, 'peripheral workers', tend not to have full-time contracts and their labour is more often required on the basis of erratic demand for special occasions such as banquets and during busy periods of seasonal demand. The terms 'core' and 'peripheral' when applied to workers are not to be confused with full-time and part-time workers. It is mainly those whose informal rewards appear quite extensive who justify the description 'core'. 'Peripheral' workers, although they are apparently paid at the same rate, do not substantially benefit from fiddled reward.

Workers can normally expect to start as peripherals and then move, in time, to become core workers – even though in less prestigious establishments, they might well occupy the same formal position within the organisation. Of course this way of allocating real rewards allows the socially stigmatised such as blacks or women to be discriminated against without any legitimate complaint and it provides management with a potent source of control over its labour. Whilst management can move people to preferred working bases within a hotel, or to bars with considerable access to fiddles, they can also move people away from such preferred work slots as a sanction, thereby taking away their access to fiddles.

Together with the distinction between high and low prestige establishments these ideas constituted the principal analytic tools through which we examined the practice of pilferage in the six hotels. The implications of these concepts for management have been recorded elsewhere (Mars, Bryant and Mitchell, 1979).

The context of hotel pilferage

All organisations invoke controls which deny people full individual autonomy. But all organisations also posess what Goffman (1961, p.56) has called 'secondary adjustments' that do not directly challenge management but which allow staff 'to obtain forbidden satisfactions or obtain permitted ones by forbidden means'. For a relative newcomer to the job, secondary adjustments might consist of nothing more than a release from the more trivial aspects of prescribed conduct. On one occasion Nicod was reprimanded because he had been seen smiling in the restaurant. Although this did not really infringe any hard and fast rule, because he was newly employed as a 'commis' (i.e. the very lowest ranked waiter), it was considered necessary for rules proscribing minor acts of physical self-involvement to be applied at all times – at least until he was judged sufficiently competent to know when rule-breaking of this kind *was* permitted. He became accustomed to receiving instructions like: 'You must never pick your nose, never scratch your hair, never stroke your chin, never touch or put your hands anywhere near your face ... and you must always try to stand straight like Prince Charles.' It was not so much intended to put him in his place, but rather to make him fully aware of the minor deprivations which he would not ordinarily be expected to sustain later on.

There are other secondary adjustments, however, such as a waiter's practice of satisfying his family's needs for food from that which he helps serve. These become so much an accepted part of the workings of an organisation that they take on the character of perquisites, indulgences, 'knock-off' or 'fiddles'. Some of these practices must always remain unofficial and cannot become a legitimate part of work activity because, as Melville Dalton has pointed out, a special capacity of the work will often have to be underwritten with unofficial rewards that are given specifically for effort or merit beyond the normal call of duty. In fact what the worker may regard as bonus or perk is often deliberately allowed – often as an ad hoc 'one-off' indulgence by management who turn a blind eye for the sake of the organisation's overall efficiency (Dalton, 1964). A great deal of conflict and hostility between management and staff is concerned with the habitual tacit understanding of what both would expect, but neither would, in most cases want to frame, even unofficially; namely, where, between the two extremes, the line is to be drawn separating the officially accepted level of tolerance from the intolerable. Much of the ambiguity concerning management's definition of 'an acceptable level' had to do with the variations which are permitted according to the class of hotel and the waiter's position within it. But before we go on to discuss this matter further, it would be better to consider first some of the techniques involved.

Techniques and types of fiddling

One of the most common forms of hotel pilferage is often simply known as 'knock-off' – a term which among hotel workers refers to illicitly obtaining food or items such as soap, toilet paper, serviettes or tablecloths, that are intended for customers' use. Almost all hotel waiting staff are permitted to indulge in this type of fiddle, but the access to these rewards has a different distribution depending on the class of hotel, the techniques used and the type of worker using them. Peripheral workers mostly take only the relatively inexpensive items such as soup, sweets, and *hors d'oeuvres* which are left unguarded in the kitchen. Core workers, on the other hand, are likely to take more valuable items of food through an informal arrangement with kitchen staff or in exchange for a drink, a lift home, money, gifts, or a favour of one kind or another. Their greater degree of involvement at work allows the development of relationships and in many respects the goods which flow along these lines of relationship are secondary to the relationship themselves (Henry, 1978 and Henry and Mars, 1978).

In most cases what is taken as knock-off is nothing more than the food which hotel staff actually consume at work. But the provision of free food for staff in canteens reduces management's acceptable level of tolerance, even to the point where, in our second high-class London hotel it was common practice for anyone caught taking food from the kitchen to be charged the same amount as a customer. One waiter for example, was charged £2 for helping himself to strawberries and cream. Some, however, try to turn their quasi-legitimate rights in knock-off to greater advantage by also taking home what can be 'knocked-off' in order to satisfy their families' needs – in particular supplying them with staple foods such as bread, butter, sugar, jam, cheese, cream, tea-bags or breakfast cereals, because these can usually be taken unnoticed and transported easily. Finally, a few go still further and make a profession out of selling the proceeds of such involvements: buying, say, steak fillets for 50p each from a 'bent' chef and re-selling them at a profit to the café down the road. To avoid detection they would strap, say, a side of smoked salmon or fillet steaks to their leg, hidden beneath their trousers. One waiter in our first high quality London hotel helped to run two restaurants of his own partly on the supplies which he managed to obtain in this way. Such characters, however, are exceptional since they run the risk that anyone caught fiddling on such a scale can often find himself being prosecuted. In the same London hotel a kitchen worker was arrested during our fieldwork period and later prosecuted for taking a 5-gallon tin of cooking oil worth about £5. But as the pastry chef pointed out, it was not so much because he had taken something which did not really belong to him, but the fact that he had exceeded long established limits without seeking social approval that accounted for him having to pay the consequences:

Everyone fiddles a little in this business ... In fact you wouldn't be considered any good as a waiter if you weren't able to make a little on the side ... It's something we all do from time to time, only some are not so good at it as others. A few don't know how far you should go ... One thing you've got to learn is that you shouldn't be too greedy ... No one is going to mind much if you take just the small things ... but when you start to nick quite expensive stuff on a regular basis, as this man was, you can't expect the head chef or sous chef [who get paid a percentage of the profits] to stand still while you walk off with half their earnings.

'Money fiddles' is a term we use to refer to a distinct class of fiddle – often involving similar techniques to those used to obtain food illicitly but quite different from the practice of knock-off in that it provides staff with a direct cash benefit. In the typical lounge or dining-room the majority of money fiddles are practised at the hotel's expense leaving the customers unaffected and unaware. Basically these fiddles involve first getting food and drink past a checker or control clerk and second, serving exactly what the customer has ordered, and then pocketing the payment for it. Since a waiter must eventually account for every cheque he presents to the kitchen or stillroom, his problem is to obtain food and beverages without a cheque. One solution is to introduce items which he has purchased outside the hotel so that a profit can be made when they are sold at the hotel's higher prices. This type of fiddle is most often practised by wine waiters. At the second north coast hotel we studied one such waiter regularly filled the boot of his car with £150 worth of wine, beer, and spirits so that he could sell them to customers. Another way round the problem is to charge customers for food or drink obtained as knock-off. An example is of a lounge waiter who had worked several years in the same hotel and who developed the practice of removing a gateau from the dining-room every Sunday, and cutting pieces from it which were then sold to the innocently unsuspecting guests in the lounge. Again this is a fiddle commonly practised by wine waiters who, for instance, pour the left-over wine from people's bottles into a carafe which they then sell as 'house-wine'.

Perhaps the most common type of fiddle, is for waiting staff to form an alliance with either kitchen staff, the restaurant manager, or a control clerk, to provide the access and support which they need for practising undetected pilferage. As already mentioned, the kitchen staff may be 'bought off', granted favours, or otherwise persuaded to provide access to food for a waiter's knock-off. This food can then be sold to hotel guests who are charged the normal price for it and the waiter pockets the full amount. More often the chef or kitchen staff who collude with waiting staff in this way receive a percentage of the illicit takings usually sharing on a 50/50 basis anything that they earn from pilferage.

Even though their awareness of much of what goes on helps to institutionalise its practice, higher management is normally outside this fiddle system. On the other hand, the more lucrative dining-room fiddles do involve one or more waiters in some kind of alliance with the restaurant manager or head waiter. He can provide both the services to facilitate pilferage and the protection against higher management if anything goes wrong. A practice which we found occurring frequently for instance, was one in which a restaurant manager encouraged some of his casual staff to give false names and addresses in order to evade tax. A similar fiddle is the practice of hiring less casual staff than the number which is actually put down on the account books and giving false names and addresses to prevent detection. The restaurant manager and the head waiter, who both have some responsibility for hiring and firing staff, can then pocket the amount which should really have gone to the extra staff they did not employ.

By and large, dining-room money fiddles primarily involve taking the cash paid by customers for the food and service they receive. But as Nailon (1978) has pointed out in the context of a discussion of tipping, the manager's allocation of customers to stations (i.e. sets of tables) may be crucial. By manoeuvering those customers seen as potentially high tippers on to a particular station a head waiter is able to benefit a particular waiter. And it is similarly so in the case of fiddles. By manoeuvering non-residents to a particular station a head waiter is able to channel fiddled benefits to the waiter of his choice. Whereas residents usually pay for their meals by cheque at the end of their stay and are therefore not good for fiddles, most non-residents pay cash to the waiter serving them. Such non-resident customers who are good for fiddling are known as 'chance'.

Sets of tables which chance customers are most likely to find attractive, such as those near a window with a view, or those away from the clatter and smell of the kitchen are therefore desirable to a waiter intent on maximising fiddles. Thus allocating these to waiters might become a matter for favouritism by the restaurant manager whose strategy is basically to provide his core workers with the best stations. 'Best' in this sense means best both for tips and for fiddles. In return for 'kickbacks', the head waiter or restaurant manager is then expected to service his chosen stations in such a way that their waiters' earnings can be maximised to their mutual benefit

Perhaps, though, the greatest opportunities for money fiddles are those practised by bar staff and wine waiters. As well as the more simple forms of pilferage, such as over-charging and short-changing, there is a wide range of fiddles of an increasingly complex and lucrative nature in which bar staff and wine waiters are able to engage. Unlike the lounge and dining-room fiddles which have been described, these fiddles are not usually at the expense of the hotel, but at the expense of customers. Most involve trying to 'short measure' or to 'pass off' less expensive beer, wine, or spirits as the more expensive kind ordered by the customer, and then charging the full amount so that the waiter can pocket the difference in price. A waiter, for instance, who receives an order for bottled beer can usually get away with serving an ordinary draught beer which costs 4p less. Similarly he can pour cheap wine into a bottle bearing the label of a more expensive one, and then again can pocket the difference in price. Or if he receives an order for an orange juice, he can easily get it from the supply kept on tap in the kitchen but charge the customer the full price of a more expensive bottle of orange.

A large number of bar fiddles are based upon short measures or watering down, but perhaps the best known and most frequently practised fiddles are at banquets. Should, for example, a table order 12 bottles of wine, only 11 bottles may in fact be served. The larger the numbers involved, the greater the ambiguity and the greater the likelihood of fiddles. Another commonly practised fiddle in bars is to dilute the bottles of spirits from which people are served so that each bottle can then be used to serve more than the number for which the hotel expects to receive payment. Alternatively if a waiter receives an order for, say, two gin and tonics, he can pour a single measure into two glasses, and then conceal the fact by adding more tonic than usual.

The enormous range of fiddles which we have found have a common feature: they are acts of dishonesty that the people involved do not consider to be dishonest. What underlies this notion is an unwritten code, not so easy to discern, in which there are limits beyond which it is considered inappropriate for a particular person in a particular situation to benefit from fiddling (Mars, 1974). This is why tacit understandings and double dealings between management and staff are often necessarily so complex. As a wine waiter in an extremely prestigious hotel put it when questioned by the restaurant manager about the loss of a bottle of wine and a corkscrew belonging to a party of VIP customers:

Well you know that I nick things . . . I know that you know that I nick things . . . but I don't nick things when it's someone important . . . or, if I do, I make bloody sure that no one knows that something has been nicked!

Implications and conclusions

Mars and Mitchell's (1976) original hypotheses about institutionalised hotel pilferage did shed light on the significance of hotel workers' fiddling and the idea of core and peripheral workers led us to examine the different careers of workers in varied kinds of setting. As our research developed, however, it became clear that the limits and choices within which individual contracts are negotiated necessarily form part of a much wider concern. What we needed was a model that would enable us to examine the idea of individual contract making, together with the values and understandings that underlie its practice. And such a model too, needs to take account of the much wider cultural and structural context of which it is a part. Though these considerations are beyond the scope of this chapter and are discussed more fully elsewhere (Mars and Nicod, 1981) we can, however, abstract from this model the variables we found that determined managements' acceptable level of tolerance and the proportion of the labour force which can be considered 'core'. The most important variables concerned the class of hotel, the individual's position within it and the degree to which rewards were bureaucratised.

In prestigious hotels the emphasis in allocating reward is based on technical skill and professional expertise and staff are graded according to these criteria. In a top class hotel for instance, there might be no fewer than five levels involved in serving a single customer. It is therefore, easy in this situation to create a system of ranks which are based on skill and through which rewards can be offered. In these hotels we find a pyramidal structure that is broad as well as tall, with the base containing the majority who are peripherals under training and with the peaks of the pyramid containing the core. It is the core and only the core who are granted significant access to fiddled benefits – as much to boost differentials as to retain their goodwill. They represent a relatively small proportion of the labour force in their hotels, and their career progressions are relatively slow.

In hotels below this top prestige level – and this covers the majority of the industry – the position is more complicated since a wider variety of structures exists, but, on the whole, the emphasis on ranking by skill levels is less pronounced. Instead the emphasis is less on service *per se* and more on *speed* of service, on the ability to cope in critical periods, on reliability and on personal loyalty. In these lower level hotels differential rewards – no less necessary to distinguish the skilled and the fast, the reliable and the loyal, from the unskilled, the slow and the erratic – are essentially offered either through informal means – that is through fiddles – or through bureaucratic ranking. With both responses we found that the proportion of core workers is higher than in the prestigious hotels and that the speed of their transition from the periphery is much greater. This is not surprising since it takes longer to learn and demonstrate that one has mastered a craft than it does to show one can work quickly, reliably and loyally.

Staff in lower class hotels were therefore found to be less 'craft' or professionally oriented than those in prestigious hotels. Where rankings were fluid and ambiguous, staff were more concerned as *entrepreneurs* to maximise their return for 'effort' in the short term — which means their return from fiddles. There are often movements from these hotels by groups of core staff who will follow a boss from one hotel to another in order to maintain their individual contracts. Loyalty therefore, tends to be to people — that is to individual contract makers — and not to the organisation.

Where managements have tried to remove the ambiguities that come from a fluid ranking structure, they have typically tightened up on fiddles and have formalised rewards. Such hotels offer a ranking system but it is one based more on length of service than on function and skill, and they tend to pay increments. These transfer loyalty from individual contract makers to the employing hotel. This response is often found where hotels are a part of larger groupings — a growing tendency in this industry. It is these hotels that are most liable to unionisation and other forms of collective action because their rewards both exclude entrepreneurial incentive and at the same time are collectively set. They may be said to develop a *bureaucratic* response to the allocation of rewards with effective control over resources often lodged outside the hotel in their group's office.

The hotels also varied considerably in the attitudes taken by their staff to work, in their staff's 'loyalty' to the hotel, and in their patterns of labour turnover. None of these features can be understood without understanding the role played by the operation of their total reward systems. Whereas 'entrepreneurs' will move *en bloc* and 'bureaucrats' will tend to stay with a particular hotel or group, we found that in the most prestigious hotels, where most of the labour force were peripheral workers, there was a short-term commitment to the hotel. These 'craftsmen' regarded their stay as an apprenticeship that deferred their greater rewards until then. They were much more likely to refer to their personal identity in terms of career progression, to emphasise their professionalism and pride in craft, to say they were working 'for the reference' and to accept their relatively low basic pay and lack of access to fiddles as part of the price of this progression.

Our preliminary findings, therefore, can be said first to emphasise variations within this industry and second to underline the importance of how total rewards are allocated within it. We are only able, here, to sketch our findings in the broadest of outlines but what we have found are at least three distinct categories of hotels each with different proportions of core and peripheral workers. These workers typically have different kinds of career, and for each there is an appropriate response to their work and its rewards. We have termed these responses craft, entrepreneurial and bureaucratic. These differences have implications for the industry's pattern of industrial relations and they vitally affect matters such as labour turnover and unionisation. Other work being carried out at the Centre for Occupational and Community Research, Middlesex Polytechnic, suggests that these implications extend also to other industries, particularly those in the personal service sector. They are implications, however, that cannot be understood if we ignore these industries' informal institutions.

4
WORK OUTSIDE EMPLOYMENT:
Some Preliminary Speculations

J. I. Gershuny and R. E. Pahl

A future without jobs?

It is now common ground that, on present trends, and without radical changes in public policy, opportunities to work in 'the economy' may be expected to decline within Britain. The rate of decline to be expected, and the time-scale over which it occurs, are both matters of debate. The decline itself is assumed even by the most optimistic participants in the debate. But what are the implications of this decline for the organisation of our society? Are we to expect rising unemployment, or may we, in the long term, hope to share out the decline in paid work through a reduction in working hours? In this chapter we go beyond that position to argue that the problem involves a radical rethinking of what we mean by 'the economy' and the nature of the different kinds of work that go on in society. Only by bringing together employment in the 'formal economy' with all the other different sorts of economic activity that take place outside it can we be in a better position to devise appropriate public policies.

It may be helpful to start by spelling out, in a rather simplified and abbreviated form, the arguments underlying the consensus about the future reductions in work opportunities. The central concept is of growth in the productivity of labour in manufacturing industry – increase in the output of manufactured products, adjusted for the number of people employed in manufacturing, holding other sorts of employment constant. It is obvious that if full employment is to be maintained, the rate of growth of productivity must be matched by a similar growth in demand for the products of employment. However, over the last two decades, throughout the developed world, productivity in manufacturing industry has grown faster than the demand for manufactured products. (Between 1960 and 1975 productivity in the UK grew by 3.6 per cent while demand grew by 2.2 per cent; in the USA productivity grew by 3.6 per cent and demand by 2.5 per cent; and in Germany 4.9 per cent as against 3.5 per cent). The result has been, in each case, a decline in the proportion of the workforce employed in manufacturing.

This decline did not lead initially to rising unemployment. As jobs were lost in manufacturing, so jobs increased in the service sector, particularly in that part which was publicly financed. There is a fairly direct casual connection here; although the interpretation of Keynesian 'demand management' policies is of spending public money in order to stimulate the economy and thereby to increase employment indirectly, a large proportion of public expenditure has gone *directly* into the establishment of permanent jobs in education, medicine, social services and administration. Thus it may be said that those countries which have in the past maintained fully employment have done so through a growing public subsidy of the service sector. However it would be less controversial to suggest that for an increasing number of developed states throughout the 1960s and for all the developed world for the first half of the 1970s, full employment has meant the transfer of jobs from the high productivity manufacturing sector into the low productivity service sector.

The economists' conventional view of the association between productivity growth of about 1.7 per cent (Clark, 1979). Growth in relationship': growth in productivity being positively correlated with growth in output. On the basis of historical data, it appears that when there is no growth in output we can expect a productivity growth of about 1.7 per cent (Clark, 1979). Growth in output per worker without growth in total output must, assuming wages and profits are maintained, mean a decline in employment. In addition, if output increases, productivity also increases, although not in strict proportion (the UK data suggests that for each 1 per cent increase in output, productivity will increase by about 0.7 per cent), so that output growth does finally catch up with productivity growth – but only at around 6 per cent per year, which is a much faster economic growth rate than we have in the past achieved, and certainly not credible for the UK in any foreseeable future. This means that employment in manufacturing could only be *stabilised* under the condition of an implausibly high economic growth rate – so we must expect the decline in employment to continue.

There are, however, reasons for suspecting that even this sad view is too optimistic. The economists' forecasts are based on historical data and therefore project past relationships between output and productivity into the future. But there are reasonable *a priori* grounds (including speculation about the implications of the 'micro-processor revolution') for assuming that this relationship is changing to give higher rates of productivity growth for a given rate of output growth – so that the rate of growth of output necessary to maintain manufacturing employment may, in the future, be even higher than the 6 per cent suggested by the historical data. Some recent empirical research does seem to support this hypothesis of an *acceleration* in productivity for any given level of output growth. The historical data may also systematically underestimate the productivity growth rates specifically associated with low rates of output growth. There is some evidence for suggesting that in the past low productivity rates reflected 'labour hoarding' – the retention of workers during a recession, either in anticipation of a future upswing in the economy, or as a result of government subsidy. But if we move into a longer term recession, voluntary hoarding becomes less likely. Since the stated intention of the present government's policy is to do without public subsidies for 'disguised under-employment', then quite apart from the effect of technical change, the future is likely to show higher rates of productivity growth associated with low output growth than our historical experience would suggest.

The Verdoorn relationship underlies the employment forecasts from both the major economic models (those of the Treasury and the Cambridge Department of Applied Economics) of the UK economy. Therefore we would suggest that forecasts from these models should be viewed as erring on the side of optimism.

We will return in a moment to consider the possibilities there may be in the future for staving off unemployment through such schemes as subsidies for manufacturing jobs or extension in the service sector. But before doing so, we should consider the possibility of a response to unemployment based on work outside the formal economy.

The informal economy

One attractive response to this view of the future is simply to deny that it constitutes a problem. Modern states have effective welfare systems, which enable people to maintain themselves without working. Technological advance, together with a large stock of productive capital equipment, means that the material necessities of life can be provided while employing only a very small proportion of the available labour. Furthermore, with technological advance have come changes in social organisation which encourage productive activity outside 'the formal economy', either on a non-monetary basis such as in housework or 'do-it-yourself' or on a very small scale, locally traded basis as with 'the black economy'; and these same technical advances have created a greatly enlarged set of options for leisure and social activity to the whole of the population. So why should we not immediately begin designing a 'culture of unemployment'?

For some time we have been developing an argument of this sort (Gershuny, 1978). Our discussion starts with the 1960s view of the future of the developed world. We have been told repeatedly that we are moving towards a 'service economy' – an economy in which the bulk of employment is in the service sector where people are employed in the production of non-material commodities which would constitute the bulk of the society's consumption, and the only growing class of consumption, desires for material goods having been satiated. But when we look carefully at the pattern of development of the service industries over the last few decades, we find that this prediction is not supported by the facts. Certainly, some service functions have been growing throughout the developed world – but these are largely functions, such as medicine and education, which are dependent on a significant proportion of public finance. Other service functions, those which are normally purchased privately by households, have not been growing as fast as predicted, and indeed in the UK have declined considerably as a proportion of household expenditure.

The reason for this change is perfectly clear. Instead of buying services, households are increasingly producing their own, or more precisely, they buy goods, which are in effect capital equipment, to which they add their own labour in the production of services. Instead of going to the laundry, or employing servants, we use our washing machines and clean our own houses with ever more efficient electrical appliances. We no longer buy transport services; but we buy motorcars and drive them ourselves. We go less frequently to the cinema and watch television instead. Moreover, these changes occur for the most rational of economic motives. As incomes become more evenly distributed, it becomes more difficult to buy other people's time to produce services for us, and service production is very labour intensive. As production gets more efficient, the price of productive capital and materials, and therefore goods, falls relative to that of labour. Under these conditions rational economic man will divert his work activities from earning money to buy services, to a combination of working for money to buy goods, and unpaid work, using the goods purchased to produce services for himself.

This pattern of development has important implications. First, as the relative prices of goods and services continue to change, so increasingly final production of services is transferred out of the money economy into the household; therefore the importance of the money economy as a generator of welfare declines as a proportion of real social welfare. The conventional indicators of production in the formal money economy such as those used to compile Gross Domestic Product become less appropriate as indicators of the population's affluence. Second, we have a transfer of work out of the money economy into the household. Work that might previously have been generated in the money economy, is instead developing outside of it. Our present stage of economic development appears to be one in which jobs are displaced, not only by automation within 'the formal economy', but also by export into an 'informal economy'.

This brings us to the second element in our argument. Household production is not the only sort of informal economic activity. The second kind of informal economy is known by a number of essentially synonomous titles: the 'black economy', the 'hidden economy', the 'subterranean economy', the 'dirty pound note economy' (recent research suggests that this should be amended to, at the least, the 'dirty fiver economy'), the 'irregular economy', and many others, all referring to the same phenomenon, which seems to be widespread throughout the developed world. This 'hidden production' of goods and services, although not entirely for money, evades, wholly or partly, the systems of public regulation and taxation.

There are a number of reasons for the development of this sort of economic activity at our present stage of development. Possibly the strongest is related to rising levels of unemployment. The classical economic view of the effects of unemployment is that wage rates should fall, lowering the price of labour intensive commodities, and thus increasing demand for labour until full employment is restored. But the institutions of the modern state prevent this process: trade unions fight to maintain wage levels; social security and unemployment payments place a floor to wage levels; and employment protection and the rising non-wage costs of employing labour dissuade employers from taking on more workers. However, since it is the institutions of the state which prevent the classical equilibrium to the extent that the institutional regulations may be evaded, this view will hold good.

Another reason for the development of hidden economic activity is closely related to the development of the household production sector. Just as with household production, a significant factor is the declining costs of tools – particularly power tools – and appliances, together with the development of new materials whose use requires lower levels of skill. High prices for productive equipment constitute a barrier to own-account working, and conversely, when equipment prices fall, it becomes easier to be self-employed. Self-employed workers find it easier to evade formal regulations. Therefore cheap tools – and cheap hiring facilities – encourage the black economy.

Finally, we must not forget the personal benefits accruing from this sort of employment. Workers in the black economy, particularly those working as contractors for households, such as construction workers, have a considerable degree of personal autonomy. Even those working in more constraining circumstances, such as outworkers in the clothing industry, still have a considerable degree of flexibility in their patterns of work, particularly where the income from this employment is supplementary rather than the main income of the household. Conversations with people working in the black economy suggest that personal autonomy is a critical factor in their choice of this way of life (see chapter 1).

Seen in the perspective we would adopt, economic development is not a one-way progress from reliance on primary production through manufacturing production to a society whose major efforts are devoted to the production of services. Nor is there a single 'great transformation' from a society in which economic relationships are based on custom, in which such processes of exchange as exist are generalised, to a modern society in which an increasing proportion of social relationships are monetised, converted from generalised to specific exchange. Rather, we argue that technical innovation, changes in capital endowments and modifications in legal institutions and in patterns of organisation combine to produce a rather less tidy pattern of development. Instead of the steady one-way flow of economic activity from the household to the industrial production system, we see a whole series of little transformations of production, perhaps taking place simultaneously, between the formal economy, the household sector and the underground sector, whose directions are determined by the particular social and technical conditions relating to the production of particular commodities at particular times (see Table 4.1).

TABLE 4.1 RELATIONSHIPS BETWEEN FORMAL, INFORMAL AND HOUSEHOLD ECONOMIES

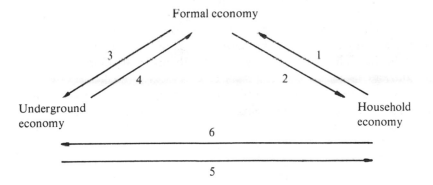

It is not possible to spell out in detail here each of the six possible categories of transformation between one sector and another, but we can provide some examples. The two-way flow between households and the formal economy is illustrated by the way in which the washing of clothes and linen moved from the wash-house at home, into the laundry and then back into the home with the technological help of a washing machine. The current prevalence of household construction work paid for in cash, may indicate a transformation (no. 3 in the Table) from formal to underground production. Similarly if unemployment levels were to rise, leading to a further lowering of prices for black construction work, we would expect a growth in demand for the products of this sector from households who otherwise might have 'done it themselves' (an example of transformation no.6). While it is still true that economies of scale and the division of labour encourage growth in the formal economy, equally, cheap consumer capital goods and high service wages encourage household production. At the same time high tax levels together with labour market inflexibilities promote the underground economy.

At a time when there is discussion about the 'de-skilling' of the work force in the formal economy, there may be a re-skilling in the informal economy. Some, who in the past might have called in a plumber or a carpenter, are more ready to try to do the job for themselves. The publication of a vast range of books on everything from re-upholstery to car-maintenance has enabled many people to acquire skills without the need to attend courses of formal instruction. 'How to' books sell well and widely and democratise skills in the informal economy. As people who sell their skills put up their rates, so those who might previously have purchased them must increasingly use and develop their own skills. Hiring a cook or a chauffeur has always been limited to a minority. The same is now coming to apply to carpenters and glaziers.

Our argument quite simply is that, at any time, the particular circumstances – of technology, labour supply, and public regulation and organisation – which pertain to the production of any commodity, may lead to a wide range of different sorts of transformation. Certainly over the last two hundred years the *aggregate* effect has been an overall transformation from household/communal production to formal industrial production. It may well be that the most significant transformations in the future will be from the formal economy to the underground economy and the household economy.

We are describing here a spontaneous process whereby working for money, in 'formal employment', is replaced by a less formal pattern – *it requires us to enlarge our notion of work to embrace a much wider set of activities than are usually considered in this context.* This might easily be seen as approaching the utopian goal of constructive, social functional unemployment. But while informal economic activity in itself presents some highly desirable characteristics – autonomy, variety, greater use of personal skills and initiative and so on – we recognise that involuntary participation for those who would prefer to be formally employed, and the growth of the criminal parts of the informal economy are highly undesirable. However, the informal economy need not necessarily have such undesirable aspects if, as we urge, appropriate public policies are formulated. We shall return to this in the concluding section.

The differential impact of unemployment

The essence of the problem that concerns us is the distribution of access to jobs in the formal economy. If it were the case that people were in practice free to choose what proportion of their time to spend in formal work, and what proportion in informal activities, then the developments we are describing could be un-equivocably welcomed as a positive response to the problem. But unfortunately this is not the case. Access to jobs in the formal economy is irregularly distributed across the population, and the impact of the current pattern of technical innovation is likely to accentuate this irregularity.

Probably the most significant irregularity is between the sexes. Women's employment is very highly concentrated into a very small range of occupations. These occupations are themselves predominantly in unskilled or semi-skilled assembly work, or in subordinate clerical functions. In service industry, the majority of employment is again in clerical jobs, and where women are found in more senior professional occupations, it is overwhelmingly in the low status professions of school teaching, nursing and social work. The part-time working pattern frequently found in female employment in manufacturing industry makes these jobs insecure. Since women's occupations in the service industries are concentrated in the public sector, the growing opposition to public expenditure makes women disproportionately vulnerable. Most importantly, technical change in production processes – particularly the micro-processor related innovations of automatic assembly in manufacturing industry and word processors in the service sector – attack the heartland of women's employment.

More generally, these inequities can be observed along

occupational – and hence class-lines. Demand for those with technical qualifications is still healthy and will continue to be so. Though demand for professional workers may from time to time be affected by events such as public spending cuts, nevertheless, we might expect jobs to become available. In aggregate, unemployment is heavily concentrated on those with redundant skills, or with no skills whatsoever. Those with low levels of education and training spend longer unemployed, and keep their jobs for shorter periods than those better provided with skills. The costs of the decline in work opportunities are borne disproportionately by those of lower status in the society. Perhaps more importantly, access to jobs is also regionally maldistributed. It is well established that economically peripheral areas are hit disproportionately hard by the downswings of economic cycles. The pattern of industrial re-organisation experienced in Britain – of industrial mergers undertaken for financial and commercial reasons rather than to take advantage of techno-economic advantages of scale – also has impacts on the regional irregularities of access to employment. This pattern of industrial concentration means that numbers of manufacturing establishments are owned by single firms; where markets decline it is frequently more rational for firms to close single establishments – so unemployment becomes locally concentrated, rather than diffused across the country.

So, rather than being able to *choose* work categories, particular social groups are forced to *accept* unemployment through the specific patterns of incidence in reduction of work opportunities. Even more seriously, those groups who are made unemployed are often those in most need of jobs in the formal economy. Women need formal jobs, not just for financial reasons, but also as an alternative to enforced participation in informal economic activity within the household. Those of low social status are often also those the least well equipped with the skills necessary for productive and rewarding informal activities. Those regions and local areas with the highest levels of unemployment are frequently those with the poorest social infrastructure – and the very fact of high unemployment means relative local poverty, and hence restricted markets for 'black economy' products and services.

Though, viewed in aggregate terms, we can speculate that the development of informal economic activities might compensate for jobs lost in the formal economy, this cannot, in the form in which it is currently encountered, be said to constitute an equitable response to unemployment. A pattern seems to be emerging in which a formal economy exists in parallel with an informal economy. Political and economic power still seems to be vested entirely within the formal economy, and we must not lose sight of the possibility that its relationship with the informal may develop along the lines of the informal's dependency on and exploitation by the formal rather like those encountered in dual economies in the third world.

We must be careful not to overstate our misgivings. We have each undertaken studies in urban areas which reveal buoyant communities coping with job losses through informal economic activity. We all know middle-class individuals who have made successful transitions from full-time formal work to some less conventional combination of job, domestic or communal production, and black economic activity. But these do not in themselves add up to a case for complacency about a future of rising unemployment. Our argument is that with appropriate public policies the informal economy may be adapted to socially progressive ends. In the next section we shall try to show that conventional policies for supporting formal employment must be either unsuccessful or politically objectionable. This leaves only the promotion of the informal economy – *undertaken simultaneously with 'job-sharing'*.

Should we protect jobs?

We can identify three different sorts of scheme currently proposed for job protection: subsidy of manufacturing jobs, subsidy of service jobs, and import controls.

Subsidising employment in manufacturing industry means supporting the inefficient use of labour. Certainly, as a short-term response to cyclical fluctuations, this could be defended, both on social grounds, and as a means of enabling firms to retain trained manpower for future efficient production. But as a longer term strategy this could only have harmful effects. Firms would institutionalise the inefficient working patterns and would rely, as technical change continues, on increasing subsidy in order to maintain their competitive position against foreign competitors, who would increasingly claim that the subsidy was an unfair commercial practice. The subsidy would become increasingly costly, demanding higher public expenditure and thus taxation and so probably provoke public opposition to the policy. We say 'probably' because there is an unknown here. Could people be persuaded to accept full employment as part of their 'social wage'? This sort of subsidy would finally emerge as a process whereby people agree to forego increases in direct welfare in order to maintain other people in work. And since these subsidies would be likely to spread right across the industrial spectrum it would be increasingly difficult to tell who is subsidising whom; the inefficiency of the production process under these conditions would eventually lead to a more or less explicit espousal of protectionism. Our guess is that full employment will not be acceptable as part of the social wage, so the extent of possible subsidies is strictly limited.

The argument for encouraging inefficiency does not apply directly to a policy of supporting employment in the service industries. Services are not in general traded internationally – so subsidies do not directly affect competitive performance. But there is already opposition to increases in public spending on services, and, if people find difficulty in accepting increases in health, education or cultural services as additions to their social wage, there is little prospect that they will be able to incorporate the provision of employment for others in producing these services into their social wage. So again, public opposition to growth in public expenditure is likely to place a limit on possibilities for this category of employment subsidy. Even if it were possible to pursue this option, the effects of the resulting high tax levels on incentives and wage claims would be such as to make manufacturing industry more inefficient more vulnerable to foreign competition, and thus produce pressures towards protectionism.

The third strategy, of maintaining jobs through protectionism, does not initially seem to raise the issue of taxation to support other people's employment, on which the first two strategies would founder. If we simply raise tariff barriers to stop the export of jobs from inefficient, low productivity British firms to efficient, high productivity foreign ones, there would be no visible payments by productive individuals to support unproductive ones in employment. But how would we run such a closed economy? If we were simply to allow market forces to work within it, then there would be every probability that we should find exactly the processes of technological unemployment that we are trying to avoid – albeit happening a little more slowly than under free trade. To avoid this we would either have to adopt some sort of job subsidy which, we have already argued will be unacceptable, or else adopt some form of direct control over labour-displacing innovation, which would theoretically be possible under protectionism. But this latter contains a hidden process of subsidy, insofar as potential innovators (and their customers) would be foregoing the potential welfare benefits of the proscribed innovations – which could only provoke public opposition and widespread evasion.

This is obviously an inadequate statement of the case against the various sorts of formal employment support. We can only hope that the brief discussion suggests to the reader the two propositions that lead us to reject these strategies: that subsidising employment leads directly or indirectly to inefficiency, loss of international competitiveness and to protectionism; and that subsidies are, and import controls lead to, processes of subsidy of the un-productively employed by the productively employed – a situation to which the productively employed will not willingly accede.

So, we cannot protect jobs, nor, as we argued in the previous section, can we accept the current pattern of distribution of unemployment. Where can we go from here?

Towards an alternative

While there may be some scope for protecting some jobs by increasing the efficiency and hence the international competitiveness of the process of productivity, this cannot be expected to make much impact on the problem. This locates the issue precisely. We cannot escape the development of some form of dual economy – so we must set about designing an acceptable form of it. If we are to avoid a society divided within itself, not only between those with well-paid work in the formal economy and those low-paid marginal workers also in the formal economy, but also between all those in formal employment and those engaged only in informal work, then a much more flexible approach to how all work gets done needs to be developed. Attempts to get a better range of mixes of different types of work, which would open up more choices for individuals and households, raise a whole range of problems and questions and it is to these we now turn.

Basically we are concerned with changes in the societal, the familial and the life-cycle division of labour. There have, of course, been substantial shifts already. No longer do we have, for example, a universal sex-linked division between the male 'chief earner' in the formal economy and his unpaid and dependent wife engaged in unremunerated housework. Nor is there such a rigidly sex-linked division of labour between men and women in the practice of domestic work. However, there are still anomalies in the way unemployment and other benefits are paid differentially to men and women, based on assumptions of the ultimate financial responsibility of the male and reflecting out-dated patriarchal values. Referring back to our diagram of the transformation between the three economic spheres, it is clear that at a societal level work must get done in the formal, the informal and the household economies. The question we are raising is how, for individuals and households, a range of satisfactory mixes of involvement in these three spheres may be arranged. Individuals and households should have a greater choice in the way they allocate their time and effort between these three spheres than they have had in the past. Certainly we would not wish to encourage the development of a world where individuals were tied, throughout their lifetime, to work in only one of these spheres.

From our perspective a policy aimed simply at greater job sharing raises more problems than it solves. *We argue that it is not possible to consider the question of sharing jobs in the formal economy without considering the sharing of jobs in the domestic economy as well.* Should jobs be kept in the formal economy, but simply reduced in time and shared amongst more employees, or should such jobs be taken over completely by the informal or communal economy? Do we, for example, create more social workers with each doing less work or do we rearrange the tasks the present social workers do to reduce their hours of employment by getting the work done informally? Do we reduce the milkman's round so that we all go and collect the milk for ourselves? Do we pay more people to look after the elderly, dependent relatives or do we get time off with pay from our formal employment to do it ourselves?

Evidently the permutations between the three different spheres for different members of a household can get very complex. But it is this very complexity that has to be explored and in which new mixes or choices have to be created. Job-sharing, seen in this light means much more than just shorter hours in the formal economy. *Which* work? in *which* economy? for *which* member of the household? for *how long*? are basically the questions at issue.

We cannot segregate work in the different spheres to different categories of people. Work in the formal economy cannot be reserved for a select group working from the time they leave the formal education system for the next 40-50 years, whilst excluding others, particularly if such exclusion obliges some to be tied to unpaid domestic work and others restricted to more or less illegal activities in the informal economy. Nor, on the other hand should we necessarily assume that unskilled employment in the formal economy is preferable to skilled work in the informal sector.

Undoubtedly the main shift has to come from men: women already have a pattern which might involve a period in the formal economy, then a period in the domestic economy with young children, followed by a period of part-time or 'voluntary' work before returning ful-time to the formal economy. This is the kind of flexibility men should aim to achieve, either through the different kinds of work following on serially one after the other, as has been the case for some women, or by dividing up daily work more equally between the three spheres.

Evidently the pattern will vary depending on whether the workers concerned are single people living separately and responsible only for themselves, or whether they live in households where part of the work includes looking after young or old dependants. The larger the domestic unit, in theory, the greater the possibility for flexibility and for fairer sharing of different kinds of work.

There are a number of obvious policy implications. Firstly it is clear that if individuals are the unit of taxation and many individuals are in systems of work rotation which reduce the number of hours they work in the formal economy, then the amount of taxation recovered would at present fall. (If six people earning, £9,000 a year are replaced by nine people earning 6,000 a year, then with a progressive system of taxation, the yield would go down.) If, at the same time more work is done with capital goods in the domestic economy, as we suggested above, and also more work is done for goods or cash in the informal, unremunerated, sector, then again tax yields would decline. Again if job-sharing is to be encouraged on a life-cycle basis then it will be necessary for those who work full-time in the formal economy for relatively short, intense, bursts of months or years to be able to carry over their earnings into the next phase of their lives outside the formal economy. Again the yields will go down if the period over which tax is assessed is lengthened to include such cyclical patterns. Evidently the whole pattern of taxation and welfare benefit payments is central to what is loosely called 'job sharing'.

There are other formidable problems involved in coming to terms with the flexible pattern of sharing work in the economic spheres which we have in mind. A second main area relates to the problem of collective organisation. Those who sell their labour power in the formal economy are supported by the Trades Unions; those who engage in domestic labour may get ideological support from the women's movement; but those who work in the informal sector are unlikely to see themselves in need of collective support and organisation. There is the possible danger that the three spheres will pull against each other instead of mutually supporting each other. New lines of political conflict may emerge both inside and outside unions and political parties. These issues are too important not to mention but also too complex to discuss in any detail here.

By now it will be obvious that we have no blueprint for an alternative society. Instead, what we have to offer is a research agenda. We feel that the most gloomy of the current employment forecasts are to be taken very seriously indeed, and that actions taken to support employment artificially are likely to be counter-productive insofar as they are likely to make British industry even less internationally competitive, and hence lose jobs. If we cannot do anything to stop this loss of work opportunities, we must learn to live with it – by sharing jobs among those who want them and by exploiting the promise of the informal economy. But we have as yet hardly started to understand the social, economic and political issues involved in this reorientation of work. Gaining this understanding is altogether the most urgent priority for research in the social sciences.

PART TWO

INFORMAL
SOCIAL ACTIVITY

5
NON-MARKET TRANSACTIONS IN AN URBAN COMMUNITY

Martin Lowenthal

[The rich] have no neighbours in the sense that the poor have neighbours. When my mother had to go out, Mrs. Craddock from next door on the right kept an eye on us children. And my mother did the same for Mrs. Craddock when it was her turn to go out. And when somebody had broken a leg, or lost his job, people helped with money and food. And how well I remember, as a little boy, being sent running around the village after the nurse, because young Mrs. Foster from next door on the left had suddenly been taken with birth pains before she expected! When you live on less than four pounds a week, you've damned well got to behave like a Christian and love your neighbour. There can be no refined and philosophical ignoring of his existence. You must either hate or love; and on the whole you'd better make a shift to love, because you may need his help in emergencies and he may need yours – so urgently, very often, that there can be no question of refusing to give it.

Aldous Huxley, *Point Counterpoint*

Survival and the problem of limited resources

One of the earliest and most thorough studies of mutual support systems among animals and among man was that of Peter Kropotkin (1888) in his work *Mutual Aid*. Kropotkin noted that he failed to find (although he was eagerly looking for it) that bitter struggle for the means of existence, among animals belonging to the same species, which was considered by most Darwinists (though not always by Darwin himself) as the dominant characteristic of struggle for life, and the main factor of evolution. Kropotkin's studies revealed a high degree of mutual support, mutual aid, and mutual defense among animals belonging to the same species or, at least, to the same society. He pointed out that in evolution those animals which acquire habits of mutual aid were the fittest in their struggle for survival. Kropotkin makes similar observations in examining the history of the development of mankind and of civilization.

In examining the histories of the United States and the nations of western Europe, it can be noted that the struggle for survival and well-being by working class families has always been a difficult one. The problems of inadequate income from employment have been noted by many commentators on the western political economic scene. The estimates of the number of persons with incomes below the poverty line in the United States vary depending upon the standard which is used; however, indicators suggest that approximately twenty per cent of the population of the country is near or below the governmental income measures for economic survival.

The question then arises of how people with inadequate income meet their needs and survive. Although many needs may go unmet and thus give rise to such problems as poor health and substandard housing, it is the argument of this chapter that many needs are provided for, not through money income but by the social networks and mutual aid systems that people participate in, and this is discussed in terms of the review of a number of studies of modern urban communities and the presentation of some findings from a study of the community of Charlestown in Boston.

Increasing attention is being given to the informal economic activities which play a role in modern industrial societies, particularly among the working class and the unemployed poor. As people confront limited income and financial insecurity, as well as the desire to maintain or create supportive relationships in their communities, they will often engage in a system of economic transactions which are embedded in networks of social relationships.

I would also suggest that this attention by middle-income professionals may be a reflection not simply of a concern for poverty and public policy, but also of an increasing awareness that even middle-income lifestyles are becoming threatened by limited resources. The inflation in the cost of material goods and of public and private services is putting restrictions on the ability of the so-called middle class to maintain their living patterns, particularly as people age. The lessons for survival that are contained in the studies of certain lower-income and poor communities are being given increasing attention and promoted through the concept of self-help. If the trend of diminishing resources and declining real wages continues (and there are many indications that it will for at least the next couple of decades in the highly developed capitalist West, see chapter 4), there will need to be many readjustments in the patterns of economic coping and support which have characterised the mainstream of western capitalist society.

At present, the problem of limited economic resources is still most obvious in the cases of dependent populations such as children, the elderly, and the physically and mentally disabled. Without sufficient income to meet their own needs and without the capability or opportunity to participate in income producing employment, these populations must depend upon social relationships and governmentally financed institutions to meet their basic needs as people and their special needs, particularly for care and protection, as dependent populations. Historically, there have been few, and generally inadequate, public institutions which are designed to meet the entire range of needs of children, the elderly and the disabled. The burden of provision, care, and protection has generally fallen upon the nuclear or extended family. In the case of children, the responsibility has been assumed primarily by women.

Economic formulations

Economists traditionally have avoided the subject of the informal aspects of livelihood and have concentrated almost exclusively on the monetised legitimate activities in what are called the 'private' and the 'public' sectors.

When referring to the 'economy', economists usually mean the sphere in which goods and services are produced for sale, are sold and are purchased. This formulation derives from the basic characteristics of the market economy. A market economy is based on the exchange of goods and services in the market for equivalent value, usually based upon a standardised monetary system. Market exchange depends upon measured payments in the buying and selling of goods and services and is the organising principle for transactions involving material products, labour, and natural resources. This means that, in general, people derive their livelihood and meet their needs from selling something in the market; for most people this is their labour.

It has been recognised by most economists that the payment of wages as an essential aspect of the organisation of the productive process is a comparatively recent development. In almost every period of recorded history there existed transactions which could be described as the hiring of labour for a contractual payment; however, such transactions were only typical for a small sector of the economic process. Generally work was done and livelihoods gained through systems of social relationships which defined the rewards and responsibilities of the participants. It is only with the breakdown of the feudal restrictions and the replacement of the domestic worker by the factory system, as well as the gradual monetisation of an increasing number of economic transactions, that the basis for a general wage system arises. Under these conditions, the 'free' but property-less worker must offer his only possession, his labour power, in order to maintain himself and his family, while the owner of the tools or land, the employer, can obtain the necessary labour force only by inducing people to work for him by offering them a wage. Labour is thus considered a particular kind of commodity, subject to the forces of supply and demand in the marketplace.

This formulation of labour power in the industrialised societies of the West has become a preoccupation of most economists to the exclusion of other perspectives. The concern of economists since the 19th century has been the development of economic models which attempt to deal with the question: what are the factors which determine the prices of labour, natural resources, and products in a national, market economy? Activities and transactions not subject to pricing mechanisms have generally been excluded from formal analysis, and thus social scientists and social planners at all levels, by accepting this traditional understanding of the economy, have tended to disregard the significance of women, the family, and the community from their economic analyses and their economic policies.

Within the classical and neoclassical framework of economic thought, a housewife cooking a meal is not performing economic activity, whereas if she were hired to cook a similar meal in a restaurant she would be. A so-called 'retired' person who looks after grandchildren during the day is not performing apparent economic activity, although if the same person were hired to care for children by a day care centre it would be economic activity. If a daughter nurses and cares for a disabled or ill parent, she is not considered to be engaged in economic activity; however, the same work performed in a nursing home or in a hospital would be considered as part of the economic sphere. This conception of 'economic' excludes activities within the family and the community, and an analysis of the economic dynamics of society based on this conception tends to exclude many economic actors, particularly women, except in their roles as wage earners. To the extent that households *are* mentioned by traditional economic theory, they are treated as a collection of individuals who are engaged in the process of production or consumption of goods in the market place.

However, if the origins of the term 'economics' are traced back to its Greek roots, a basic concern becomes evident. The Greeks gave us the term 'oikonomos' which is a compound of the word 'oikos', meaning house, and a derivative of 'nemein', meaning to distribute or to manage. Thus the word meant household management. The Latin word 'œconomis' meant specifically household management. When economics is approached from the question of how households are managed and maintained, the limitations of the market economy in our modern industrial society become obvious. For example, the poor know that the market system provides them with limited amounts of income through their wages and that this is often insufficient to meet their normal needs for goods and services and provides little protection in times of crisis. They know that only high income persons can purchase many of the services they provide for themselves in the maintenance of their households, such as child care and household management. They know the importance of relatives, friends, and neighbours in time of illness, family problems, and loss of the job for the survival of the people in the family and the maintenance of the household over time.

In searching for alternative economic theories to explain the nature, the extent and the significance of non-market, non-governmental economic transactions, a clue is suggested by Karl Marx. Marx, at one point, made reference to a larger conception of the economy in the preface to the *Critique of Political Economy* (1867) when he described the economic structure as the total ensemble of social relations entered into in the social production of existence. However, from this broad starting point, Marx narrowed his concern to the study and critique of market capitalist economies. The bulk of his theory and concern revolved around the class structure as it is derived from the operations of capitalism.

Network studies

While many sociologists and anthropologists have accepted the focus and formulations of economists in their discussions of modern economies (Smelser, 1963), others who have done field studies of families, communities, and tribes have examined the economic significance of *all* forms of social relationships. They also describe the units of social relations in terms of the factors which make them cohesive and in terms of how the units themselves are bound economically, socially, and politically into larger systems.

Some of the research on lower-income working class communities has identified many of the informal helping systems which are crucial for the survival of families in these communities and for the survival of particular dependent populations. In her work, *Blue Collar Marriage,* Mirra Komarovsky (1967) found that among the families included in her study, the extended family played a crucially important role. In addition to the part played by relatives in the socialisation of their children, in providing emotional support, and in being companions in recreation, parents were also economically important to the survival of the young family. Although they were usually in no position to help their children to buy a home or establish a business, some financial aid was frequently provided in emergencies. Komarovsky notes that these economic arrangements among kin were often of the form 'reciprocal aid'.

Thus, a widowed father shares his home with a married son who pays no rent but is responsible for household expenses; a widowed mother residing with her daughter works as a waitress, paying rent and her share of the grocery bill; a widow and her bachelor brother inherited the parental home and rented rooms to a married daughter who is the homemaker for the whole group and expenses are shared . . .

Apart from such more-or-less permanent arrangements, relatives frequently exchange services which among wealthier families are purchased from specialists – such as housepainting, carpentry, repair,

laying linoleum, building partitions, and help in moving.
(Komarovsky, 1967, p.237)

In their work *Family and Kinship in East London,* Young and Willmott (1957) also discussed the exchange of services between members of working-class families. Among the most important services that were noted, the ones provided by mothers for their daughters received particular emphasis. In most cases the mother would look after the home when her daughter was in bed preparing to give birth to a child. Usually there was at least one other child, as well as a husband to provide for. The child had to be looked after, food bought, meals cooked, clothes washed, housecleaning to be done, arrangements and schedules to be coordinated, and preparations made for the care of the new baby. Young and Willmott note 'the wife's dependence for help on her kin, and especially upon her mother, does not end with the confinement and its aftermath (at times of childbirth). Whatever the emergency, and whether her need is big or small, the wife looks to her mother for advice and for aid' (Young and Willlmott, 1957, p.54).

In his study of widows and their families, Marris (1958) examined the manner in which social relationships were continued, altered or eliminated after the death of the husband. Most of the women in the study were young and had children. He found that immediately after the death of the husband, parents, brothers, sisters, and children all helped to provide companionship which served to distract the widow from her loss and, at the appropriate time, to insist that she had grieved long enough. During this period, relatives helped in protecting her from harrassing practical problems, such as the funeral arrangements, and often helped to defray the cost. Money was tight in many cases, particularly if the husband had been ill for a length of time. Some help in money came from relatives and sometimes from neighbourhood groups and the workmates of the husband. The extended family tended to be the most important in providing for widows with children by giving meals, clothes and financial assistance.

The issue of the importance of the kin group for older people was the focus of Townsend's study (1957) in a small working-class borough near London. He found that old people saw themselves first as members of a family and secondarily as elderly individuals. Forty-five per cent of his sample lived with relatives and only twenty-one per cent lived by themselves. Most of his population had children who lived in the same household or nearby. Townsend indicated that many activities and transactions were involved in the kin relations of older people. For instance, if a widow lived with her married daughter and her grandchildren, many of the chores would be shared. The grandmother would do much of the cooking and babysitting in return for having her washing and shopping done by her daughter. This pattern was evident in most of the cases; the older people were helped with shopping, cleaning, washing and transportation and they assisted with cooking and watching after grandchildren.

Townsend points out that the major problems of old age and retirement centred around the fall in income and subsequent drop in the standard of living at a time when needs tended to increase. New expenses grew out of the need for medicines, additional fuel, and home entertainment in the form of radios and televisions. Many received help from their children in meeting their expenses; however, others who were the most isolated from their families were socially and financially the poorest. Townsend concludes by postulating that those who are socially isolated in old age, particularly those with fewest contacts with relatives, tend to make greater claims on hospitals and other health and social services and to die earlier.

Fried, in his study of the West End in Boston, notes that the finding 'which emerges most consistently from studies of the working class is the central importance of locally based social relationships . . . ' (Fried, 1965, p.132). He characterises the pattern of the social relationships as being 'close knit networks' (1965, p.132). These close knit networks may include family, extended kin, neighbours, community workers, local shopkeepers, and people who work and live in the community.

What is common to the various close knit networks is not their bases in kinship or common enterprises but rather the ready availability of members and the binding set of expectations for a mutual dependence and dependability in emergencies and in daily encounters, in sorrow and in joy, in routine contact and in the presence of conflict.
Fried, 1965, p.133

One of the most revealing studies of how social relationships and networks operate to meet economic needs was conducted by

Carol Stack and reported in her book *All Our Kin: Strategies for Survival in a Black Community* (1974). Stack lived and studied in a community suffering from severe economic depression and found that extensive friend and kinship networks supported and reinforced each other in devising schemes for self-help and strategies for survival. Lacking the material resources to meet family needs at a subsistence level,

People in the Flats borrow and trade with each other in order to obtain daily necessities. The most important form of distribution and exchange of the limited resources available to the poor in the Flats is by means of trading, or what people usually call 'swapping'. As people swap, the limited supply of finished material goods in the community is perpetually redistributed among networks of kinsmen and throughout the community.
Stack, 1974, p.33

Charlestown
In 1974 and 1975 we carried out a study of the material coping patterns of families and individuals who live in a section of Boston called Charlestown. We sought to examine the ways in which families utilise the goods and services which are provided outside the monetised market and which we termed 'social economic transactions'. This community has been an Irish-American neighbourhood for well over a hundred years and has a highly developed system which provides structure and organisation to the community. Although this historical continuity may be atypical for urban neighbourhoods, the people were chosen because their network patterns were such an integral part of every day life.

The findings in the study were not so surprising but did reveal much of the intricacy and complexity of the networks of social relationships which most people in Charlestown maintain. For example, while households may contain a number of people as part of an immediate family, each adult member will have some-what distinct, individually orientated networks. The networks are open relationships in which there is overlap between relationships, but no precise coincidence. Each individual tends to have a number of people in his/her network but will tend to count on only selected close relationships for regular support. Wellman (1979) found similar patterns in his study of the intimate networks of the residents of East Yonkers.

Non-market activities tend to transpire more between kin than between friends and neighbours. In these reciprocal transactions, particularly between kin, a material good or service may flow from one individual to another but may be reciprocated by the provision of emotional or psychological support. The proximity of kin tended to be an important variable in the ability of persons in need to receive support and for persons as providers to carry out many of the types of non-monetised activities.

The most commonly exchanged goods and services in Charlestown included: child care, financial assistance, meals, employment information and placement, repairs, clothing, solicited information and advice, housing information and assistance in rental or purchase, food, care for the sick, elder care, shopping, temporary home for children, cleaning services and political favours.

Women tend to have primary responsibility for performing much of the social economic activities in Charlestown and generally take care of the obligations to kin. Partly owing to this pivotal role, the dependency on kin tends to revolve more around the kin network of the wife than that of the husband.

It was also found that the larger networks of kin and friends were rarely used for material support except in times of crisis, such as prolonged illness, death or unemployment and that this support would come from only a selected number of close people within the wider network. The wider circle also becomes operative for support during times of celebration.

The psychological aspects of transactions were not specifically studied in the research, but these factors emerged from our data and reports as being very important. The networks of relationships and the systems of support within them provide an important sense of security and psychological well being to the participants. These also provide many people with the sense that they belong to a larger community and that there is a larger community that will share in the burdens of life. This sense of belonging also defines their relationship to the larger society.

Those people who did not have networks of relationships and support tended to be in much greater need and tended to perceive that they had many fewer alternatives open to them. They not only lacked the support that networks can provide, but in many cases, lacked the information linkages through which networks hook people up with needed goods and services from governmental agencies. The reasons why some people had few or limited networks were difficult to determine but the data suggest some factors. These include the mobility of the person, the geographic mobility of the family, the closeness of ties that the person maintained with kin and friends at earlier times, the network skills the person had acquired (usually during adolescence and early adulthood), and the extent to which the person participated in the larger community.

Other anthropological works, particularly those concerned with tribal societies, contain many observations and descriptions about the operation of social economic systems which are primarily non-monetised. The works of Richards (1932), Watson (1958), Epstein (1962), Ishwaran (1966), Bohannan and Dalton (1962) and others are examples of such studies. However, there have been few attempts to treat the economies of these societies outside the framework of classical western economics.

Sociological and anthropological formulations: towards a theory of the social economy

Although these and other studies touch upon the material importance of social relationships in modern urban communities, there has been only limited development of coherent theory which incorporates the economic functions which these helping systems and social relationships perform.

Polanyi (1968) and Dalton (1971) have noted the limitations of the analytic power of traditional economic theory in anthropology and have suggested some alternative categories for a better comparative analysis of economic systems. Polyani suggested that economic activities fall into three main patterns. The first he calls 'reciprocity', which is illustrated by the ritualised gift giving among families, clans, and tribes – as can be seen in the works of Malinowski (1922) and Mauss (1954), for example. Another illustration of reciprocity is the cooperation among farming families to assist each other in the building of barns, known as 'barn raising', and the mutual assistance they lend to each other at harvest times. In patterns of reciprocity, goods and services are given because of bonds which mutually obligate the parties involved. The rights and obligations of each party are usually determined according to some traditional concept of how they are supposed to relate socially.

The second pattern noted by Polanyi was 'redistribution'. This involves the gathering of economic goods and services to some form of central place – usually controlled by governmental or religious agents – and then redistributing the goods and services throughout the populace. Polanyi notes that many Asian societies and African tribes utilise this economic pattern of behaviour and that, like reciprocity, redistributive patterns are characterised by the absence of equivalency calculations and price mechanisms. The principle of calculation in redistribution patterns seems to be one of a kind of 'justice' – namely determining what each class in the population traditionally deserves.

The third pattern noted by Polanyi is that of 'exchange', by which he means the exchange of economic goods and services within some form of market context. Under exchange, prices and distribution are not determined on the basis of tradition but they are the result of bargaining mechanisms which adjust and match supply and demand.

Although Polanyi and his associates and followers applied these categories to the study of primitive and non-industrial systems, this type of analysis was not extended into the investigation of modern industrial society. Polanyi argued, particularly in his work *The Great Transformation* (1957), that the non-market patterns of economic integration which prevailed in archaic economies were supplanted in the 19th century by the growth of the market economy under capitalism. Polanyi argued that the market economy transformed the whole of society and harnessed the economic and productive dimensions entirely to the institutional mechanism of the market.

In an attempt to incorporate the historical, sociological and anthropological evidence that a large portion of goods and services in contemporary western industrial society are produced and distributed through mechanisms other than the market and governmental intervention, I developed some initial formulations of a theory of the 'social economy' (Lowenthal, 1975). I argued that the economic transactions which are imbedded in and based on the network of social relationships which people maintain over time have characteristics which suggest that they be treated as a system. They are a structured set of arrangements for providing material goods and services. In addition they are governed by certain rules which integrate the transactions and interdependencies and assure the continued cooperation of those involved in the provision of goods and services.

The economic aspects of social relationships in the social economy are usually not primary; the relationships are based on other principles of organisation which give their primary significance and meaning, such as kinship, tradition, religion, friendship, community or neighbourhood. This is not to say that the economic dimension is not important, for it may play a vital role in maintaining the ties between the participants. The rules for the initiation and maintenance of relationships in the social economy derive from the cultural values and social norms of the relationship in which the participant is engaged. For example, among some ethnic groups, as with the working-class communities we looked at above, it is expected that grandparents will assist in the care and socialisation of grandchildren. In many communities neighbours who are friendly with the corner grocer or pharmacist may purchase items on credit without interest or collateral, and without a credit check. Neighbours may borrow food or share appliances. Parents may provide a newlywed couple with some funds to begin a household, and sons and daughters may provide money to help their parents in their old age.

One of the operating principles of the social economy is that of reciprocity. Reciprocity is the mutual recognition of rights, responsibilities, and privileges. This means that a party in a relationship had certain rights to goods and services from others in meeting his/her needs. The others in the relationship have the responsibility to respond to that need. In return the party is obligated to respond to certain needs of the others in the relationship.

In complex situations, the patterns of reciprocity may not be so obviously two-way. For example, members of a particular kin group need not reciprocate with one another but may do so with the corresponding members of a third kin group toward which they stand in an analogous relationship. Among the Trobriand islanders, the man's responsibility is toward his sister's husband. If he is married, he is assisted by his own wife's brother – a member of a third family. The point is that the rights and the corresponding responsibilities apply to all participants in the network of social relationships according to mutually accepted implicit criteria.

The principle of reciprocity involves anther principle for effective operation – the principle of adequacy of response. Unlike market exchange transactions in which mathematical equivalencies are computed and in which the value of the good or service you give in an exchange is theoretically equivalent to the good or service you receive and is standardised in money terms, the principle of adequacy of response requires that those responding to a need do so as fully as they are able even though the person in need may not have responded to others to the same extent, owing to his own limitations. For example, a family may pass on outgrown children's clothing to relatives with a newly born baby and the recipient family, responding to the donor's needs during a time of illness of the mother for a few days, may do the cooking for the donor family. In another instance a grandmother may care for the children of her daughter during the day while the daughter works and in turn may be able to turn to the daughter for extra cash when the rent is due, or utility bills must be paid, or when medical bills arise.

Cohesive stable working-class communities have generally developed intricate and complex systems of reciprocal arrangements which can be effective as redistribution mechanisms within the community. These reciprocal arrangements are also important for the survival and integration of the community itself over time and help cement the social relationships themselves. The redistributional aspect of the social economy is particularly important in integrating groups in communities and assuring the permanence of the arrangement. The participants in the relationships are able to derive a measure of security within a larger society in which they are considered marginal by wage market standards.

Some conclusions

The personal networks that most people maintain provide direct and indirect links to a wide range of people and resources. There is extensive and vital economic activity that takes place within this complicated system of relationships, which not only is essential to the material and emotional well being of individuals but provides an informal but underlying structure to modern urban society. Even within the formal organisations of the workplace, it is the informal networks of relationships which provide much of the meaning and support for people on the job. People derive much of their security and sense of relationship to the larger society through their participation and belonging in various informal personal networks.

As the personal networks of a number of people are traced, another dimension of networks begins to emerge which might be called a 'network of networks' connecting many individuals and groups into larger social wholes. From a systematic viewpoint, these complex linkages represent and maintain a social order which has great social and economic significance and which allocates many resources outside of the market and governmental mechanisms.

6
ALTERNATIVE HOUSING

Stephen Platt

My house is an ugly thing.
It has broken windows.
And all of the houses are much
Better than my house.
People laugh at my house,
And they say to me,
Why not fix it?
One morning I got up,
And the Town Hall man came.
And he said,
Your house must be knocked down.
And I said,
Can I rebuild it?
And the Town Hall man said
Yes.
And I built it.

Hakeem, aged 11, from *Fire Words,* compiled by Chris Searle, 1978

Normal housing

The majority of the world's people house themselves. The tradition of personalised, informal provision of housing remains dominant over large sections of the globe. Few Third World rural-dwellers, for example, would even consider not building their own homes; and when, attracted by the greater opportunities offered by urban life, they join the massive migrations to urban centres, they generally provide shelter for themselves as best they can. Their 'shanty town' settlements, constructed on land over which they have no legal right or title, are characteristic features of growing towns and cities throughout the Third World:

90,000 persons were living in shanty towns in Lusaka in 1969 . . . One quarter of the population of Baghdad was living in squatter settlements in 1960; the figure for Istanbul was 21%. At the same time such settlements were accommodating half of Ankara's population. In Latin America recent estimates have included a figure of 800,000 squatters, or one fifth of the total urban population in Rio de Janeiro . . . while the figure for Lima, the capital of Peru, shows 800,000 in the 'barriadas' in 1970 (one third of the total urban population) . . . Over 40% of Mexico City is currently living in 'colonias proletarias'.

(Dwyer, 1975, pp.18-19)

In many cases the majority of the inhabitants of a city are squatting. According to the 1974 World Housing Survey (see Ward, 1976), there were 1,380,000 squatters, comprising 60 per cent of the total population, in Bogota, 569,000 (75 per cent) in Ibadan, 5,330,000 (67 per cent) in Calcutta, and similarly large numbers in many other towns and cities of all sizes. Throughout virtually the whole of the Third World, the non-regulated self-provision of shelter is a major source of accommodation, sometimes outstripping the efforts of both the private construction industry and the state. By making use of their own labour and locally available materials, be they corrugated iron sheets or bamboo canes and mud, people provide themselves with shelter quickly and at minimal expense. The large numbers of squatters and the absence of alternative ways of housing often compel the authorities to recognise the settlements and assist in the provision of water and electricity supplies, drainage and other public services. The squatters improve their homes gradually over a period of years until their settlements become established within the cities. The recently established refugee encampments in South East Asia demonstrate the speed at which self-organised self-built settlements develop in response to the absence of more formal systems of provision. In the island refugee camp of Bidong, off the coast of Malaya, for example, thousands of Vietnamese live in huts that are almost invariably self-constructed. The camp has developed its own health, sanitation and education services; it has a market place and shops; and it is already evolving rudimentary forms of policing, social organisation and decision-making.

The sheer scale of the refugee problem in South East Asia imposes such strains upon the existing institutions and economies of the countries receiving refugees that they simply cannot cope with the kind of mass housing programmes needed to meet even a fraction of the demand for shelter. Self-provision is the only immediately practicable and economical solution.

Indeed, many Third World cities which are not the recipients of large refugee influxes have already had to come to terms with this fact. Many have experienced, in the period of just a few years, population increases equal in magnitude to the entire refugee exodus from Vietnam since the communist victory. The population of Nairobi, for instance, doubled during the 1970s, and cities such as Lagos and Lusaka, both growing at a rate of 14 per cent per year, have doubled in size in a little over five years. Such cities live with a permanent 'refugee' crisis, created by the combination of explosive population growth and rapid urbanisation. Their fledgling housing institutions do not have the organisational capacity to meet demand on such a scale, even if they had the political will or access to the necessary resources. In this context, informal approaches to housing provision are not so much an 'alternative' to formal provision as a necessity brought about by the failure of formal housing systems.

Squatters in the developed world

It is not only in Third World countries that an informal housing sector exists. Estimates of the number of squatters in 'bidonvilles' on the outskirts of French cities, for example, vary from 75,000 to over 150,000 (Clout, 1972) and according to the *New York Times* (1968) 'Authorities estimate that 500,000 illegal dwellings worth some 15 billion drachmas (500 million dollars) have literally cropped up on the outskirts of Greek cities over the last twenty years.' The number of squatters in empty dwellings in London has been put at between 20-25,000 (SHHRL, 1978), while for Paris a figure of 10,000 is not unreasonable and for Amsterdam 3-8,000 has been suggested (Van Tijen, 1978). In most developed countries the informal housing sector is swelled by thousands of dossers, gypsies and unlawful occupants who provide for their own housing needs independently of the state and market systems. According to the Minority Rights Group, for instance, there are around 250,000 Romany travellers in Western Europe.

In Italy, one commentator estimated that by 1976 some 70,000 people had obtained accommodation through squatting, and he commented that 'Squatting has become such a frequent affair, especially in the large cities, that it is no longer news' (Pucci, 1976). In the UK, where organised squatting re-emerged at the end of the 1960s, it has been estimated that at least 150,000 people have squatted during the last decade (Wates, forthcoming); usually for just a few months at a time to provide for short-term housing needs, but sometimes for several years on end. These people are not the 'politically-motivated scroungers' of media mythology, and it is difficult to categorise them succinctly at all.

Characteristics of UK squatters

Squatters are not a homogeneous group. Some, whether families or single people, have a geniune need for housing; they may well have gone through the mill of trying to find somewhere to live and turned to squatting only as a last resort when other alternatives, including bed and breakfast, proved unacceptable. Some have political objectives – either to influence central and local government housing policies, or to bring about more far-reaching changes. Others may prefer the lifestyle of squatting and its cheapness; or they may be existing council tenants trying to force the council to give them a transfer, or the children of tenants trying to obtain their own tenancy. Yet others may be disaffected groups or individuals who welcome the freedom and anonymity of squatting, may be passing through, or tourists. The list could go on.

DoE, 1975, p.3

What statistical information is available suggests that the majority of squatters in the UK are single, childless and below the age of thirty (though the majority of *squatted properties* do contain people with children). They make up a relatively mobile population, with a large proportion coming from outside the area in which they are squatting, and a disproportionately high number have low incomes, few savings and limited educational or vocational qualifications or skills. Almost 75 per cent of squatters come from manual occupational groups.

Many of them were assisted to squat by the variety of informal advisory agencies spawned by the squatting movement. The Advisory Service for Squatters, for instance, originally established with a grant from a national housing charity, regularly handles 30-40 enquiries daily, all of which are dealt with by volunteer workers, most of whom are squatters or ex-squatters. Among the formal bodies which refer homeless people to them are local authority housing and social service departments, the probation service, housing aid centres, and even the police. The Brixton Women's Centre, in south London, which acted as an unofficial organising centre for squatters in the area during the mid-1970s, sometimes received as many as 20 referrals from statutory agencies in a single day. In one north London borough the local squatting group set up an 'Alternative Housing Aid Centre', which dealt with all kinds of enquiries about housing, and countless individual squats have acted as unofficial community centres, not only helping people to squat, but also providing advice, support and assistance in other ways. Many council representatives and officials concede privately that they have to tolerate squatting because they would be unable to cope with the problems of homelessness which would arise if it was completely suppressed, and some commentators even refer to it as a 'de facto' tenure form (Smith, 1975, and Gimson et al, 1976). At least half a dozen local authorities in London currently permit squatters to remain in properties which they do not require immediately, and even in some areas where this is not the formal policy, there exists a degree of acceptance of squatting in otherwise unused dwellings.

The failure of formal housing

In large part, the continued existence of a sizeable informal housing sector is simply a reflection of the failure of formal housing systems to provide everyone with a home. Thus, for example, in France the 'bidonvilles' are mainly inhabited by poor migrant workers denied access to any other form of housing, and most squatters in the UK would gladly take up legitimate tenancies if only they were available. Fifty-nine per cent of those interviewed for a DOE-commissioned survey stated that the main reason they were squatting was that they 'couldn't find anywhere at a rent (they) could afford' (Kinghan, 1977, p.46). One interviewee, who had previously been housed in a short-life local authority property, described the circumstances which led her to squat:

When I first moved into the flat they (the local council) said I'd only be there a week: I ended up eleven months there. It was terrible ... You couldn't live there – it was so bad. The walls were damp and water

coming in made a hole in the roof. It was very small – just one room divided into two, and the baby was always cold . . .
Kinghan, 1977, p.50.

Other squatters told of having come from still more brutal housing conditions, or of having had no home at all, and spoke of the institutional indifference they had met and the difficulties they had faced in finding somewhere decent to live. Between 1969, when the current squatting movement started, and 1976, when the number of people squatting reached a peak of around 50,000, the number of homeless families applying for emergency accommodation from local authorities in London alone increased more than threefold, to over 30,000 (GLC, 1977). For single people the position was even worse. During the 1960s the number of single person households in England and Wales increased from 12.1 per cent to 18.1 per cent of all households (Drake and Biebuych, 1977), but over the same period the private rented sector, in which they would traditionally have been housed, declined by almost three million dwellings. Nor was access to public housing accommodation or home ownership made significantly easier for single people, who tended to be excluded from the former by allocation systems which discriminated against them and from the latter by their limited savings and incomes. In a survey of squatters in Haringey, one group of single people, all of whom were in full-time employment, told of having been refused a mortgage by five different building societies and the local authority, and of having tried for no fewer than 45 privately-rented flats and houses before, in desperation, they decided to squat in empty council property (Platt, 1977).

What happened to produce the massive upsurge in the number of people squatting during the 1970s was not that the *overall* housing situation worsened, but that it did worsen for *some* people in *some* areas, most notably for single people in London and other major cities. At the same time, the number of empty dwellings was large, and probably rising. The 1971 Census identified 675,000 empty homes in England and Wales, 100,000 of them in London, and by 1977 the National Empty Homes Campaign was claiming that the figure was approaching one million and that in parts of London one house in every ten was empty (National Empty Homes Campaign, 1977). The failure of the formal housing system to bring these dwellings into use was a major contributing factor to the shortage of *available* dwellings which emerged during the 1960s and 1970s. This shortage was something unusual in the UK, where overcrowding and the condition of housing had tended to be more a problem than its absolute availability. On the last occasion the UK experienced a major absolute shortage of housing – at the end of the Second World War – tens of thousands of squatters, mainly ex-servicemen and their families, seized disused army camps and other empty buildings throughout the country (Ward, 1976), and so it is perhaps unsurprising that people in dire housing need 25-30 years later should turn their attention towards the empty, but habitable, homes that were to be found in large numbers, often in precisely those areas where housing stress was greatest.

Although the re-emergence of a substantial informal housing sector during the 1970s in the UK was primarily a consequence of the inadequacies of the formal housing institutions, and particularly of their inability to provide some people with a home of any kind, this is only part of the explanation.

Flexibility, self-control and freedom

The popularity of informal options also owes itself to more positive factors. One of the lessons derived from self-built squatter settlements in the Third World has been that self-builders can achieve something that is currently beyond the state and big business – they can provide adequate homes in sufficient numbers, in the desired location, quickly and at little cost. What is more, the homes that people provide for themselves with limited resources and largely unskilled labour, are often more satisfactory to the people who live in them than those built to far higher standards by government or private enterprise. Between 1954 and 1958, for example, the authorities in Caracas rehoused over 100,000 squatters in massive blocks of municipal flats specially built for the purpose in an attempt to put an end to the squatting in the city. They failed, not only because a further 160,000 migrants arrived in the city during the period, but also because the flats did not satisfy the needs and desires of the rehoused squatters. They could not be adapted for use by extended family households; there was no possibility of self-improvement over a period of years; they were distant from sources of income and employment; and countless squatters had to give up their small businesses or trades as a result of the rule that the flats could only be used for residential purposes. Rent arrears soon became an intractable problem, the physical condition of the flats deteriorated rapidly, and petty crime and other forms of social disorganisation were rife. In their attempt to bring squatting under control and to provide housing of a better physical standard the autorities had torn apart cohesive communities and stripped the proverty-stricken occupants of their last vestiges of peronal autonomy, dignity and freedom.

In this context, self-provision is the product of what J.F.C. Turner (1972, p.511) calls 'the difference between the *nature* of the popular demand for dwellings and those supplied by institutionalised society'. To draw on Turner again, the importance of housing in people's lives consists not just of what it *is,* but also of what it *does.* That is to say that the occupants of a house judge it not only by physical standards, such as whether it has a bathroom, a full-fitted kitchen, or whatever, but also by way of other factors such as proximity to work, friends, relatives, shops or entertainment, or by *the degree of control that one has over it and the freedom one has to shape and use it according to one's needs or desires?* Self-provision offers various freedoms which are simply not available when housing is provided as a fully-finished product to be *consumed* by dwellers who have not direct control over their homes and their personal resources, including income. As one squatter in Haringey told me:

I suppose that I could have afforded to rent a small room or two if I'd really wanted to, and have had all the usual creature comforts and security . . . but I wanted to be free to choose who I live with and what colour I paint the walls . . . and to be able to fix bikes in the basement if I want to, without some landlord breathing down my neck all the time.

Other squatters have spoken of the importance of the extra freedom to budget their own resources. Where previously they may have been paying a third of their income in rent, some of which perhaps went to provide facilities which they did not want, they were now free to choose how much they spent on other things, such as food, clothing, travel or leisure. The imposed standards and regulations which have been so important in raising the condition of the housing stock in the UK have also had the unfortunate effect of removing a whole layer of low-rent accommodation altogether, with the result that this kind of budgetary choice has been denied to the urban poor, who usually have to accept whatever accommodation they can find, with the relevant choices concerning standards and cost having already been made for them.

Squatting has also offered other freedoms. In Tolmers Square, a large central London squat which at one time housed over 200 people, it enabled residents to set up all manner of workshops and small enterprises, including a café, a poster workshop, a monthly magazine, a bookshop, a motorcycle repair shop, a fruit and vegetable co-operative and an artist's studio:

One middle-aged couple renovated a Georgian house, thought previously beyond repair, and called it a 'Community House'. In one room they built a workshop which any resident was free to use, and in another room they built a grain store and ran a wholefood shop selling muesli, nutbutter, honey, grains and dried fruits. In the basement they started a bakery which produced 30 loaves of bread every day made with handground wholemeal flour, as well as small pies and cakes. They also constructed a storeroom for plaster, cement, sand, recycled timber, nails and other building materials for use on repairing the houses. The whole enterprise was non profit making and everyone was encouraged to be involved so as to break down alienation between producer and consumer; almost a return to a rural peasant economy, where craftsmanship and barter replace mechanisation and money. Squatting was the only way that enough space could be obtained to experiment with alternative lifestyles. Wates, 1976, p.164

Squatting was also the only tenure form that provided the control and freedom necessary to permit experimentation with such enterprises. Even ownership, bound up as it is by regulations and controls that apply equally to property companies and individual householders, profit-maximising businesses and co-operative enterprises, cannot offer quite the same degree of freedom. Nonetheless, it remains true that the appeal of home ownership is inextricably linked with the desire for control over one's home, and not merely with the economic benefits which accrue from it. The practice of squatting extends the possibility for such control and its associated freedom to those poorer sections of society normally denied it. In that squatting is so much more commonplace in Third World Countries, then, the urban poor in those countries have a greater freedom of housing choice than in developed countries where dependence upon institutional provision is almost total. In those wealthier countries where squatting does occur, the rediscovery of personal autonomy, self-reliance and self-help, and the associated knowledge and co-operative spirit, is often an exciting and liberating experience. It is also an experience which squatters have constantly attempted to transfer to a more secure, longer-term setting.

Integration and interdependence

As early as 1969 squatters in Lewisham, South London, reached an agreement with the local authority whereby they were given licences to use and administer empty property awaiting demolition or modernisation. The Lewisham Family Squatters Association thus became the first 'licensed' squatting group in the UK. It still operates today, providing homes for, on average, in the region of 100 households at any given time, and it has been joined by at least 20 other such groups, housing in the region of 5-6,000 people. The success of these groups, which are controlled by the people living in their houses, in utilising short-life properties which local government bureaucracies would be unable to let, has won them official encouragement and support from central government. A government circular on empty property, for example, recommends that more authorities should licence 'short life and similar properties' to 'responsible groups' (DOE, 1977). Their informal and flexible approach and structures, and their ability to make use of the varied skills and resources of their members, make them infinitely more capable of handling short-term empty dwellings than the most efficient and sensitive council housing department could ever be.

They have also provided working examples of democratic tenant self-management in practice, and played no small part in persuading the authorities of the viability of tenant-controlled schemes in permanent housing. The development of housing co-operatives during the 1970s, for example, owes a great deal to the experience and work of squatters and ex-squatters. Indeed, of 161 housing co-ops and interested groups listed in the Co-operative Housing Agency's (1978) Directory, eight had been formed by 'licensed' squatting groups, eleven by previously unlicensed squatting groups, and thirteen had a substantial input from squatters or ex-squatters. A tentative, but growing commitment to self-help approaches to housing on the part of the authorities had enabled a significant number of squatters to re-enter the mainstream of the formal housing system, while retaining some of the freedoms offered by squatting.

In addition to their interest in housing co-operatives and other forms of tenant self-management, local authorities have also made use of self-help possibilities in other ways. The Greater London Council's homesteading scheme, for example, offers young people rundown properties rent-free for three years on condition that they carry out necessary repairs and improvements to a standard specified by the Council. A hundred per cent local authority mortgage is made available to enable participants in the scheme to purchase the property at the end of the period. While the scheme may well be primarily a means of selling off substandard council properties, it certainly takes account of the policy potential in promoting self-help approaches, and it is an indication of the way in which the informal sector has contributed ideas and understanding to public housing policy.

Why alternative housing now?

The growing belief in and practice of self-help approaches and the integration of elements of the informal housing sector within the formal housing system has occurred as a result of two factors. First, there has been an ideological change in society. Since the 1960s – and this is closely associated with the failures of Labour governments during the period – there has developed a growing disillusionment with the welfare state and state provision generally. An increasing number of people have come to doubt that, however well intentioned it may be, or however admirable the visions of social planners, the paternalistic state will ever be able to provide the services that people require, largely because a hierarchical decision-making structure is too remote to respond sensitively and efficiently to diverse human needs and preferences.

Secondly, there has been an economic change. The economic depression of the 1970s has led to massive cuts in public spending at a time when, because of rising unemployment and falling living standards, the need for welfare provision is actually increasing. The former change has led to an unprecedented willingness to accept the devolution of responsibility from the state, and the latter has led to an unprecedented determination on the part of the state to hand over responsibility. One consequence in the field of housing has been that the state – both locally and centrally – has sought to offload the burden that housing imposes upon its coffers as far as possible. The growth of the housing association movement (which now accounts for 25 per cent of all central government spending on housing) is partly due to this effort, as is the heightened government interest in self-help and the policy options it makes available.

Conclusion: the importance of self-help for social change

Given the preoccupation of government with cost cutting and economies, and given that right-wing politicians describe self-help as a 'cornerstone' of their philosophy (not to mention the anti-trade union body which names itself 'Self-Help Organisation'), it is not surprising that social radicals should regard the concept with much scepticism. It is associated with the selfish, individualist philosophy which owes so much to Samuel Smiles, capitalist laissez-faire, and the Victorian ethos of the 'deserving poor' pulling themselves up by their own bootstrings.

But the fact that the emergent middle class of Victorian England took the concept of self-help, divorced it from the complementary notion of mutual aid, and turned it into an ideology to justify their private affluence amidst poverty and squalor, does not mean that it should be abandoned wholesale. Nor does it mean that the only alternative to a society governed by the market is one governed by a paternalistic, highly centralised state apparatus. Indeed, there exists a different and collectivist tradition of self-help – or non-reliance upon institutional society – which has roots in the Victorian friendly societies, the forerunners of today's trade unions. Many of the most radical social movements of recent times have embraced self-help as an important strand of their political philosophies. The reclamation of self-help from capitalist ideology has been an important element in the success of the women's movement, whose desire for independence from the male-dominated institutions of society has caused the development of self-help health care and treatment, consciousness raising, refuges for battered wives and countless other autonomous activities and structures. Employed in this kind of collective context, self-help need not be at variance with principles of social justice or equality; indeed, it enhances social, as well as individual, wellbeing and satisfaction.

What the women's movement, the informal housing sector and

other groups employing self-help approaches to common needs and problems have demonstrated is that self-help can be a preferable option, *even when institutional alternatives exist.* Indeed, for many of these groups self-help is an *essential* part of the changes they are seeking in society. One squatter in St. Agnes Place, south London, has referred to squatters repairing their own homes as 'not just to do with mending one's own living space', but as a 'central part' of 'confrontation with the existing culture . . . Practical tasks are carried out as far as possible by squatters themselves. People learn how to do their own wiring, plumbing, glazing, guttering. Expertise as such is not rejected, but it is demystified. It is rejected as an instrument of control and bureaucracy. . .' The same person went on to develop his own belief in the importance of self-help:

Learning what other people need and what each of us needs ourselves; facing one's fear in a confrontation with the Council or with police; getting on with it when you want something and finding out for yourself what can be done, practically or in terms of other people's sensitivities — the true meaning of self-help or helping yourself; accepting other people's differences, having your own accepted . . . This 'therapeutic' aspect of squatting seems to me inseparable from the growth of new ownership or decision-making structures.
Osborne, 1980

Of course this kind of interpretation has little in common with the motives behind government interest in self-help initiatives. But the informal housing sector has much to teach government, and not only in terms of revealing the inadequacies of formal systems of housing provision. As well as providing an invaluable, perhaps essential, stop-gap source of accommodation for people whose housing need is not being met by the formal housing system, it also tells us a great deal about the *nature* of housing need itself. The personal autonomy, control and freedom that the growth of state intervention and the advent of social planning have taken away from the poor of developed countries is every bit as important an aspect of the housing process as cost or standards.

According to Colin Ward, 20 per cent of all single family dwellings constructed in the USA are now self-built by the people who intend to live in them (Ward, 1976). That so many people in the world's wealthiest nation should choose to construct their own homes is indication enough of the demand for self-provision. Of course not everyone wants, or is able, to build their own home. Many, perhaps most, people would prefer not to, and theirs is a perfectly reasonable choice to make. But that the poor of developed countries should be denied almost all choice in housing – and not just as to whether they build their own home or not – is as damning an indictment of the housing systems of those countries as the fact that they have all failed, without exception, to provide decent homes for everyone. Indeed, in the absence of dweller control and freedom in the housing process, it is doubtful whether 'decent homes for all' will ever be more than a hopeful slogan on a distant horizon.

7
COMMUNITY EDUCATION

Colin Ward

My neighbour Alan is a farm mechanic who maintains the equipment for a group of farms in Suffolk, England. Like most country people with a patch of land of their own, he and his wife keep poultry and geese, rear pigs and grow fruit and vegetables. In his spare time Alan fells trees, uses his pond as a fish-farm, and repairs other people's cars and mowers. Feeling the need to undertake the kind of jobs that used to be done by the blacksmith, he has built himself a forge. One day he decided to make a traditional copper coal scuttle. So he went to the sheet metal merchants in Ipswich and asked if they could put him in touch with a coppersmith. They gave him the address of the last practitioner of the trade in that town and he went to see the old man, who discussed with him the techniques of cutting and shaping the metal, the appropriate gauge to use, and the method of riveting. He lent Alan an example to copy and suggested that he should bring it back, together with his own effort. Alan returned to the metal merchants, bought his materials and went home. After making the object he took it back for inspection by the old craftsman, who examined it and pronounced it 'not bad'.

Alan's experience illustrates perfectly the ideal of 'learning webs' or networks expounded by Ivan Illich; in particular the notion of 'skill exchanges' in which people 'list their skills, the condition under which they are willing to serve as models for others who want to learn these skills, and the addresses at which they can be reached' (Illich, 1971, p.79). It would never occur to Alan that he was part of a learning web: it is as natural for him to seek out someone with the knowledge he needs, as it is for him to pass on to others the information that Fullers Earth may sometimes improve the performance of brake linings.

Why, in a decade of unprecedented expansion of technical education throughout the world, should Illich exalt to the status of a theory of education, that ordinary propensity for sharing skills and knowledge which is, and always has been, the way in which most people learn most of their wisdom? Why, for that matter, should the same decade – the period roughly of 1965 to 1975 – see a group of highly educated people in North and South America make the distinction between education and schooling, a distinction previously made only by the unschooled? Why, above all, in the same period, did a number of gifted and dedicated teachers abandon the security of the official education systems, not for the less exacting, though similarly paid, life of the 'private sector' in education, but for the hazards and poverty of unofficial educational adventures in the poorest parts of our cities? I am thinking of, for example, the First Street School in New York, the Barrowfields Community School in Glasgow, the Scotland Road Free School in Liverpool and the White Lion Free School in North London.

Experiments in alternative education

The teachers involved in these experiments had a number of beliefs of which the most immediately important was that the proportion of children who reject the official system of education, and who express this rejection in truancy or disruption, are in fact right. As Newell (1975, p.400) says, 'When offered a radical alternative, children are the quickest to see that the conventional state school was not designed with their interests at heart.' Likewise these teachers concluded that the aims of the official system were not relevant for the children who had been prejudged as educational failures, and they sought, in an informal setting, to provide learning experiences which were closer to the children's needs.

One of the earliest British experiments of this kind, in Liverpool, soon found itself appealing for help from the local education authority. This was thought hilariously funny by the educational journalists, but was completely logical in terms of British educational finance. Schools are provided by local education authorities and financed, theoretically, at a local level, though in fact through grants to local authorities from central government. Parents, and everyone else, are without scrutiny paying for the official education system. But if the parents had opted for a

Catholic, or Jewish education for their children, it would have been provided by the religious institutions and financed by the local authority. Why should not the Free School, or any other experiment in education outside the official system, qualify for the money which would have been spent on the education of the children for which it catered? What the Liverpool Free School asked for was accommodation, furniture and the statutory school meals. What it got was the loan of second-hand tables and chairs. One member of the Education Committee declared that, 'If we are being asked to support the school we are being asked to weaken the fabric of what we ourselves are supposed to be supporting . . . We might finish up with the fact that no children will want to go to our schools.'

There were similar misgivings in London on the question of aid to unofficial school provision there. Having benefited for several crucial years from the voluntarily established 'truancy centre', the Inner London Education Authority decided to set up its own versions, described with a variety of euphemisms, though known to the press as 'sin bins'. In a sense this is the tribute that the formal system of education pays to the informal alternative, for every city in Britain has established some kind of informal provision for those children that the schools cannot contain, and has leaned heavily on the experience and personnel of the alternative providers. The fact that schools provided by various religious enterprises are financed by the official system has led a number of would-be enablers of unofficial education to seek ways of exploiting the legislation to finance parent-controlled educational alternatives on the model of the *Friskoler* in Denmark, which make use of the provision for religious schools to obtain public finance for local community educational experiments.

The de-schoolers

But the challenge to educational orthodoxy made by that small group of critics which we label as 'de-schoolers' went beyond Ivan Illich's rejection of the school as an 'age-specific, teacher-related process requiring full-time attendance at an obligatory curriculum' (Illich, 1973, p.10). They pointed out that in the postwar decades throughout the world, education had been grotesquely oversold. Every new school or college building, every increase in educational spending, every extension of the minimum permissable age for leaving school, every increase in student numbers at the upper and more expensive end of the system, had been seen as a step towards some great social goal of a universally educated population, a goal which was further justified in economic terms. Gross National Product, the needs of industry, the balance of payments, the arms race and the space race would all be enhanced by increased educational investment.

In practice, the de-scholars insisted, the greater the sums of money that are poured into the education industries of the world, the smaller the benefit to the people at the bottom of the educational, occupational and social hierarchy. The universal education system turns out to be yet another way in which the poor subsidise the rich. It is, in Everett Reimer's words, 'an almost perfectly regressive form of taxation' (Reimer, 1971, p.63). Not only this, but the professionalism of knowledge represents a conspiracy against the community as a whole. Illich, the most influential of the de-schooling critics, describes the effect of this with devastating clarity:

It makes people dependent on having their knowledge produced for them. It leads to a paralysis of the moral and political imagination. This cognitive disorder rests on the illusion that the knowledge of the individual citizen is of less value than the 'knowledge' of science. The former is the opinion of individuals. It is merely subjective and is excluded from policies. The latter is 'objective' – defined by science and promulgated by expert spokesmen ... Overconfidence in 'better knowledge' becomes a self-fulfilling prophecy. People first cease to trust their own judgement and then want to be told the truth about what they know. Over-confidence in 'better decision-making' first hampers people's ability to decide for themselves and then undermines their belief that they can decide.
Illich, 1976, p.79

The notion that a formal and governmental system of education operates against the interests of the community is much older than the de-schooling ideology of the 1970s. It was at the end of the 18th century that William Godwin set out his objections to the idea of an official education system:

The injuries that result from a system of national education are, in the first place, that all public establishments include in them the idea of permanence ... public education has always expended its energies in the support of prejudice; it teaches its pupils not the fortitude that shall bring every proposition to the test of examination, but the art of

vindicating such tenets as may chance to be previously established . . . Secondly, the idea of national education is founded in an inattention to the nature of mind. Whatever each man does for himself is done well; whatever his neighbours or his country undertakes to do for him is done ill . . .He that learns because he desires to learn will listen to the instructions he receives and apprehend their meaning. He that teaches because he desires to teach will discharge his occupation with enthusiasm and energy. But the moment political institution undertakes to assign to every man his place, the functions of all will be discharged with supineness and indifference . . . Thirdly, the project of a national education ought uniformly to be discouraged on account of its obvious alliance with national government . . . Government will not fail to employ it to strengthen its hand and perpetuate its institutions . . . Their view as instigator of a system of education will not fail to be analogous to their views in their political capacity.
Godwin, 1793, p.616-7

Contemporary critics of the alliances between government and education would agree, and would argue that it is in the *nature* of public authorities to run coercive and hierarchical institutions whose ultimate function is to perpetuate social inequality and to brainwash the young into the acceptance of their particular slot in the official economy. Over a century ago, the anarchist Michael Bakunin (1872, p.38) characterised 'the people' in the eyes of the government as 'the eternal minor, the pupil confessedly incompetent to pass his examinations, rise to the knowledge of his teachers, and dispense with their discipline.' Bakunin made the same comparison that is made today by Everett Reimer and Ivan Illich, between the teaching profession and a priestly caste, and he declared that, 'Like conditions, like causes, always produce like effects. It will, then, be the same with the professors of the modern school, divinely inspired and licensed by the State. They will necessarily become . . . teachers of the doctrine of popular sacrifice to the power of the State and to the profit of the privileged classes.' (Bakunin, 1872, p.40.) Must we then, he asked, eliminate from society all instruction and abolish all schools? Far from it, Bakunin replied, but he demanded schools from which the *principle* of authority will have been eliminated: He called for, 'popular academies in which neither pupils nor masters will be known, where the people will come freely to get, if they need it, free instruction, and in which, rich in their own expertise, they will teach in their turn many things to the professors who shall bring them knowledge which they lack.' (Bakunin, 1872, p.42.) This conception of the school as an informal institution had already been envisaged by Godwin as a plan 'calculated to change the face of education.' He saw distinctions between teacher and pupil being dissolved and that, 'The boy, like the man, studies because he desires it. He proceeds upon a plan of his own invention, or which, by adopting, he has made his own.' (Godwin, 1797, p.80.)

In setting out the polarities between ideal types of formal and informal education, Godwin and Bakunin anticipated the recent efforts by Tim Simkins to list these differences. He finds the purpose of formal education to be long-term and general, while those of non-formal education are short-term and specific. Admission to formal education is based on previous credentials, admission to non-formal education is not. In terms of timing, formal education is 'long-cycle preparatory and full-time' while non-formal education is 'short-cycle, recurrent and part-time.' In terms of content, Simkins finds formal education to be 'input-centred and standardised' while non-formal education is 'output-centred and individualised'. The formal sector is academic, while the informal sector is practical. The clientele of the formal sector is 'determined by entry requirements' while in the non-formal sector the 'entry requirements are determined by the clientele'. In terms of its delivery system the formal sector is institution-based and isolated from the environment and the community, while the non-formal sector is 'environment-based and community-related'. Formal education, Simkins found to be rigidly structured, teacher-centred and resource-intensive, while non-formal education is flexibly structured, learner-centred and resource-saving. In terms of control, formal education is externally controlled and hierarchical, while non-formal education is self-governing and democratic (Simkins, 1976, p.16).

It is true that some people will be able to recognise in Simkins' non-formal section of education some particular enterprise which has all the characteristics which he ascribes to the formal sector. It would be equally possible to identify a formal provision which had all his informal characteristics. But as a typology, his distinctions are shrewd and accurate. In practice the influence of individuals with no particular reason for identifying with either of these polarities has a considerable effect on educational provision which is hard to identify with either of the ideal types. For example, in the inter-war and immediate post-war years, the director of education for one English county was Henry Morris, a sherry and silver-spoons aesthete, as remote as one could imagine from ideals of community-based education. He nevertheless had a vision of the local secondary school as a centre of enlightenment for the whole community, and persuaded his county council that its new shcools should provide every kind of educational opportunity for the local population. When the budget of his department did not match up with his ambitions, he brought in, at his own expense, outsiders like Maxwell Fry, Jack Pritchard and Walter Gropius to ensure that the right physical provision was made.

The school as a community resource

Henry Morris' example led other directors of education, like Stuart Mason, to elaborate the concept of the school as an education and leisure resource for the whole community. At one level this expresses itself in the demand for the provision of educational facilities for people who happen to be beyond the statutory minimum leaving age for compulsory education, i.e. adult education. At another level it demands that the expensively provided school premises should be available for out-of-school activities by people of school age. This demand for 'opening up' schools is powerfully expressed in the propaganda of one of the crusading groups:

For some years now, parents like myself have felt that there just isn't enough positive opportunity for children and teenagers to get together and enjoy themselves in a constructive way. We're told on the one hand that Britain can't afford to spend much money on children's play, regardless of the need for it; and on the other hand, as taxpayers and ratepayers, we're asked to pay £2½ billion a year for an education service ... from the point of view of the average parent, like myelf, you've got magnificent resources here that are shockingly under-used: playing fields, a gymnasium with all the showers and changing rooms, classrooms, an art room, a kitchen, a big assembly hall with a stage, and so on. By my arithmetic, your schools shut at four o'clock during the week, and over each weekend, you have three weeks' holiday at Christmas, another three at Easter, six weeks in the summer, and another good fortnight for half-terms, special holidays, polling days and so on. I make that a seven-hour day on only 190 days in the year, leaving all the evenings and 175 full days when all those magnificent resources are locked up, and our kids are in empty houses or on the streets with nowhere to go.
Fair Play for Children, 1979, p.11

This parent had an unanswerable case, and it is a case which is just as valid in terms of adult education. The combination of this variety of demands had led, even within the official provision, to a changed concept of the school. It is no longer an isolated building surrounded by playgrounds and fences. It is instead a community facility, located among the shops and public buildings in the centre of a district. There is no school hall: a hall used for a variety of purposes by the public is used by the school when necessary. There is no dining room; the children use, like anyone else, a cafe open to the public. There is no gymnasium, they use the sports hall, open to all. There is no school library: the public library has a far greater stock. Among the shops and offices of the district are scattered the classrooms and laboratories which are also used by other organisations. The daily lives of the community and those of its children are inextricably mixed. It goes without saying that the traditional distinctions between the different stages of schooling are equally blurred: day nursery, infant and junior school, middle and secondary school, further education centre and adult education centre, are, in terms of their physical use of the environment, simply fellow users of the same space.

The vision of the school as a community resource has been realised in varying degrees in different places. Just because it is outside the mandatory sector of local authority education provision, adult education, like preschool education, has been one of the easiest aspects of publicly funded education to curtail when times are hard, though its curtailment is pointless since it takes up much less than two per cent of the total of local authority education budgets.

This precious two per cent has nevertheless been most responsive to community pressures. Barbara Dinham and Michael Norton draw our attention to the variety of 'community-orientated courses' which have arisen, precisely because this particular branch of the education industry is outside the statutory area. They report, for example, how Holloway Institute in London, in conjunction with a local tenants' association, ran a course which prepared plans for a proposed new community centre, and put forward a proposal that the management of the estate should be handed over to the tenants, as well as devising a summer holiday programme and the means for funding it. They describe how at other centres, at Brighton and Bethnal Green, courses have been held that have prepared and presented alternative plans for road and redevelopment proposals, and taught how to fight the compulsory purchase orders (Dinham and Norton, 1977).

Another group of teachers has described their work in the suburbs of a southern English city, where, in pursuit of a relevant programme of *adult* education, they found themselves organising pre-school playgroups. Their scene was Leigh Park, outside Portsmouth, and the assumption of their New Communities Project was that 'adult education should seek to serve the whole community and not merely those sectors of it who currently take advantage of what is provided.' (Fordham, Poulton and Randle, 1979, p.2.)

Following this principle, Michael Newman found employment as an 'outreach worker' for The Addison Institute, London, and he describes, with a host of graphic examples, the experience of providing a service for that majority of the population who never thought that 'night school' had anything relevant or useful for them, and whose needs for education as a tool for social action were neglected by every other agency.

Newman reminds us that the origins of the adult education movement, like the origins of so many other aspects of education in Britain, were in a tradition of working-class self-help, 'community-based' as the current jargon goes, and revolving around literacy, numeracy and technical skills, and around the urge to study and discuss history, politics and economics. With the development in the twentieth century of statutory local education authorities, the emphasis of the voluntary sector moved to hobbies, recreational and leisure interests. However, he claims, it could be argued that the dressmaking, pottery and flower-arranging period in adult education was in fact a brief aberration, 'from which the service is only now showing fitful signs of recovery.' (Newman, 1979, p.120).

And, paradoxically, it was during the 'hobbies' period of adult education that the principles and practices arose, which are most valuable in the effort to respond actively and vitally to community needs. Classes were opened or closed on the criterion of consumer interest, the principle was established that tutors might be people with experience or skill in a particular activity, rather than professional teachers, and the idea grew up that the group itself should steer the course the way in which it wanted to go.

When, by the end of the 1960s, the demand actually arose among people signing on for evening classes for courses on welfare rights, community action, planning and housing matters and similar community issues, the practices of the system enabled it to respond. Adult education is moving perceptibly into the world of informal learning networks and skill exchanges, out of the classroom and into the community.

Conclusion

In education we are very far from a situation where the informal sector is gaining ground from the official sector. As attendance at an approved institution to gain the requisite educational qualifications becomes the passport to a continually widening range of occupations, the education industry is more strongly entrenched than at any time in history. Even when the myths have been swept away, its strength rests in its function as a filter to status and income. Those with the fewest years of schooling are destined to the least esteemed, least enjoyable and lowest paid jobs.

Informal education is however, rich in ideas and experiment, and powerfully influences the formal system. This is most evident in the aspirations for breaking down the walls between the school and the community. Harry Rée, when professor of education at the University of York, told a conference of young teachers that, 'I think we are going to see in your lifetime the end of schools as we know them. Instead there will be a community centre with the doors open twelve hours a day, seven days a week, where anybody can wander in and out of the library, workshops, sports centre, self-service store and bar. In a hundred years the compulsory laws for children to go to school may have gone the same way as the compulsory laws for attendance at church.' (Rée, 1972, p.8.)

As ideas borrowed from the de-schoolers become absorbed into the conventional wisdom, the professional and institutional vested interests ensure, of course, that *they* continue to dominate education. This has already happened to the notion of 'continuing education' or 'lifelong learning' which the professional educators have taken over to ensure that they are to be considered as the providers of education from the cradle to the grave. In this sense the official system lives off the ideas and practices evolved in the seedbed of educational alternatives.

8
INFORMAL CARING INSTITUTIONS

Stephen Hatch

The British economy is not providing jobs for all those seeking employment, and high levels of unemployment do not seem to be a temporary phenomenon. The effects of this shortfall in the demand for labour may remain concentrated on the unskilled and the least employable. Should the economy improve sufficiently to allow greater public expenditure on the social services, more personnel will be taken on. These people will be mostly women carrying out relatively low-skilled caring that they might otherwise have been doing on an informal basis. Thus the transfer of functions to the state will be resumed: and the natural logic of statutory action combined with the reasonable aspirations of the employees concerned will bureaucratise and professionalise this kind of work. Alternatively, leisure, or perhaps one should say discretionary time, might be spread about more widely. This would create opportunities for much more extensive participation in informal institutions of all kinds and involve a change in the balance between formal and informal activity: people would place less emphasis on earning the money to purchase goods and services from the formal economy and pay taxes for services from the State. Instead they would rely more on doing things for themselves on a self-help or reciprocal basis.

In these ways, by reintegrating production and consumption and asserting an active instead of a passive role for the consumer and by back-stepping towards the dream of a simpler, more innocent world, informal institutions might offer a new direction for the development of industrialised societies. However, the political and economic life of industrial countries is presently dominated by, and polarised around, the organised forces of production. What prospect, therefore, is there that informal institutions will ever be allowed anything but a marginal, interstitial role, or offer anything more than a few perks for the affluent and a means of survival for the poor? The present discussion is concerned with social and health care, and will attempt to answer this question only for that field.

Dominance of the state

Public discussion of social welfare is nearly all about the role of the state. The relevant statistical information is mostly about what the state does to people, and argument concentrates on ways in which statutory services should be extended or cut back. The great volume of caring activities carried on by families, neighbours and voluntary organisations lies in the shadow of this Leviathan and is little studied and little recognised.

The terminology available reflects the bias in our preoccupations. The terms social services and health services are in frequent use and denote clearly the formal, bureaucratically administered activities that are the focal point of public attention. Although not all provided directly by the state, they form part of a system of which the state is the lynch-pin. In contrast, there is no term in wide currency that covers all forms of looking after people. Yet a generic expression is essential if one is to place the formal, organised services in a wider perspective. The terms 'social care' and 'health care' will be used here to fill this gap.

The reasons for the preoccupation with statutory services and for the lack of a widely used terminology that embraces the more informal as well as the formal sorts of caring are obvious enough. Public policies are rightly the object of debate and the state is the predominant instrument for collective action. It is the source of legislation and, through taxation, the medium for mobilising most large scale financial resources. Social services all involve some transfer of resources, from the healthy to the sick, from those at work to children and the retired, and from rich to poor. Public expenditure on the health and personal social services now amounts to over six per cent of the Gross National Product while that of all the social services combined exceeds a quarter of the GNP. Whatever the limitations of statutory action, the state alone is in the position to determine priorities and to provide a framework that establishes the extent and direction of the transfers and minimal levels of standards and coverage.

However, the state is far from the only source of care, nor is it the main source of care even for many of the people in the greatest need. Thus a majority of the severely handicapped elderly and of severely mentally handicapped children are looked after by their families (Moroney, 1976). The relationship between the family and the state has recently become a subject of renewed debate. But in between and not a part of either the family or the state there exists a spectrum of other sources of care. The various elements in this spectrum need to be distinguished before the discussion can be taken much further.

The range of informal caring institutions

One element is the services provided on a commercial basis, that is, in return for payment by individuals. Private health care is controversial and significant as a means whereby the better off can obtain preferential treatment. However, in Britain expenditure on it still amounts to only a small proportion of that spent on the National Health Service. Another source of care is voluntary organisations. These are very diverse in form and in the kinds of service they provide. Thus some voluntary organisations like Barnardo's and the National Society for the Prevention of Cruelty to Children depend almost entirely on paid staff to carry out their work and provide a professional service akin to that of the statutory social services departments. More numerous are the voluntary organisations that rely mainly on unpaid workers. These are the third in the spectrum of non-statutory, non-family sources of care and can be further sub-divided in various ways. One significant distinction is between organisations providing a service for others, like the Samaritans and the Red Cross, and organisations which operate through self-help or mutual aid. The latter exist to serve their members or their members' dependants. Alcoholics Anonymous and Gingerbread, the self-help group for one-parent families, are well known examples of this kind of organisation.

The fourth element in the spectrum is the care given quite independently of any organisation by friends and neighbours. This most properly merits the term informal. However, although a boundary can be drawn between the informal group and the organisation, it is not a sharply defined one. As Henry and Robinson (1978) have shown, for example, in the case of Alcoholics Anonymous, people who are brought together as a result of their problem situation, solve their difficulties partly by forming friendships with fellow members which are ongoing outside the formal activities of the group and which continue long after formal membership of the group ceases. Hence in applying the term informal institutions to the field of social and health care it will be interpreted so as to include both care provided outside the family without any organisational basis and care provided by organisations, the participants in which receive no financial remuneration for their work. Thus, though none of the non-statutory sources of care can be excluded from the present discussion, the main focus will be on care outside the family for which the giver is not paid.

Prevalence and functions of informal care

As with other kinds of informal institutions, there is a dearth of evidence about the incidence and functions of informal caring institutions. This is partly because little interest has been taken during the past two decades and is only now beginning to revive, and partly because by their nature they are elusive and difficult to study. This applies particularly to the care provided by friends and neighbours. The good neighbour is the subject of frequent anecdotes and exhortation, indeed almost a mythology. People not infrequently bewail the decline of community and neighbourliness and have an image of a golden past of communities whose members truly cared for each other. Out of all this the truth is difficult to disinter. Certainly there have existed communities such as those described by Young, Willmott and Townsend (Young and Willmott, 1957; Townsend, 1957) in Bethnal Green in the 1950s where people were embedded in strong helping networks, the members being often relatives as well as neighbours. How many people are today part of such networks it is difficult to say. A survey of the elderly carried out by Mark Abrams for Age Concern indicated a rather modest level of informal help. Less than half of those living alone and aged 75 or more said they were visited more than once a week by friends and relatives, and less than one in ten at least once a week by voluntary workers (Abrams, M. 1978). However, there was considerable variation between the four places studied. Caring networks are likely to be strongest where there is a long settled population with little geographical mobility and a history of shared adversity. But the modern norm is more that of a mobile society where the desire for better housing and better jobs encourages frequent moves and where a home-centred life puts a premium on privacy and on the maintenance with neighbours of no more than a limited friendliness. Certainly this is what Willmott and Young found when they surveyed the suburbs to which Bethnal Greeners had moved (Willmott and Young, 1960). However, it does not preclude the possibility that friends and neighbours may do a lot to help each other when help is really needed. Cartwright's study of people at the end of their lives suggests that this does in fact happen:

The overwhelming impression of the data presented . . . is of the extent of support provided by relatives, friends and neighbours to people in the last year of their lives . . . It is perhaps surprising that this informal network of relatives and friends seems to work in such an effective way: wives and husbands care for the married, daughters for the widowed, sisters and more distant relatives for the single. Friends and neighbours generally give less intimate types of care, but if there are no relatives to help they often step into the breach. And the more things people need help with, the more people there seem to be who rally round and help. Cartwright, *et al* 1973, p.162

The important questions which cannot at present be answered concern who does and does not get cared for in this way, in what circumstances and in what sorts of neighbourhood people are willing to behave like this.

The same issues can be given a more practical slant by asking about the ways in which neighbourhood caring can be supported and encouraged. Collins and Pancoast, two American social workers, argue that natural helping networks are widespread and often arrange themselves around a key natural helper (Collins and Pancoast, 1976). They go on to advocate a strategy for social work based on identifying, supporting and working with such networks. The British counterpart to this American approach is the interest currently being taken in 'patchwork' — that is in making the basic geographical unit for the delivery of social services a patch or neighbourhood, where the social worker has the job of linking with and supporting whatever caring arrangements exist within the community. This involves a reinterpretation of the role of social workers, giving the main emphasis to a community approach instead of to that of a specialist professional service directed at individuals or families in isolation from their communities. So far, however, patchwork of this kind has not got beyond the experimental stage.

Another way of developing less formal, less professional kinds of care is to put them on an organised or semi-organised basis. This can be seen as turning caring networks into voluntary organisations, and has found expression in the growth over the past decade or so of numerous 'good neighbour' schemes. These are currently being researched by Philip Abrams who has identified several hundred schemes and whose preliminary findings indicate that they are aimed mainly at the isolated elderly and usually involve visiting, combined sometimes with other services (Abrams, P. *et al,* 1979).

Rather more evidence is available about the activities of voluntary organisations and volunteers. Indeed in the past decade two committees of enquiry have deliberated on them – Aves (1969) and Wolfenden (1977). The extent of these activities is substantial. Recent surveys (Hatch, 1978, and General Household Survey, 1977) indicate that some 10 per cent of adults in this country take part in organised voluntary work at least once a month. Estimates of the time worked by them suggest that in terms of man hours, volunteers may be making as large a contribution as the paid staff of the local authority Social Services Departments. Voluntary organisations are numerous and varied, and it seems that there is at least one relevant to the social services for every thousand people in the population.

The Wolfenden Committee sought to define the roles played by voluntary organisations in relation to the statutory services. As pioneers, they have a distinguished record; a large proportion of the present social and health services can be traced back to initiatives taken by voluntary organisations and subsequently adopted and extended by government. The pressure group activities of voluntary organisations are also prominent and have generally been linked to the pioneering role. Since the establishment of the Welfare State these two roles have tended to be seen as the main justification for voluntary action. Voluntary organisations, it is argued, cannot match the resources available to the state; nor can they provide services universally available to all those eligible. Today, however, there is a renewed awareness that there are other valuable functions for voluntary organisations besides simply blazing a trail and creating a demand for statutory action.

Thus volunteering is being extensively promoted as a means of extending and supporting statutory services, in such forms as meals on wheels, helping in hospitals, organising holidays for the handicapped, running social clubs for the elderly and so on. Most of these are the kind of activities which the state could carry out itself if it was prepared to raise the necessary resources. To say this is not to imply reservations about voluntary action, since the activities are of value in themselves and represent a form of community involvement in caring; and whatever the government's attitude to the level of public expenditure on social services there will always be a gap between the volume of needs and the resources available to meet them.

Special features of informal care

Some voluntary activities could not be taken on by statutory agencies whatever the level of resources available. This seems to be particularly true of those carried out by self-help organisations. A recent study of Alcoholics Anonymous and other self-help health groups, (Robinson and Henry 1977; Robinson, 1979), concentrates attention on the self-help process: it shows that many of the participants are enabled to cope more successfully with their problem through the sharing and involvement with others in the same situation as themselves. This can only happen in an organisation of and for the sufferers themselves, since only in that context do problem sufferers have the opportunity of taking control over their own lives and drawing on the benefits of the 'helper principle' (Riesman, 1965).

In recent years, there has been a proliferation of self help organisations for people afflicted with specific mental or physical problems, and there is now a widespread network of local branches of such organisations as the Spastics Society, the Ileostomy Association, the Disabled Drivers' Association and the Association for Spina Bifida and Hydrocephalus. Those concerned with addictions, compulsive behaviour, phobias and other mental problems tend to be influenced by the A.A. model. More numerous are those that place their main emphasis on providing services themselves, offering practical advice and information and representing the interests of their members to the statutory authorities; but, in so doing, they can also bring considerable psychological benefit to participants through sharing problems and coping with stigma. Some of these functions the state might be able to carry out, but others arise uniquely from the voluntary, mutual-aid basis of the organisations.

Another recent field of growth for voluntary organisations has been in the provision of advice and counselling. Citizens Advice Bureaux are long established in this field, but they have been joined by Samaritans, Marriage Guidance and recently by a variety of local legal and housing advice centres. The latter tend to be run by paid staff, but in the field as a whole, trained volunteers play a major part. The desirability of an independent source of advice is a strong justification for the predominant role of voluntary organisations in this context. It is also worth noting that people have been taking personal problems as well as ones to do with the statutory services to voluntary organisations, rather than to the local authority social workers. The result is that the voluntary sector has become not just an extension of the statutory services, but the main provider of advice and counselling.

The third field where voluntary action cannot readily be replaced by statutory services is community care. Looking after people in the community requires a variety of services: for some of these, like home helps and sheltered housing, the state is bound to be the main provider, but the state cannot be the source of the more informal, day-by-day care and company. The good neighbour schemes mentioned earlier are one way of enlisting the community in meeting these needs, and there are other arrangements like pensioners' clubs and street warden schemes which serve a similar integrative function.

The future of informal care

The discussion so far has concentrated on the present role of informal caring institutions. What of the future? Present trends in the care provided by friends and neighbours cannot be gauged with any assurance. There can be little doubt that there is less informal care in new as compared to old communities, and this may be why people tend to think that these kinds of caring relationships are on the decline generally. However, one cannot tell to what extent caring networks develop as new communities get older. On the other hand, there are good grounds for thinking that care provided through voluntary organisations is increasing. The General Household Survey in 1977 recorded a figure of 9.6 per cent for participation in voluntary work compared to 8.3 per cent in 1973, and in those localities studied for the Wolfenden Committee, the number of voluntary organisations seemed to be rising at the rate of two or three per cent a year (Hatch, 1980). Thus voluntary organisations appear to be on a steady if undramatic upward trend.

Why should this be? The answers can only be speculative. One line of interpretation might be that participation in organised activities is a substitute for more informal kinds of caring; as the neighbours cease to act spontaneously, more organised efforts are required to elicit the same willingness to help and to meet the same needs.

Another set of explanations relates more to the development of statutory services. The growth of statutory services is evidence of an increasing demand for social services in some form and of rising expectations. What the state can offer is constrained partly by the availability of resources, but also by the nature of the bureaucratic machinery through which statutory services are delivered. Remoteness, impersonality, departmentalisation and lack of sensitivity and responsiveness are complaints frequently heard of the extended statutory services of today. Such shortcomings create openings for more informal and direct ways of helping people.

Related to these negative aspects of statutory services are changes in the pattern of needs. Demographic factors mean that in future there will be increasing numbers of infirm elderly; and while medical knowledge has made great advances in dealing with infectious diseases and various acute conditions, growing numbers with chronic, sometimes degenerate, conditions such as arthritis, strokes and mental handicap are surviving and requiring a mixture of social and medical care. This raises questions as to the assumptions underlying the organisation of caring services. A highly professional service, one where an essentially passive client or patient is ministered to and given instructions by an omniscient professional may be appropriate for acute illnesses which can be cured by technical administration of drugs or surgery. It is less appropriate for helping people live with chronic conditions. This is a matter of self-care, mutual aid and community care, and makes an issue not so much of the availability of specialised professional expertise, equipment and facilities in distant institutions, but of the knowledge and support available to the sufferers and those who care for them on a day-to-day basis. In other words, it is about enhancing the capabilities of informal caring institutions.

Another way of looking at the growth of voluntary organisations is to see participation in them as a form of leisure-time activity, which itself is affected by changing roles within the family. In *The Symmetrical Family,* Young and Willmott (1973) argue that there is a trend towards more active forms of leisure, towards participant as opposed to spectator sports for example. Voluntary work is one of the more active forms of leisure likely to benefit from this trend. However, there is another more marked trend for married women to take paid jobs. This may not detract from the proporiton of the population who take some part in voluntary work, but it is likely to reduce the proportion of women who give a great deal of time to voluntary work and who effectively treat voluntary work as a part-time job. These contrary trends seem to be finding expression in the increasing level of participation in voluntary action combined with the expansion of such paid posts as volunteer organisers and administrators.

Conclusion

Informal caring institutions share, with other kinds of informal institution, the characteristics of not being widely recognised, recorded or regulated, of being outside the state and outside the mainstream of capitalist enterprise. However, they differ from much of the informal economy in being perfectly legal and publicly regarded as laudable rather than culpable. They cannot be condemned as hustles or fiddles. Also, whereas the informal economy generally provides goods and services that would have to be paid for if obtained through the formal economy, informal careers generally provide services that would be free if obtained from the state. This obviously affects people's willingness to exchange the one for the other and the character of the relationships between the formal and the informal. Whereas the rising cost of housing repairs provides an obvious incentive to do it yourself, and the higher rates of income tax and VAT an incentive to providing services on a reciprocal basis without formal cash payments, there is no such obvious impetus behind the offering of socal care.

One significant result of this difference is that whereas much of the informal economy subverts and conflicts with the formal economy, this is less the case with social care. Some occupational groups fear displacement by volunteers; the pretensions of some professionals can be exposed by greater community involvement and voluntary organisations rightly act as critics of inadequate performance by statutory services. Thus there are tensions, especially when voluntary organisations step out of docile and supportive roles. But the conflict is perhaps less fundamental than in other fields. Consequently, the idea of a closer integration of formal and informal sources of care is not a nonsensical one.

The role of the state in social welfare is bound to be a major one: it can hardly avoid being the dominant partner in any relationship with informal institutions. The question is what part it encourages or allows informal institutions to play. At present the spokesmen of the statutory services can be relied upon to give public accolades to the value of voluntary action: but there is often a patronising tone in such accolades, and in practice, in allocating resources and everyday decision-making, the voluntary sector is usually accorded only a marginal role, one exemplified by the tendency to tack on at the end of policy statements sentences like 'voluntary organisations too have an important part to play'. The statutory services are now retreating from some of the grander pretensions and expectations of a decade ago. It is an important question for the future of social policy whether this is simply a tactical withdrawal, or the starting point for a new strategy. Such a strategy would seek to support rather than supplant informal institutions and to develop a more integral relationship between the formal and the informal.

PART THREE

INFORMAL
SOCIAL INSTITUTIONS

9
INFORMAL MARRIAGE

Petrine Macdonald and Gerald Mars

Jane Austen's often quoted remark that a single man in possession of a good fortune must be in want of a wife is just one example of society's preoccupation with marriage. In recent history, the academic study of marriage owes much to social anthropologists who have provided descriptions and analyses of the institution and comparative studies of marriage and kinship in various non-industrial societies. Most modern anthropologists would agree with Douglas' definition of marriage as 'arrangements approved in society with special reference to the institutionalised relationships of husband and wife' (Douglas, 1964, p.409). But she points out that in ordinary usage 'marriage' includes two distinct ideas: 'that a man and woman cohabit, generally with the intention of founding a family; and that some distinction can be drawn between marriage and other forms of sexual union qualifiable as pre-marital, extra-marital, adultery etc.' With this limited focus of attention shared as much by other social commentators as by anthropologists, it is perhaps not surprising that serious academic research has neglected what has become an important aspect of the subject: the increasing tendency for partners to live together without formal, legal or religious sanctions.

Admittedly, there has been some discussion, in describing Eskimo and American Indian cultures, for instance, of a failure to distinguish the status of husband and wife from other casual, temporary unions, and Evans Pritchard (1951, p.116) showed that the Nuer have a system of concubinage which is not disapproved of in the case of widows cohabiting with lovers of their choosing. Also in industrial societies some attention has been given to alternative collective forms of living as in Israel's Kibbutzim (Spiro, 1970), and the North American experiments in 'group marriage' (Constantine and Constantine, 1977) and communal living (Fairfield, 1971; Speck, *et al,* 1972). But generally there have been no more than a few dozen articles and the odd unpublished paper or thesis (Macklin, 1974; 1976; Lewis and Spanier, 1975; Lewis, *et al,* 1975) on 'cohabitation', 'common law marriages' or men and women who 'live together'.

Scanning magazines and newspapers, which often reflect popular preoccupations more immediately than acadmeic literature, one is aware of problem-page letters which seek advice on unmarried cohabitation, short stories concerning couples living together who are not married and newspaper articles reporting the details of, and examining the implications of, episodes such as the 'Lee Marvin case'. It may be that this increased interest is not the result of a great increase in the number of unmarried people living together but merely a reflection of an increased number of people living together openly. As Bowman and Spanier (1978, p.34) say, 'What is new perhaps, is a growing acceptance and tolerance of these life styles and sometimes a recommendation of them as a solution to certain problems of living.'

Nevertheless, if the statistics are examined there is evidence of a real increase in the numbers of people who enter some form of unmarried co-habitation. For example, according to British government statistics on *Changing Patterns of Family Formation and Dissolution in England and Wales* (OPCS, 1979) the number of couples who live together before their first marriage more than tripled between the late 1960s and 1975. Similarly, analysis of American census data for 1960 -70 suggests that cohabitation increased number of people living together openly. As Bowman of the Census Study (1979) showed the number of unmarried couples living together has more than doubled since 1970. And while single people make up one-fifth of the nation's households, cohabiting couples make up two per cent of some 48 million marriages. In Sweden, the number of unmarried cohabiting couples also seems to have increased recently. Whereas ten to twenty years ago, they comprised only one per cent of the total of married and unmarried cohabiting couples, the number of unmarried couples living together in 1970 was about seven per cent of the total, while in 1974 the figure seemed to have increased to about 12 per cent (Trost, 1978).

For some sections of the population, notably the young and the old, these proportions are much higher. In 1974 a national study of a representative sample of American men between 20 and 30 years of age, found that 18 per cent reported living with a woman for six months or more without being married to her (Clayton and Voss, 1977). As Bowman and Spanier (1978, p.4) say, 'Cohabitation . . . is one of the more remarkable trends in modern social life since few social activities of such great personal significance have accelerated so dramatically in a span of only a few years.'

The relative paucity of research in the context of this apparent rise in the number of cohabiting unmarried people prompted the study on which this chapter is based. According to the evidence available, cohabitation seems to take three forms. First, it is seen as a temporary arrangement without any commitment to formal marriage. Second, it has been defined as a 'trial marriage' (Berger, 1971) in which people see if they are compatible for formal marriage. Third it might be seen as an intended permanent and lasting alternative to marriage. It is this third form of cohabitation which we call 'informal marriage' and to which our study is orientated. While such a form of marriage is informal in attitude and not bound by legal constraints, it may be said to be becoming institutionalised in terms of the numbers of people taking part and the longevity of their relationships. The general aim of our study has been to document the underlying patterns which apply to different socio-cultural groups; to examine any extensive, though unformulated understandings and to uncover any generally accepted and taken for granted rules which govern this form of cohabitation.

As anthropologists, the starting point for our research has been that 'a marriage is essentially a re-arrangement of social structure' (Radcliffe-Brown and Forde, 1958, p.48) and, therefore, one of the main aims of our study is to try to relate the specific social phenomenon of informal marriage to a wider social context. Since any developing institution must be seen as intimately interrelated with the wider social structure, our study is attempting to examine both the effects these alliances have on existing structures and the effects the social structure has on the form and duration of the informal marriage.

This preliminary report has been written after six months of a three year study carried out at the Centre for Occupational and Community Research, Middlesex Polytechnic, and is based on depth interviews with 18 couples whose ages range from 20-33. In most cases both parties to the cohabiting relationship were interviewed. We are using a network system similar to Irwin's (1972) method of 'snowball sampling' to find cohabiting couples who have been living together for one year or more. Informally married couples are asked to take part in the study and also asked if they have friends who would be willing to cooperate. We are aware of the fact that this method may produce an atypical sample and, therefore, a national survey determined by geographical and class factors is planned to test out the hypotheses raised by our initial investigation.

The major questions when considering informal marriage are: who enters into such relationships and why do they do so; how do such relationships develop; what problems are experienced by the participants; and how do the characteristics of the relationship differ, if indeed they do so, from conventional formal marriage? We will address each of these in turn, drawing on our own findings to date and placing these in the context of existing research findings.

Who takes part?

The initial findings of our study suggest few clear answers to the first question: who is likely to enter into an informal marriage? There are two approaches possible here: the first would look at respondents from the viewpoint of their background; the second from the viewpoint of their 'foregrounds'. We found that the backgrounds of the people we interviewed varied: they came from different parts of the country and from all social classes. The structure of the interviewee's families of origin also varied ranging from large, 'extended' and close-knit families to small, relatively isolated nuclear families. Most of the parents of those interviewed still lived together while some had divorced and in some cases remarried. None of the participants, however, was raised in an orphanage or other institution.

These sample characteristics, however, correspond with those of several American studies, Henze and Hudson (1974), for example, who interviewed 291 students at Arizona State University in 1971-72. Their study compared the personal and family characteristics of a random sample of both cohabiting and non-cohabiting college students. Questions were asked about where the participants were brought up, whether their parents were ever divorced, who was the principle disciplinarian in the home and whether the discipline was strict. They found that 29 per cent of males and 18 per cent of females admitted currently cohabitating or that they had cohabited. They concluded that as far as the families of origin were concerned they 'failed to differentiate between cohabitors and non-cohabitors.'

Another study carried out by Peterman, Ridley and Anderson (1974) also supports these findings. Using a questionnaire, eleven hundred under-graduates at Pennsylvania State University were asked about parents' occupation, marital status, education, income, religion and the size of their hometown. This study concluded that 'the cohabiting students differ little from their non-cohabiting counterparts on family and community background or their level of intellectual and emotional functioning.' (Peterman, Ridley and Anderson, 1974, p.344.)

A number of American studies (Henze and Hudson, 1974; Bower and Christopherson, 1977; Groves Conference, 1974) do, however, suggest some general differences between the lifestyles and experiences of cohabitors as compared to non-cohabitors. What cohabitors seem to share in common is that they are less apt to attend church, are more likely to identify with a liberal lifestyle, more likely to indicate a willingness to engage in a variety of nontraditional lifestyles and are more apt to be drug users. Like the American research, a significant feature of our sample is that they have all undergone some form of tertiary education. However, unlike much of the American material few of the people in our sample were involved in full-time education when we first interviewed them because we were specifically interested in informal marriages where at least one of the partners was in full-time employment. They had either been to university at some time since leaving school, or had attended art school, or had been to a teachers' training college.

When we come to consider what we have termed 'foreground' factors we are finding that the common characteristic of tertiary education in our sample is of great significance. It can be argued of course that 'foreground' factors become overemphasised as the result of using a network approach to finding suitable subjects for the study, rather than being indicative of the general characteristics of participants of informal marriage in Britain as a whole. Equally likely, however, is the possibility that people who enter into informal marriage will have already moved from the parental home before they enter such an arrangement, which is usually the case among those who have some tertiary education. The major reason for this is that informal marriage is still not regarded by social commentators as a respectable alternative to marriage. There is still a degree of social disapproval reflecting the idea that it comprises 'matings of inferior status in the social scheme of values' (Lowie, 1933, p.146), even though this may be changing gradually. Most parents want their children to marry eventually; to conform to what they believe are society's norms. Therefore, it is likely that people who enter into an informal marriage need to have been somewhat independent of the influence of their family before they can consider taking such a step.

In the case of our study, we would further argue that since educational establishments like universities are often isolated from the rest of society, peers are likely to become more important reference groups to those attending them. As Bowman and Spanier (1978, p.39) say, 'College campuses appear to have an insulating effect on students. It is possible to live together at college without much negative sanction whereas such a relationship might be frowned upon and avoided in the student's home town.' Indeed, it is significant that the majority of students who live together do not tell their parents about the relationship, at least early on, but that they readily tell their friends (Macklin, 1974). This insulation, isolation and the change of reference group that goes with it, further weakens the parental generation's control and encourages the rejection of its influence in favour of the student's own peer group. It must be pointed out, however, that although people might leave the parental home to cohabit, we feel it worth examining our data when we have more case studies, to see if such people had previously lived away from the parental home and, therefore, had already established their independence.

Why informal marriage?

The second question, what are the reasons for people living together without marriage, is discussed by Jan Trost (1978) in 'Married and Unmarried Cohabitation in Sweden'. He says that reasons can be broadly classified as: legal, economic and ideological although, as he points out, the legal and economic reasons that people give may be based on 'erroneous' beliefs and assumptions. An interesting example of an economic motive for not legally marrying is discussed in an American paper by K. A. Yllo (1978). The study was based on a national, random sample survey of 2143 men and women and showed that, while the rate of cohabitation declines sharply with age, there is a marked rise for those over 60. This is due to the social security laws which penalise widowers who remarry by withdrawing their rights to claim survivors' benefit. We would question whether fifteen years ago such an economic motive would have been sufficient on its own to deter many people from marrying.

According to yet other American research (Groves Conference, 1974) the most common reason given by respondents for why they cohabit is emotional attachment to their partner, just as in formal marriage. We did not directly ask the people in our sample why they did not marry but through a number of indirect questions, reasons emerged which would broadly fit into Trost's ideological category. Most of our respondents gave negative rather than positive reasons for not getting married; they could not see that formalising their relationshp would grant them any benefits which they did not already enjoy. But as C. Wright Mills (1969, p.440) has said, 'the differing reasons men give for their actions are not themselves without reason'. Indeed, the changing attitude to informal marriage, the fact that sexual codes now make permissiveness with affection more acceptable and the availability and increased usage of various means of contraception, especially the pill and sterilisation are all factors which contribute to this feeling.

A number of couples in our study expressed a disenchantment with traditional courtship and marriage because of the high divorce rate and the feeling that those who avoid divorce are often less than happy. Several people said that they strongly objected to the hypocracy involved in having a church wedding when they were not church goers and of promising to stay together even though the divorce rate was rising. One man said: 'People go into it (marriage) without thinking enough. They make vows, "to have and to hold" and then spit fire at each other.' Interestingly a number of women interviewed objected to the implied dependence which being married suggests. Several said that even if they did marry, they would not change their name.

We feel that two things have been overlooked in Trost's analysis. First he seems to have neglected the possibility that cohabitation is, in many cases, a 'trial marriage' rather than an informal marriage as we have defined it, and that a major reason why people live together without marriage is to assess whether or not the relationship will work on a longer, more intimate basis than just dating. Henze and Hudson for example, conclude: 'We believe that cohabitation patterns on the college campus are, in the 1970s, what dating patterns were in the 1920s; that is expanding dimensions of the courtship process.' (Henze and Hudson, 1974, p.726.)

A number of American researchers believe that increased unmarried cohabitation is unlikely to significantly reduce the marriage rate in the long run because the majority of people surveyed by them saw informal marriage as a stage in the relationship and marriage as the ultimate goal. In this sense it might reflect changing patterns of formal marriage and result in 'bunching' in the marriage statistics in later years, rather like the changing patterns of women's work which has resulted in 'delayed families' as opposed to a real decline in the birth rate as was first suggested. Indeed one of the reasons why studies have identified informal marriages as being of shorter duration than legal marriage could be that many of these relationships are really trial marriages which are ended by the couples concerned marrying legally. A couple may decide that their 'trial marriage' is a success and that, therefore, legal marriage is the obvious next step. Equally, if it is considered a failure they might seek out a new cohabiting relationship, again with the object of long-term formal marriage.

The second point overlooked by Trost arises from our own research; he ignores the possibility that reasons for not formally marrying can change during a relationship. In a number of our cases the couple's initial reason for moving in together could be described as an uncertainty about whether their relationship would be successful. Having discovered, after several months or years, that the relationship is satisfactory, a couple may still decide not to marry if they feel that the legal fact of being married will not improve their life together or might even risk changing or threatening it. However, *all* those interviewed by us said that they would marry in the event of children because they felt that their unmarried status would make life difficult for and reflect badly on any offspring. When questioned more closely on this point, it was clear that in most cases these feelings were not based on a specific understanding of the laws concerning illegitimate children, on their inheritance rights for instance, but were based on a concern for the *social* acceptance of the children. Several women, did make the point that having children implied total dependence on the man if only for a short time and they felt they would like to feel legally protected at such a vulnerable time.

Becoming informally married

The question of why people live together without being married proves to be important when one examines and tries to understand the initial stages of informal marriage. Diana Barker (1978) in 'A Proper Wedding' notes that, whatever the pros and cons of marriage, the wedding ceremony itself is significant both to the couple concerned and to their relations and friends. Most weddings involve some organisation and planning; the wedding is an event anticipated by the people concerned for several weeks, and in some cases for several months, before it actually takes place. This period is renowned for short tempers, arguments and last minute second thoughts, as the many separate elements of the event are organised and arrangements made. However, it is an important period, for it gives the participants time to absorb and discuss the implications of the wedding and what marriage will involve. This element of a 'proper wedding' or the lack of it, is also important when one considers informal marriage.

At the beginning of our research we suspected that informal marriage might also be marked by tension in the parallel period between the decision to live together and actually moving in with a partner. Since this period can be seen as a 'safety gap', we suggested that informal marriages involving such a period would be likely to be more stable and longer lasting than informal marriages which were less well considered. This suspicion, however, has so far proved unfounded. In only a very few cases did we find couples with anything like a waiting period between their decision to live together and its implementation. The great majority of people interviewed revealed that their initial moving in together had been either somewhat casual: 'We didn't discuss it but it seemed silly to pay two rents'; or due to force of circumstances: 'I didn't have anywhere to live and she said that I could stay with her'. But this set of findings needs further examination. It may be said that our original suspicion has some foundation and that the couples we interviewed who are still together, are together in spite of the lack of forethought. To answer this question we need to interview couples who have lived together but who later separate and see whether their relationships began in a different way. This material will be obtained during the course of our study.

More importantly, assuming the significance of the initial planning and decision-making phase, we suggest that informal marriage can be seen as one alternative to marriage; that it is the same as formal marriage without the legal and religious sanctions. If the distinction between trial marriage and informal marriage is maintained this does not ignore other interpretations of cohabitation. If the participants viewed their relationship at an early stage as trial marriage then our findings regarding the lack of formalisation of the beginning of the arrangement are much less surprising in the same way that one would not expect a couple to plan and discuss their first date at great length or see it as a necessarily significant step. Alternatively, however, should we find evidence of such a prior waiting period before a couple decide to live together then this would support our notion of their cohabitation as informal marriage.

We do not mean to suggest by this that all cohabitation must be seen as an informal alternative to marriage. It is obvious that this is not the case. Some cohabiting relationships are clearly a reaction against rising divorce rates; some arise from legal wrangles between those separated from their spouses; while others have to do with changing notions of conjugal rights in a context of the growth of the women's movement. Yet others are the result of changing courtship patterns and will be ended by traditional marriage or by the couple separating because they feel that they are not suited.

Ambiguity in social relationships: The problems of informal marriage

When considering the effects that informal marriage has on the existing social structure, one major point seems to us of particular interest: informal marriage creates ambiguities in the relationships of the couple with the outside world. While both formal and informal marriages involve a rearrangement of the partners' immediate relationships with their families of origin, the lack of public ceremony in the case of an informal marriage adds to the ambiguity of their situation and further bedevils the relationships between the generations.

As we have said, legal marriage generally involves a number of pre-arranged steps which culminate in a ceremony. This ceremony marks, among other things, that control of the couple has passed from the senior to the junior generation; the sexuality of the couple is no longer under the nominal control of their parents and any services which the couple performed for their parents, such as contributing money to the household, helping around the house, are formally withdrawn in favour of the new household which the couple will set up. In the case of informal marriage, however, there are no socially marked demonstrations indicating that this has happened and, from the point of view of the parental generation, the change of control from one generation to the next appears to happen without their fore-knowledge, consent or even involvement. The fact that all but one of those interviewed by us had already left the parental home before they cohabited, suggests that in these cases parental control had already been relaxed, surrendered or displaced before the start of the informal marriages. Despite this, ambiguities still remained, perhaps because there was no formal or conscious expression of what the new situation involved for the parties concerned.

This amibguity is reflected in the fact that approximately half those interviewed admitted to never actually telling their parents of their informal marriage. This is not to say that the parents of these people were unaware of the situation but that they were left to glean the information for themselves: 'I never actually told them but they are not daft, they worked it out.' 'They knew we lived in the same flat and I was always talking about him so, eventually, they must have put two and two together.' When asked why they had not told their parents, some of those interviewed said that it was a private arrangement and, therefore, did not concern their parents. In the case of a number of women, the reason given was that they felt it would upset and disappoint their parents and so the situation was left deliberately vague or not admitted. In several cases the pretence was carried to the extent that parents visiting one partner caused the other to move out of the home temporarily so that the parents would be unaware of the nature of the relationship. Of those people who did tell their parents about the arrangement, we found that women tended to want to tell their parents in person while men were more unconcerned about the method of breaking the news. There is therefore a suggestion here that control over procreation by the senior generation is regarded as significant by their juniors.

We found the ambiguity further reflected in answers to questions about sleeping arrangements during overnight visits to parents and relations. In cases where couples did not sleep together at their parents' home, the reason given was that either their parents would not permit it or that the couple themselves were reluctant to raise the matter. In some cases, after a time parents changed the sleeping arrangements without prompting, which the couple took as a sign that their relationship had become more acceptable to their parents.

On the other hand, in all cases but one, where it was applicable, parents staying overnight at the couple's home assumed that the couple would sleep together there. In the one case where this did not apply, the mother, who was a regular churchgoer, refused to visit the couple. However, she did permit both her husband and her daughter to visit and stay overnight. It would seem from this that people respect and abide by the informal rules operating in the home that they are visiting and that, if they feel unable to do this, they avoid the situation altogether.

The ambiguous nature of informal marriage extends to the couple's relationship with the wider social structure and it does so in a variety of ways. For example, where both unmarried partners work they are typically taxed as two single people and, therefore, pay higher tax than a married couple. In the UK this aspect of informal marriage costs them £195 per annum. On the other hand, if one of the partners applies for social security, the earnings of the other will be taken into account when the case is being assessed, as is the case with a married couple. Legally, the status of an unmarried couple varies with the particular law invoked. In the UK, in the absence of a will, one unmarried partner cannot automatically inherit from the other because they are not legally next of kin. However, in several cases recently, the ownership of the home has been awarded to the surviving partner where they have been able to prove that this was the deceased's intention.

While the colloquial term for informal marriage is the same as that for cohabitation, namely 'living together', the ambiguity of the institution is perhaps most obviously represented by the fact that there is no commonly used, unambiguous word in the English language to describe the partners of an informal marriage. Most of the people interviewed by us said that they found referring to their partner when talking to strangers difficult because of the absence of a suitable word. The words 'boyfriend' and 'girlfriend' were used in the main, although all said that if a shopkeeper or tradesman referred to their partner as husband or wife, they rarely corrected the misunderstanding since it was not important to do so, and indeed it may be important not to do so. It is interesting that the English language has responded so quickly to the women's movement by the introduction, if not widespread acceptance of, the term 'Ms' for both married and unmarried women, and yet no word has so far emerged to describe the partners of an informal marriage. It may be argued, however, that the women's movement has existed in one form or another for many years and in comparison, the institutionalisation of informal marriage is relatively new. Of course, people living together in a permanent arrangement without marriage is not a new phenomenon in itself. In the recent past, couples in such a relationship tended to live *as though* they were married; the women used their partner's name, wedding rings were worn and, generally, the impression given to outsiders was that the couple had actually married. The phenomenon of living together relatively permanently without the pretence of religious or legal sanctions as with informal marriage is of relatively recent origin and it is this that perhaps accounts for this linguistic gap.

The normality of informal marriage

When considering the effect social structure has on the form and duration of informal marriage, the point which stands out, perhaps surprisingly, is the similarity between informal marriage and its formal counterpart. We argue that this similarity can be accounted for by the influence of existing social pressures and the strength of existing formal institutions.

Although informal marriage may seem to many a radical and somewhat shocking departure from traditional legal marriage, we found the couples we interviewed remarkably conformist in their approach to their relationship and that the pattern of most of their informal marriages paralleled traditional ones in major ways. At its most basic, the influence of formal marriage can be seen in the fact that all those interviewed had chosen to live as part of a couple rather than as part of a threesome, foursome etc. (We realise, of course, that there is a relatively small number of people who have chosen to live in large sexual groups as in 'group marriage' or in certain communes.) Further, we found that the informal marriages we studied entailed the same kind of sexual obligation as in traditional marriage in that the ideal of sexual exclusivity was subscribed to. In several cases interviewees said that they felt this exclusivity was important and that it entailed rejecting other boyfriends/girlfriends at the beginning of the relationship. As we said earlier, all those interviewed said they would marry if they had children and thus the duration of informal marriages seems to be greatly affected by the social pressures regarding illegitimacy. The legal position of illegitimate children does not, in itself, appear a major factor in determining the duration of informal marriages.

As far as domestic duties are concerned, while equal sharing tended to be seen as the ideal, in fact the women interviewed did more than the men and, more importantly, took more of the responsibility for such work. This finding echoes those of an American study by Stafford, Backman and Dibona (1977, p.41) which compared the division of labour among married and unmarried couples. The authors of this study conclude: 'the persistence of the traditional division of labour among both the cohabiting and married couples is neither the outcome of a power struggle nor the differential availability of time. Rather it is the nonconscious ideology developed from parental modeling that preserves traditional sex roles.'

Finally, the normality of informal marriage is underlined when the couples split-up. Current research being conducted by Kitty Mika of the University of Colorado suggests that couples who live together can find breaking up as traumatic as do married couples getting a divorce. Indeed, since commitment has been found to be as critical a variable in the adjustment of cohabiting couples as it is in formal marriages (Lewis, *et al*, 1975; Dean and Spanier, 1974; Spanier, 1976), it is perhaps not surprising that couples find opting out of the relationship less easy than they originally believed.

So far our tentative findings would confirm that, in spite of what people might think or fear, and not discounting the minor interactual difficulties faced by all kinds of cohabiting partners, informal marriage is rather less radical than it is often described. As Bowman and Spanier (1978, p.35) have said, 'It is sometimes assumed not only by the individuals involved but by outside observers, that every seeming innovation represents the point of a wedge of social change. If we learn anything from history we learn that many such apparent innovations either remain as the lifestyles of small minorities or are gradually phased out.' To this we might add that even if such innovations become established as an institution they take on a form not so dissimilar from existing comparable institutions. Thus informal marriage seems far less a reflection of major new directions in social organisation and more a reminder of the strength of existing social forces.

10
THE EXTRA-MARITAL AFFAIR

Tony Lake

It seems almost impossible to obtain reliable statistics of the prevalence of affairs in contemporary Britain. This is partly due to practical problems of methodology, and partly the result of wide differences of opinion as to what constitutes an affair.

Broadly defined, an extra-marital affair occurs whenever a married person sets up a private sexual relationship which takes over some of the functions of the marriage. Affairs are, by their nature, personal and intimate matters which men and women are often reluctant to discuss except in general terms. Surveys which are normally reliable, including those which employ trained interviewers who visit respondents in their homes, cannot be depended upon to provide reliable data on such matters.

It is widely believed that affairs affect a great many marriages. Thirty per cent of all current divorces cite adultery as causing the irretrievable breakdown which the law accepts as being a necessary precondition of divorce. Wilson and Nias (1976, p.128) state: 'Surveys show that around 50 per cent of men have extra marital relations at some time in their lives, and about 25 per cent of women.'

Perhaps the best UK statistics, however, were achieved by Gorer (1970), in an ORC quota sample poll of 1,986 people aged 16 to 46, interviewed at home by trained staff. Eighty-one per cent of his total sample were married, of whom eight per cent admitted 'full extra-marital affairs'. Twice as many husbands as wives made these admissions. A further distinction was made between those five per cent who said they had 'gone all the way', and the remaining three per cent who had not. That the survey

157

included this additional question is an interesting illustration of the problem of definition.

Gorer's survey also posed the question: 'Apart from kissing people in greeting or in fun (such as under the mistletoe) have you ever kissed anybody except your husband/wife since marriage?' Twenty-two per cent of his married informants answered 'yes', amongst them more husbands than wives, and with a greater concentration among the early school leavers, and in the lower middle and skilled working classes. If it is argued that about five per cent of marriages are between people of whom at least one partner has an affair, then this figure seems rather lower than the other surveys would suggest. A low figure might arise in situations where the interviewee did not wish to make admissions of a personal nature with a spouse nearby. It would therefore be reasonable to suppose that the 22 per cent figure is nearer to a true estimate, at least for this age-group.

The more intractable difficulty lies in defining an affair. A brief appraisal of some of the variables will help to show why this is so. First, there can be disagreement about whether an extra-marital relationship is an affair if there is no 'full' sexual intercourse. Two people may be very strongly attracted to one another, and form a romantic attachment which is equivalent to a courtship, but still manage to avoid sexual intercourse. Yet others will have no love for one another, and indulge in a variety of sexual actions. So the question arises as to whether it is love or sex which defines the 'full' affair. At the same time, sexual intercourse is itself a loose phrase, lacking in clear definition. For some people, full intercourse means coitus; and sex play resulting in oral intercourse and multiple orgasm is not regarded as full intercourse. This distinction is used by some to differentiate between 'going all the way' and not doing so. There are, of course, wide differences in tolerance on the part of married people. Actions which would be seen as minor infidelities to some will be regarded as full adultery by others and treated as sufficient to end a marriage.

Ultimately the distinction as to whether or not a relationship is or is not an affair has to be left to individual judgements. The lack of reliable statistics on the prevalence of affairs is not, however, an insurmountable obstacle to the study of the phenomenon. Case-work methods and, in particular, the use of the highly confidential interview employing counselling techniques, reveal many of the factors which cause affairs, and many of the ways people cope with the resultant conflicts in themselves and within their marriage. The material upon which the following comments are based was derived from nearly two hundred interviews and some forty letters. These investigations have been more fully reported in *Affairs – The Anatomy of Extra Marital Relationships* (Lake and Hills, 1979).

The nature of affairs as alternative marriages

My wife continued to feel a lot for me after I had stopped feeling anything much for her . . . I wanted things to go on, and I was moving more away. It was immensely distressing for her. I felt guilt about the children. I never felt I was withdrawing from them . . . My lover came on the scene about then. She was a friend of the working sort at first, and I became more and more fond of her, and it was impossible to allocate how much the relationship between her and me affected my marriage. I still can't sort that out.
'Oliver', Lake and Hills, 1979, p.88

Oliver's dilemma – an inability to resolve a multidimensional conflict between a deeply involving extra-marital affair and an unhappy marriage which is not totally unsupportable – typifies the central problem posed by the affair which becomes an alternative marriage. The conflict is partly between the person having the affair and his spouse, partly between the lovers, and partly within the person being considered – which might be any one of four people as the partners of two marriages. The conflict arises in the first place as a result of the nature of formal marriage.

If the essence of formal marriage can be described – and there are those who would aruge that it cannot – then it probably lies in the *exclusive mutuality* of the contract between man and wife, in the scope of this mutuality, and in the ideal nature of the aspirations upon which marriage is founded. In the ideal marriage nothing of importance happens to either partner which is not then shared as part of an overt process of mutual enrichment and growth. Individual need-fulfilment can be seen to encompass the meeting of many objectives in the social, economic, sexual, emotional, and intellectual life of the person. When a couple marry, they publicly declare their commitment to achieve all their individual objectives together, in the interests of the furtherance of their unity as man and wife.

It is arguable that this ideal task is a practical impossibility. Few people are sufficiently resourceful and well matched to become an unlimited source of growth for one another for the rest of their lives. Even where this happens, they are unlikely to be able to act as the exclusive source of growth for one another. People require stimulation from other company outside marriage. Most marriage is therefore based on a series of compromises which falls short of the ideal, but which maintains certain elements of exclusivity acceptable to both partners. For example, it is common for the husband to take the major share of economic and intellectual growth and to share the benefits of this growth vicariously with his wife. It appears to be normative, also, for the husband to have more social enrichment than the wife, although this norm is probably less rigid now than it was two decades ago. The view is still widely held, however, that sexual enrichment, and to some extent emotional enrichment should be a joint activity. In marriages which are seen as 'stable', it is generally assumed that the marital relationship is built upon inter-related compromises – give and take – of the homeostatic nature. When the balance is disturbed by a breech of mutuality, the couple discuss this and stabilise their feelings by affirming the nature of their homeostatic contract.

Such an analysis is incomplete, however, unless account is also taken of the part played by marriage in socialisation. Traditionally marriage is the final stage in the socialisation of the adolescent. Marriage is therefore a continuation of the aims and purposes of the parental marriages – an extension of the objectives of the family of origin of the husband and of the wife. These vary widely from class to class, and from family to family. Broadly, they are concerned with the achievement of *survival and physical growth* – a person is 'old enough' to get married; the achievement of *economic self-sufficiency,* and the attainment of *responsible fertility* – often expressed as 'time to settle down'. The status of 'being married' marks people out as socially adult. In the middle-classes emotional and intellectual maturity are particularly stressed as an indication of a sufficient socialisation for marriage. In all classes the continuity between family of origin and family of marriage is a major influence upon whom one marries, when, and where. People choose as spouse a person who seems most likely to be able to contribute to the meeting of the ideals of marriage with the minimum of effort, and this usually means someone who is like the parent so that continuity of socialsation will proceed.

Extra-marital affairs disrupt this continuity by contravening the mutuality of the marital contract. An extra-marital affair is a sexual relationship between two people in which either partner or both is actively married to somebody else, and in which deceit is used to conceal the relationship from the spouse so as to produce or preserve the appearance of stability in the marriage. Seen from the point of view of the marriage, an affair is an act of individual enrichment which robs the spouse of what is rightfully his or her own. For example, time which could have been spent with the spouse is spent with the lover instead. Money which could have been spent on joint comforts is used privately on another person. Love, sexual pleasure, and enhanced self-esteem, which the legitimate partner has a right to expect exclusively is shared with an illicit partner. Intellectual respect towards the spouse is seen as diminished because more is given to a lover. Indeed, the ideal mutuality of marriage is so all-encompassing that any private enrichment can be seen as an *ipso facto* deprivation of the official partner. An affair is also a breech of the continuity of socialisation with the family of origin. People who have affairs therefore not only hide them from the spouse, but usually also from their own parents.

But it frequently happens that affairs take on many of the qualities of marriage, and that the mutuality of the illicit couple becomes more significant to them than the life experiences they continue to share with their partners in the extant marriages. It is in this sense that some affairs act as alternative marriages. The lover replaces the spouse to a significant degree in the individual growth and socialisation of the person having the affair, but not necessarily to the extent that the affair replaces and destroys the marriage. It is not uncommon for an affair to be the ultimate stimulus for a divorce which is then followed by the marriage of the two people having the affair. But it may be far more usual than is commonly recognised for affairs to last for many years as undiscovered and unrevealed parallel or alternative marriages, skilfully concealed by each lover from their spouse. The individual having the affair sees it in terms of the continuity of his or her own private growth, and the conflict arises because he or she sees this growth, in terms of objectives which are not conceded by the 'official' partner, (and often the family of origin), to be legitimate aims on his part.

Oliver's dilemma, in the passage quoted above, is that he needs to go beyond the agenda of socialisation which was drawn up for him by his parents and peers during childhood and adolescence. In setting out to meet their expectations he undertook a formal marriage which proved he was qualified for the status of adult male parent. The experiences of the marriage enabled him to grow economically, sexually, emotionally, socially and intellectually. Now that growth is complete he has continued to grow through his affair and through his work. But this growth itself threatens his wife and children because resources they expect to be shared with them are being taken away from them, thus jeopardising their own growth.

The affairs which become alternative marriages arise as alternative strategies of individual development within the continuity of growth from childhood to adolescence and beyond to the wider objectives of adult self-realisation. This usually means that an affair enables the married person to tackle again those aspects of the adolescent agenda which were left uncompleted at the time of the marriage, and which were abandoned early in the marriage as incompatible with its total mutuality. People cheat in order to grow. In doing so they are often repeating behaviour required of them during childhood. For this reason, further insight into the nature of affairs can be gained from an analysis of why and how people justify their deceit.

Why people cheat

In producing justifications for lying and cheating the three or four principle actors in the drama of an affair frequently give away clues as to the attitudes they learned in childhood from their own parents. The following are six of the most commonly encountered groups of justifications.

Love justifies everything: deceit is justified on the grounds that love transforms the sordid business of cheating into something noble, or something beyond the control of the deceiver because a person who is in love lives on a higher plane than normal. Underlying this type of justification is a defence against guilt about sex. It is not only the sordid business of lying, but also the sordid business of sex which becomes sacred and pure by the addition of love. The myth of the one true love, often carefully fostered by adults during the deceiver's childhood and adolescence can clearly be seen as a parental way of controlling both the child and the parent's own fears about sex. The same controlling myth can be seen in the argument that for two people to be truly right for one another the 'chemistry' must be right. Many affairs are justified as alternative marriages because they continue to meet the objectives of socialisation laid down by the parents in controlling myths of this kind. For example, a woman who has an affair with a person who makes a better lover than potential husband will justify it on the grounds that it makes her 'happy' – thus meeting the criterion of marriage set her by her parents, but meeting it outside marriage. "Happiness' and 'love' are transmuting processes which help her cope with a fear of sex transmitted to her by her parents during socialisation.

It was nothing to do with my wife/husband: Children are often made aware of the fact that if it was not for them their parents would separate. The child's role in holding the marriage together actively involves him in producing two sets of acceptable behaviour – one for each parent – which differ in several respects. This can lead to conflicting agendas in adolescence, typified by conspiracy with one parent against the other – for example, 'I shouldn't tell your father just yet' – and then the reverse conspiracy: 'Mummy said I shouldn't tell you, so please do not let her know I have.' When such a person marries it is often to suit one parent rather more than the other. The affairs which follow then meet the objectives on the list of the parent who least approved of the marriage. They are 'nothing to do with the spouse' in the same way that covert arrangements with one parent were nothing to do with the other parent.

He lies about his affairs – why shouldn't I about mine?: the competitive 'tit-for-tat' affair, in which a married person gives the impression of his marriage as a race to score the most extra-marital scalps, is probably the cruellest of marital 'games'. The lover is used as a pawn in the power struggle between the married partners. In the same way the child is often used as a pawn in its parent's marriage, being given extremes of attention – neglected and spoiled by turns. The child's method of coping is to resort to tantrums, which are then rewarded with massive attention. Very often, however, the child is competing with a parent who also throws tantrums. Two wrongs are seen to be an effective substitute for justice. When affairs start they are often justified on the grounds that the other spouse started it first.

I make it right in other ways: the idea that a marriage depends on the happiness of both partners individually, and that how this is achieved matters less than its effects lies behind this group of justifications for cheating. Similar justifications include: 'What he/she doesn't know can't hurt him/her' and 'as long as she knows I'll never leave her, she will trust me.' The affairs in question are often seen as props to the marriage, and the lies are 'white' lies. Provided that the lover accepts this role, affairs of this kind often have a rock-like quality, and last for years as alternative marriages. The guilt is assuaged by careful, and as far as possible, equal attention and love from the person having the affair to both lover and the spouse. Often in cases of this kind lover and spouse are socially connected and accept one another as friends, neighbours, or colleagues. The lover has the major disadvantage, in that he or she carries the burden of jealousy to save the spouse from feeling it, and to avoid upsetting the carefully constructed balance of power. The adulterous spouse is, however, usually very jealous if his or her quasi-wife takes a second lover. 'Making things right in other ways' usually applies from the person having the affair to both the official and unofficial spouse, and if the latter is unfaithful this often hurts more than if the former were so. The childhood equivalent behaviour is that of keeping both parents happy, by following a jointly agreed agenda of socialisation.

He/she just could not take it: to tell about an affair which is serious, or to have one discovered is often the most difficult crisis a married person can face. The partner having an affair, therefore, often justifies deceit on the grounds that he is afraid to hurt the spouse in this way. Not only will all the trust and faith on which a marriage has been built be destroyed, but it seems also asl though the spouse will be irreparably hurt. In many marriages there is a one-sided emotional development which leads to extremes of dependence. But the roots of this justification probably go deeper, to the parental control of the child through the stricture that some things are totally unforgiveable. The child is led to believe that there is a special category of sin which would physically harm the parent, which would be 'the death of me', as some parents put it. Yet others are told they would 'never' be forgiven for some transgressions. To a young child, 'never' is difficult to grasp, but utterly terrifying. The fear of permanent rejection lies deep within many children who have been banished under indeterminate sentences before they were old enough to understand time. The fear that a spouse would never forgive, or be totally destroyed by revelations of infidelity seems to be a reliving of such punishments.

It doesn't mean anything: the reduction of the status of the affair from serious to casual – at least, as far as the spouse is concerned – is another form of deceit. In one or two cases the interviewee said that the spouse suspected an affair, and that suspicions had been allayed by saying it had been casual and was now over. More usually, this form of deceit was used for affairs which really were casual, but here the adultery took the form of a long series of relatively petty infidelities in the form of 'one-night stands', rather like some forms of teenage rebellion.

Conclusion: the function of the affair

The structure of marriage acquires its cohesion from the mutual behaviour of the partners. Mutual behaviour is made up of actions which cannot be separately apportioned to the individual participants without doing damage to the relationship – for example, joint ownership of property, joint status as man and wife, emotional interdependence, the conception and upbringing of children, parenthood itself, etc... In perhaps the majority of marriages, the partners love one another sufficiently for many such mutual activities to bind them together too far for divorce ever to appear likely. To the extent that divorce and separation are traumatic this is due to the necessity of apportionment of mutual behaviours and the products of mutuality. The structure of many serious affairs is also reinforced by mutuality.

The affair often resembles marriage for this reason. There is also, however, a functional homogeneity between affair and marriage in that both are extensions of the socialisation process which is the primary task of the family of origin in the life of the individual. The affair seems to continue the objectives of marriage by other, alternative means. In part this shows in the way so many people having serious affairs return to the unfinished agenda of their adolescent growth. In part it also shows in the extent to which deceit is justified by arguments repeating the self-control mechanisms imposed by parents on the person during childhood. The affair often becomes a re-enacted drama in which the unknowing spouse stands in for the punitive parent.

11
INFORMALISING
JUDICIAL PROCEDURES

Christopher J. Whelan

There is an issue that overpowers and encompasses all others in the history of the modern Western rule of law. It is the problem of formality in law.
R. M. Unger, 1976, p.203

Traditionally, the study of the legal system in Western countries has been characterised by an emphasis on its more formal aspects. Lawyers have been concerned with the exceptional rather than the typical; the few rather than the many. While the law may have applied to the whole population, only a few exercised their rights under it. Thus, while a famous legal commentator could write in 1926 that 'Procedure lies at the heart of the law' (Amos, 1926, p.340), very few were concerned in practice with aspects of 'procedural justice', that is, the ways in which substantive legal rights are enforced, and how the legal system actually operates. Factors such as the background, significance or efficiency of judicial procedures were secondary to arguments concerning grand notions of 'justice', and the 'rule of law', and to the quest for what the law actually said. As Cappelletti and Garth (1978, p.7) have observed, 'Formal, not effective, access to justice – formal, not effective, equality – was all that was sought.'

Since the second world war, however, the judicial process has undergone a remarkable change. The consistent thread in this quiet revolution has been the move towards greater informality in the judicial process. This trend, which may be described as the 'delegalisation' of judicial procedures, has recently accelerated under the pressure of a variety of 'reform movements'. These include the campaigns for improved legal services which have led to the appointment in Britain of a Royal Commission on Legal Services; the 'access to justice' movement, the 'justice with a human face' group and the studies in dispute processing, particularly alternatives to the traditional judicial process.

This chapter will attempt to chart the growth of informality by showing how the 'delegalisation' of judicial procedure has emerged in the face of formal justice to consider some particular examples of informality, and finally to draw briefly some implications and conclusions.

The formality of justice

The traditional dominance of formal justice in the history of law in industrial societies has had a number of obvious consequences for the majority of members of the legal profession. They have been conditioned by their work to think in the marginal, the exceptional, or the abnormal situation. The historical development of law has led to an emphasis by lawyers on 'case law' – that is, on individual cases. The result is what may be described as the 'pyramid' approach to the judicial process: attention is confined to those few cases which reach the pinnacle of the system – the courts. Cynics might prefer to characterise this more as the 'iceberg' approach, with lawyers blind to the bulk hidden below the surface.

The dominance of formal justice has also had a number of consequences for the law itself. In particular, it can be argued that since the time of the Industrial Revolution or thereabouts, reforms in the judicial process were based on an ideal of formal justice. This is not surprising, given the predilections of many of the reformers. Moreover, legal formalism rests with notions of the uniform application of general rules and of the use of independent or impartial principles. For many, this has been, and indeed remains, synonymous with the ideals of 'justice'. But there are a number of difficulties with the traditional formal approach.

The formal judicial process has proved to be very expensive. Not only does a party in an action risk losing his case if he goes to court, he may also have to pay the costs of the other side. Both sides' costs are 'notoriously impossible' to predict since they are based on the amount of work done, which in the High Court will increase the further the case proceeds (Evershed Committee

1954, para. 684). In the County Court, costs are more predictable as there is a scale which is directly related to the amounts involved. Furthermore, the overriding principle concerning the award of costs in civil proceedings is that costs are determined after the event, since the loser pays ('indemnifies') the winner (to the extent of his necessary costs).

Accordingly, the smaller the amount in dispute, the greater the barrier of cost, and the question of costs may itself become part of the dispute. As Zander (1976, p.323) has observed, regarding personal injury litigation in England, 'in about a third of all contested cases, the total costs were greater than the amount in dispute'. At any rate, uncertainty over costs makes the litigation process a gamble, in which risk-averse parties may prefer to settle.

The formal process is also very time-consuming. In 1977, in the Queen's Bench Division of the High Court in London, which deals primarily with disputes arising from contracts and torts, 43 per cent of actions took between two and four years from the date the action arose to the date of the start of the trial or its disposal; another 44 per cent took over four years. The respective figures outside London were 48 per cent and 34 per cent (*Judicial Statistics*, 1977).

Although the administration of justice is not the sole cause of delays, it is possible to locate lengthy delays through court overloading. In London, for example, after a case is fully prepared for trial and has been set down for a hearing, there is still a gap before the date of the start of the trial or its disposal. This amounts to 7 to 12 months in 39 per cent of cases, 13 to 24 months in 24 per cent of cases and over 24 months in 15 per cent of cases. Once again, delays are less outside London, but even here, over 50 per cent of cases are not heard for at least 7 months after they are ready (*Judicial Statistics*, 1977). While delays in other courts may be less than these, seeking justice within the formal judicial process remains a lengthy process.

There are two observations concerning the traditional civil justice system that need to be made in the context of this chapter. First, concerning the High Court, despite the emphasis on adjudication, case analyses and the trial that exists in the rhetoric of civil justice, in quantitative terms, settlement and not adjudication is the predominant outcome of civil litigation. Whatever the reason (including delay and expense), in the High Court in 1977, of the 168,968 writs issued (proceedings commenced), only 8,933 (5.3 per cent) of cases were sent down for trial, of which 7,692 were disposed of during the year. Of these, only 2,497 (32.5 per cent) were determined after a hearing and 5,049 (65.6 per cent) were withdrawn before a hearing (*Judicial Statistics*, 1977).

Second, concerning the County Court, again in quantitative terms, administration and not adjudication is the predominant outcome of litigation. For although out of the 1,852,920 proceedings commenced in 1977, 5 per cent (943,736) reached the stage of judgment, over 800,000 (85 per cent) of these occurred without a contest of any kind. In other words, the vast majority of cases which were not settled before trial only went for formal disposition to the court to receive the rubber stamp.

Given the above limitations on the operation of the formal judicial process, it is perhaps not surprising that when the explosion of new legal rights occurred after 1945, a more informal process was required in which these rights could be enforced.

The growth of informality: tribunals and legal representation

Since 1945, there has been a vast increase in the amount of administrative social and financial legislation. New laws concerning social security, taxation, planning and consumers have resulted in a growth of bureaucracy, and have created a mass of social rights and duties. One feature common to most of these new laws is that they have granted specific rights to individuals against organisations. Thus, 'on the one hand, they involve efforts to bolster the power of citizens against governments, consumers against merchants, people against polluters, tenants against landlords, and employees against employers and unions, and, on the other hand, the monetary interest of any one individual – as plaintiff or defendant – is likely to be small' (Cappelletti and Garth, 1978, p.20). Accompanying this development has been 'a veritable explosion in the development of tribunals other than courts of law, resulting from the great expansion of governmental activities and responsibilities and the enormous extension of welfare services' (Jacob, 1978, p.456).

There are over 2,000 tribunals in existence today. According to the Franks Report in 1957, whose recommendations were incorporated into the Tribunals and Inquiries Act 1958 (now 1971), 'openness, fairness and impartiality' should be the keystones of tribunal procedure (Franks Report, 1957, p.9). In general, tribunals, which have become 'an essential feature of the English judicial process' (Jacob, 1978, p.457), are cheap, accessible, free from many technicalities and speedy. Contrasted with the traditional judicial process, they are informal: they are not usually bound by strict rules of evidence, participants and representatives do not wear special robes, yet they adjudicate a variety of disputes and they administer justice in a form which is as binding as that dispensed in traditional judicial settings.

Indeed, tribunals operate in such areas of society as social security, rents and employment. A useful example of the developing role of tribunals is the case of industrial tribunals. These were established originally under the Industrial Training Act 1964. But since then their jurisdiction has been greatly extended, and they now form the nucleus of a system of labour courts. Today their jurisdiction includes redundancy payments and related matters and complaints and appeals under the various employment Acts. In this way, industrial tribunals have become a fundamental part of the judicial process in this country. In 1976, there were 43,166 applications, and in 1977, 41,995 applications made before industrial tribunals. Moreover specific groups in society, such as racial minorities, are continuing to be granted legal rights which may require enforcement, often by way of tribunals.

Accompanying the apparent increase in laws of this kind has been an improvement in legal representation for the underprivileged. This now includes assistance in all criminal and some civil cases, although it is not usually available in cases before tribunals. The attainment of what may be called 'social justice' (Scarman, 1974, p.29) through the civil justice system was the objective of many of the reforms which have provided for legal assistance, beginning with the Legal Aid and Advice Act 1949 up until the Legal Aid Act 1979, and including the establishement of about 30 neighbourhood law centres, legal advice centres (and citizens' advice bureaux), and duty solicitor schemes, whereby solicitors offer their services in Magistrates' Courts (criminal cases) on a rota basis to assist unrepresented defendants.

Legal representation and advice has also been provided specifically for the new emergent collective interests referred to above. There is now a range of agencies, as well as the numerous pressure groups which often have lawyers attached to them, such as the National Council for Civil Liberties, the Child Povery Action Group and the National Association for Mental Health.

Despite the growth of tribunals, and the extension of legal representation and legal services, the reaction of the legal profession to these and other developments has been painfully slow. But the changing structure of the sources of law, from casuistic (common law, case by case) to statutory, and the needs for which it caters, is having an effect. The positive attitude of organisations like the Law Commission, which considers reforms of the law, has filtered through into legal training. The tempo of change has accelerated as the profession is slowly getting involved in law concerning the many rather than the few (through legal aid in particular), and the law for the many has been increasing through satisfactory enactment.

However, in some ways, greater awareness by lawyers and increased legal representation are synonymous with formal, rather than substantive, change. New legal needs may be remedied by legal rights which do not require legal representatives in order to enforce them. They may be remedied by a restructuring of the judicial system itself. Accordingly, one of the most fundamental developments in recent years has been the creation or encouragement of alternatives to the formal judicial process. In the civil area of law, the most important examples have been the use of conciliation and arbitration as alternatives to or integrated within the normal procedures.

Delegalisation: conciliation and arbitration

Although formality and justice may have been viewed traditionally as synonymous, the system of justice has always been supplemented by informal institutions. Whether it be the family, trade unions, the church or whatever, their role at the base of the judicial pyramid undoubtedly has been and remains significant, despite the failure of most obsrvers to consider them. They perform a variety of functions including advice, negotiation and bargaining, conciliation and arbitration. Attention will be paid here to two informal devices which have been introduced to process and indeed, to prevent, disputes in modern society: conciliation and arbitration.

Conciliation
According to Eckhoff (1966, p.161), the task of the judge is 'not to try to reconcile the parties, but to reach a decision about which

of them is right.' In contrast, 'The mediator should preferably look forward, toward the consequences which may follow from the various solutions, and he must work on the parties to get them to accept a solution.' The advantage of conciliation (or mediation) therefore, is not only that it can save expense and time, but that settlements can occur through compromise and negotiation.

Basically, conciliation takes two forms: as prevention, it is the involvement of neutral third parties to advise parties generally regarding relations between them with the intention of avoiding disputes and aiding agreement; as intervention, it is the mediation of a neutral third party in a specific dispute, with the intention of helping the parties to reach a mutually acceptable outcome through their own efforts. Conciliation has been a feature of procedures to deal with labour-management disputes in the UK for some time. Recently, however, it has been extended to other areas, such as industrial, marital, civil courts and consumer agencies. It is not possible to consider these in great detail, but some will be outlined briefly.

For about a century, collective bargaining between employers and employees has been an increasingly important method of dispute resolution. To assist the parties, since the Conciliation Act 1896, government has provided conciliation services. Today, this takes the form of the independent Advisory, Conciliation and Arbitration Service (ACAS) which has an advisory as well as a conciliatory role and has been given the power to conduct inquiries or attempt to reconcile conflicting parties in a trade dispute.

The development of conciliation as a technique for resolving disputes involving individual employees is a more recent phenomenon, and one which has important implications. For many of the proceedings brought before industrial tribunals, there is a requirement that conciliation be attempted; that is, conciliation has been built into the judicial process. Indeed, during the life of the Industrial Relations Act 1971, the rules of the National Industrial Relations Court, which was equivalent to a branch of the High Court, obliged it to 'use its best endeavours to ensure that, where there is a reasonable prospect of agreement being reached between the parties, they are enabled to avail themselves of the service of conciliation officers or of other opportunities for conciliation.' The Court also had to regulate its procedure so as to avoid formality. For the first time since the creation of formal courts and a legal profession, anyone could appear before a court.

Today, ACAS has conciliation officers who have a duty to try to negotiate a settlement of complaints by individual employees, whether it be about unfair dismissal; guaranteed pay, maternity pay, trade union membership or activity, time-off, or complaints under the Equal Pay Act 1970 or Sex Discrimination Act 1975. There is evidence that the conciliation services have had a high rate of success. In 1976, 18,030 (52 per cent) of the 34,778 unfair dismissal cases were settled or withdrawn by conciliation.

The general use of conciliation processes in matrimonial disputes is well-known, although of fairly recent origin, dating from the Royal Commission on Marriages and Divorce, 1956. Until recently, apart from the probation service, marital counselling was a matter for voluntary organisations. In the Divorce Reform Act 1969 however, reconciliation provisions were written in and now the Matrimonial Causes Act 1973 provides for the solicitor acting for the divorce petitioner to certify he had discussed with the petitioner the possibility of a reconciliation and given the names and addresses of persons qualified to help effect reconciliation between estranged spouses.

The range of conciliation agencies in this field today is vast: marriage guidance counsellors, probation officers, social workers, health visitors, as well as doctors, clergymen, family friends and the like. The Finer Commission (1974, p.176) defined conciliation as 'assisting the parties to deal with the consequences of the established breakdown of their marriage, whether resulting in divorce or separation, by reaching agreements or giving consents or reducing the area of conflict upon custody, support, access to and education of the children, financial provision, the disposition of the matrimonial home, lawyers' fees and every other matter arising from the breakdown which calls for a decision on future arrangements.'

Although the trial procedure within the traditional judicial machinery remains formal, there have been some interesting developments in the pre-trial processes of the High Court and the County Court. In English civil procedure there is a sharp and marked division between the stages of pre-trial. To operate the pre-trial processes in both courts, there has evolved the office of Masters and Registrars to deal with virtually all the stages before trial. A 'new and revolutionary' summons for directions process was recently introduced, whereby Masters, when giving directions to secure the 'just, expeditious and economic' disposal of the action, have a duty to take a 'robust initiative.' The purpose of these pre-trial conferences is to reduce the number of issues between the parties and prepare the case for trial. It is thus 'trial-orientated.' There is no attempt to resolve the underlying dispute. Thus, settlements that may occur following these pre-trial processes are merely by-products of them.

A number of County Court Rules do grant the Registrar a discretion somewhat wider than that of the High Court Master. In particular, under a new procedure introduced in March 1972 the Registrar gives preliminary consideration to cases in a 'pre-trial review.' This is a discussion, held in the office of the Registrar between one or both parties and the Registrar. It is intended that Registrars assist unrepresented parties in a more relaxed and informal setting, where, in the place of the adversarial process, the Registrar can secure admissions from parties and extract more information from either side. He can take advantage of the fact that the parties (or their legal advisers) are present, which encourages concessions to be made at this stage before the actual hearing, thus promoting the possibility of settlement.

The pre-trial review occurs in ordinary actions, and also, at the Registrar's discretion, in default actions and in originating summons. At the review, the Registrar has the same guidelines as the Master: to give directions as necessary to secure the just, expeditious and economic disposal of the action. But he has wider and less formal powers than the Master. Thus, if one or other party does not turn up, he can order that the action be struck out, or that judgment be granted after the claimant (the plaintiff) proves his case.

There is now a vast range of private and public conciliation processes for consumers, covering an incredible variety of subject areas. Some of these have been established following the involvement of the Director-General of Fair Trading. He is empowered under the Fair Trading Act 1973, to encourage trade associations to adopt voluntary codes of practice in the interests of consumers, and to encourage the establishment of complaints machinery. Examples of these include the Advertising Standards Authority which handles objections to advertisements, the Post Office Users National Council and the Family Practitioners Committee of the General Medical Council. The procedures which have been adopted usually include conciliation as a preliminary stage before eventual arbitration.

This development indicates that a variety of institutional bodies are involved in informal judicial processing. When considered as a group, they have an increasing role to play in the judicial process. As an example, the Association of British Travel Agents Scheme uses a Code of Practice involving 1,750 travel agents and 304 tour operators. It aims to deal with the 'more intractable' complaints by conciliation and in the last resort, by arbitration. In 1976 there was a total of 2,698 complaints regarding travel services received by consumer advice centres, citizens' advice bureaux and Trading Standard Officers. Around the same number of complaints are received annually by ABTA. ABTA intervenes in cases of disagreement or breakdown in negotiations. Settlement rates are very high, for only about 85 cases are arbitrated each year.

Arbitration
Arbitration involves the submission of a claim to a neutral third party whose decision is usually final and binding. It is not a new idea, but it has usually been associated with commercial, financial and shipping disputes. Its virtue, as an alternative to the formal judicial process, is that it aims to be cheap, speedy and informal. These are virtues which may have disappeared somewhat in commercial arbitration, and which the new Arbitration Act 1979 has been designed at least in part to restore. Given the expectation that these virtues are part of an arbitration process, it is perhaps not surprising that this should be seen as the best process for dealing with small claims. The problems of litigating small claims within the formal judicial process have proved to be overwhelming for individuals. As noted earlier, the costs of legal representation and of the courts themselves compared with the claim, have been too great. The result has been that 'delinquent buyers are commonly hauled into court. Delinquent sellers are not' (Ison, 1972, p.22).

The response in many countries has been to establish small claims courts. In the UK, this has taken the form of what is in effect a small claims division of the County Court. This was established in 1973 by adapting the existing arbitration system under the County Courts Act 1959 to small claims, so that a Registrar could refer a small claim to arbitration with or without the parties' consent (Administration of Justice Act, 1973). Since 1978, a reference to arbitration can be made by either party to the proceedings (Administration of Justice Act, 1977). In addition, the 'no-costs' rule, whereby no legal costs, other than those fixed on the summons, could be recovered for cases involving less than £5 was extended in 1972 to £20, in 1973 to £75, and it is now £200 which is the current definition of a small claim.

At the hearing, the key to which is informality, strict rules of evidence do not apply; the arbitrator (who is a Registrar) may adopt any procedure which he considers to be convenient and to afford a fair and equal opportunity to each party to present his case. Apparently, the Lord Chancellor's Office regard the new procedure as a 'very considerable success' (Appleby, 1978, p.4). Certainly, a number of objectives have been achieved. Small claims are heard about eight weeks after the claim is made. According to Appleby the use of lawyers has been reduced: 34 per cent of plaintiffs, 8 per cent of defendants, and 7 per cent of both are represented; in 51 per cent of cases, both parties appeared in person. On the other hand 52 per cent of cases are brought by corporations or firms, who make up only 24 per cent of defendants. Moreover, the majority of individuals acting in person are defendants.

Appleby reported that Registrars considered the 'primary advantage' of small claims arbitration was its 'informality': 'This helped people to talk more freely, and enabled the Registrar to gain the confidence of the litigants. Holding proceedings in private was less awe-inspiring for the average person. The informal atmosphere enabled the arbitrator to take a more active role in the proceedings' (Appleby 1978, p.38). Appleby added that arbitration could be hard work, partly because people did not always know what to do: and that regarding the effectiveness of litigants in person presenting their own case, there seems to be some doubt. He concluded that informality in the hearings themselves has been achieved, to a large extent' (Appleby, 1978, p.42).

In addition to the state provision of procedures for small claims, and indeed preceding their provision, at Manchester in 1971, and at Westminster in 1973, small claims courts were established as 'experiments', totally independent of the state system. Another, at Lewisham, closed down after one year. Both courts provide voluntary arbitration – that is, both parties must consent to it – in a setting free of formal rules of procedure of evidence. The procedure in these courts is different from that occurring in the County Court scheme. Legal representation is usually prohibited; a case proceeds only if the defendant is willing to be bound by the decision; the claimant must be a private individual; a company or a firm or an individual bringing a claim connected with his business are all excluded; and finally, the hearing may be held at a time that is as convenient as possible for the parties, such as in the evening. Like the County Court scheme, the hearings should be informal, and the arbitrator, who is usually a lawyer, can adopt any procedure and admit any evidence that he deems appropriate.

Referring to these experiments Jacob has observed that 'There can be little doubt that in these small claims procedures we have sown in England the germ of what may be a great and crucial development in the field of access to justice' (Jacob, 1978, p.453).

Implications and conclusions

Although advocates of small claims courts and of conciliation may point to greater informality and accessibility as a major asset, such procedures are not without critics. In particular, there is a fear that these procedures might represent a 'second class' type of justice. Thus, small claims courts may be used by businesses, who have legal representation, against individuals, who do not.

Most fundamental criticisms would point out the danger that informality will reduce the limited protection that exists for individuals through formal judicial procedures, and that informal institutions will be ignored. Thus, in 1977, of the one and a half million cases commenced in the County Court, nearly one million (75 per cent) involved amounts of £100 or less, 94 per cent involved amounts of £500 or less (*Judicial Statistics*, 1977). Yet despite the fact that the County Court is essentially a small debts court, the more informal process of the arbitration scheme was rarely used. Out of the 943,000 judgements in 1977, only 10,000 occurred after arbitration.

Lack of use is also a problem regarding conciliation services in cases of matrimonial disputes. A common criticism both in the UK and in the US is that there is a lack of commitment on the part of the court system and all those who work within it to the concept of conciliation as an essential tool for the welfare of the family which they must promote (Manchester and Whetton, 1974; Foster, 1966). In addition there is the problem of the essential conflict of interests which exists when a lawyer who promotes conciliation may greatly increase the amount of time and trouble spent on a client while depriving himself of at least part of his fee.

Moreover, it would be easy to over-emphasise the trends towards greater informality. After all, the system of justice is still trying to fulfil the promise 'To no one will we sell, to no one will we refuse or delay, right or justice' that it made over 750 years ago in the Magna Carta! But if, instead of considering merely the formal constituents of the judicial process, one considers 'the full panoply of institutions and devices, personnel and procedures, used to process, and even prevent, disputes in modern societies' (Cappelletti and Garth, 1978, p.49), then the conclusion is inescapable that, particularly with reference to the new substantive rights being granted, the increase in informality is an irreversible trend of fundamental importance to the legal system.

The major benefit of a judicial system which incorporates informality is that if it is restructured, then a greater flexibility in reform is allowed. Procedures can be altered, new courts or tribunals established, the personnel of the law can include lay persons, and the use of private or informal mechanisms of dispute processing can be encouraged. Placed in this kind of context, the trend towards informality, if it is continued, is nothing less than revolutionary. While formal machinery may remain as a vital constituent for the resolution of large-scale disputes in particular, it is likely that for other disputes, especially those which involve individuals, there will be a growing dependence on informal judicial procedures.

12
DECENTRALISED JUSTICE:
Private v Democratic Informality

Stuart Henry

It is increasingly becoming accepted that the existing judicial systems of the Western world have *failed* to control or deter crime. This criticism has arisen because the apparent escalation of conventional property crime has occurred *in spite* of an extension of formal control methods and increased law and order budgets. These have been unable to cope with the growing number of offenders: the police are undermanned, criminal courts are over burdened with a back-log of cases;and trials are themselves becoming long, cumbersome and excessively expensive.

In addition, the formal system for administering criminal justice is charged with becoming impersonal and bureaucratic and increasingly less controllable by ordinary people. In the course of its development formal criminal justice has become so *divorced* from people that it is now 'complacently isolated in an ivory tower, clothing a moralistic approach in logical garb. It prides itself on a haughty independence which causes it to turn its back on society' (Versele, 1969, p.9).

As a result, people have lost interest in official justice and are powerless to change it. It is argued that the increasing denial and subversion of citizen power by bureaucratisation and professionalisation of the justice system, and the progressive elimination of ordinary people from it, have made it less account-able. This has led to distrust and to an increased reliance on discretion and pressure by nameless agencies (Christie, 1976; Reiss, 1974; Baldwin and McConville, 1977). In this context the formal system for administering justice has been indicted with causing the disintegration of community life, for it is argued that disputes which arise in communities are generally exacerbated rather than healed by the formal machinery of justice (Christie, 1976; Conn and Hippler, 1974).

It is for these reasons then that a section of academic opinion is taking the view that the existing administration of justice is no longer adequately equipped to deal with current trends in crime. As Danzig puts it, 'A strong case can be made out that the . . . criminal justice systems neither control, nor consider, nor correct criminality' (Danzig, 1973, p.2). What is proposed instead by these critics is that both crime and criminal justice are managed through some form of democratic, decentralised system of community justice and control. In this chapter I will argue that such a critique places too much emphasis on the use of formal courts as the main form of judicial machinery. In doing so it overlooks the very important area of informal disciplinary procedure. It will be my point, that rather than having a formal system of justice, the majority of 'judicial' decision within our society take place *informally* and privately within particular social institutions. In some ways this renders the decentralisation critique misplaced since we already have decentralised criminal processing. What we do not have, however, is decentralised *justice* and it is toward correcting that anomaly that I am concerned.

The argument for community justice and popular control

A number of commentators have come to the conclusion that only people *involved in,* and *aware of,* the community can act as effective forces in crime prevention and that simply increasing police and court capacity will not solve the problems presently plaguing criminal justice systems (Fisher, 1975, Ferdinand, 1977). It is felt that the only way out of the present situation is for criminal justice and the community to be brought closer together so that those who judge and those who are judged are part of the *same* 'society'. Public participation in the administration of justice and intervention by community representatives in both criminal court proceedings and the execution of sentences are seen as the only direct and reliable means of achieving such integration (Versele, 1969; Christie, 1976).

It is claimed that decentralisation and popularisation of criminal justice would have major advantages over the present system. These measures would improve the operation of various controlling agencies, such as police and courts, because, by integrating the responsibility of these institutions with the community, people would be made directly responsible for their own offences, thereby releasing the formal system to handle only the most serious offences. In addition, greater use of non-specialist personnel would not only close the gap between those who administer justice and those who receive it, bringing back trust and respect for the law, but would also be economically advantageous.

Most importantly, a decentralised system of community justice would, it is argued, be more efficient and effective in preventing people from committing major offences, and more just in its handling of those people who commit minor ones. A main aim of the decentralisation movement, then, is the establishment of community control over justice.

The fallacy of decentralisation is the importance that it places on the formal system. The critics take as their 'straw man' formal justice and maintain that it is out of touch and unable to cope. While this is certainly supported by much recent evidence, what such criticism does is to accept unquestioningly the notion that formal justice is *significant* in handling judicial decisions. But many would argue that the formal system handles only the tip of the iceberg of criminal offences. The majority of offences never get as far as the formal system because they are handled *within* the contexts in which they occur by various forms of informal disciplinary procedure. To illustrate my argument I will concentrate on one offence: property theft.

The hidden economy

It is now established criminological wisdom that a major proportion of all property offences remain hidden. In a year when theft loss totals in Britain for all offences such as robbery, burglary, and theft amounted to £100 million (*Security Gazette,* 1975) the comparable figure for the losses due to pilfering, fiddling and tax evasion were estimated to be thirteen times higher at £1305 million (Ditton, 1977a; OCPU, 1978).

Whatever the actual size of hidden property offences, the important point for our purposes is that even when such offences are known to companies and organisations they are unlikely to be reported to the authorities. For example, Martin's Home Office study found that in large firms the police were contacted in only 31 per cent of cases of theft and in small firms this rate was a mere 21 per cent (Martin, 1962, p.90). In addition he found that prosecution for discovered employee property theft was considerably lower than for other crimes. He found that large firms in his sample prosecuted only 41 per cent of the cases and smaller firms in only 24 per cent (Martin, 1962, p.86). Gerald Robin produced similar findings in his study of the way employee theft is dealt with in the USA. Basing his study on occupational crimes committed in three large independent store companies, he found that overall, only 17 per cent of the 1,681 apprehended employees were eventually prosecuted. He points to considerable variation in attitude towards prosecution among different companies. Only 2 per cent were prosecuted in one company and 8 per cent in another, but 34 per cent were prosecuted in a third (Robin, 1970).

Both these studies show that there exists a sizeable number of hidden property offences which do not get to the formal system of criminal justice. But the studies also reflect something else which has long been recognised by observers of employee theft. As Jerome Hall put it, 'The most salient feature of the entire embezzlement situation is the widespread practice of private justice – private individuals deciding who shall be prosecuted, who condemned and what if any sanctions shall be applied' (Hall. 1952, p.340).

Private justice

In many cases if an offence is discovered while it is in progress it is often dealt with summarily. A verbal warning by management may only be followed with a formal written warning if the original offence is repeated. In the case of theft, whether more serious action follows depends firstly on whether the offence is identified as theft and secondly upon the value of the goods stolen. Interpretation of an act as theft may be linked to the value and the quantity of the goods stolen. For example, a worker interviewed by Horning told him that if someone was caught pilfering on the plant, 'It depends on the item. You're fired it it's large – warned if its small . . . If you take often and you're caught, you're fired. If you do it occasionally then you are just warned' (Horning, 1970, p.61). As Martin showed, half the firms in his sample stated that theft only began when the goods were worth five pounds or more. Robin similarly found that the critical value for a crime to be seen as theft and worthy of prosecution was $100. Only 19 per cent of those who stole less that $100 were prosecuted compared with 57 per cent of those who stole more (Robin, 1970, p.128).

Settling the matter privately can involve various levels of activity depending upon the company or organisation. In making his decision, the first thing a manager might do is obtain copies of any company records on the employee. Then having considered the case in the context of the employee's record he may decide to discipline the employee.

The disciplinary procedure for this form of private justice can vary enormously from the small firm in which the owner/manager simply calls an employee into his office and sacks him, to the large organisation that has a written disciplinary procedure following the government's Advisory Concilliation and Arbitration Services' eleven point Code of Practice. The company or organisation might in addition operate a sophisticated disciplinary panel composed of members of management, personnel officers, trade union advocates and workers' representatives, which, having the power to suspend or dismiss an employee, may also make provisions for him to appeal to a separate 'independent' hearing.

Why is it, then, that the preferred course of action taken by employers in cases of discovered theft is to settle the matter 'privately'? Martin found that on almost 70 per cent of occasions when an employer failed to report the offence to an outside agency he was attempting to minimise the unpleasantness for both himself and his employees. He argues that, in general, the employers' control policy 'may be described as a mixture of humanity and expediency' (Martin, 1962, p.104). However, rather than the historically protective, and paternalistic view of employee/employer relationships as being like that between servant and master, this may have more to do with good business sense. A company's reputation might be questioned by bad publicity should it be revealed that people in the company are fiddling or stealing. A court might also criticise a company for poor supervision or inadequate security. Besides this employers fear costly reprisals through union strikes and counter charges of 'wrongful dismissal', 'malicious prosecution' or 'victimisation'. Finally, irrespective of the high success rate of prosecutions (Robin, 1970 found a 99 per cent conviction rate), clearly, taking people to court is a costly and time consuming venture and as Jason Ditton has said, 'Whilst there may be specific cases where court action might secure restitution, in general . . . there is no room for civic sentimentality in business' (Ditton, 1977c, p.7). Through the system of private justice, the employer is not only able to make good his economic loss, but his action has a considerable deterrent impact within the company.

Perhaps the most disturbing reason why private settlement is preferred is because it can be used to control the workforce. Institutionalised pilferage and fiddling can be considered 'perks' to reward employees in place of salary increases or promotion. This is particularly popular in times of government wage policy as a means of rewarding managers and executives. But it can also be used to provide additional incentive to workers. A report by London Transport's Chief Secretary on ticket-barrier fiddles says that the 'fraud' has a 'bonus effect' by keeping staff interested in checking tickets and therefore preventing more widespread fiddles by passengers.

But the 'rights' to fiddles and perks can also be withdrawn in order to sustain a charge of serious misconduct in cases where wages are free from constraints, where 'troublemakers' are concerned, or where unionisation is threatened. A good example occurs in the hotel and catering industry where individual contracts are made between employers and employees allowing flexibility over manpower in order to cope with the erratic nature of the catering market. Mars and Mitchell have shown how catering managements manipulate opportunities for hidden economy activities in this low unionised industry in favour of core staff. 'A man making extra or untaxed income is unlikely to respond to calls by union officials to join in collective action if he suspects that his individual contract benefits will decrease in the process and that any benefits gained by union action might be taxed at a high marginal rate' (Mars and Mitchell, 1977, p.9). To seal the issue of unionisation, catering managements can sack any emergent union organiser on a charge of pilfering, or fiddling, activities which are normally allowed as part of a catering workers' hidden wage. It is for these reasons, then, that employers prefer private justice when handling internal property offences. However, not only is private justice based on expedience rather than moral and legal principle: it is also open to abuse.

Abuses of private justice

While private disciplinary proceedings have been said by some to be 'an enlightened private individualisation of treatment which overcomes the crudities of exposure and punishment and, in sum, is superior to official administration of the criminal law' (Hall, 1952, pp. 340-1), it also provides a very rough jsutice for the accused since the employer is often the victim, prosecutor, judge and jury. It is 'rough justice' because employers still have the choice of whether to prosecute offenders. They can pass sentences based on personal knowledge of the offender and there is still a variation in what is considered a tolerable level of pilfering as well as there being an inconsistent policy regarding dismissal. In spite of the Employment Protection Act, an employer still need only satisfy and industrial tribunal that he had reasonable grounds for believing an employee guilty in order to sack him. As Lord Denning said in a 1978 Court of Appeal case, 'If a man is dismissed for stealing, as long as an employer honestly believes it on reasonable grounds, that is enough to justify dismissal'. The ACAS (1977) Code of Practice makes it clear that employees should not be dismissed until the matter has been investigated and a disciplinary hearing has been completed. So, although an employee offender can no longer be sacked on the spot, there is no obligation to allow him to remain at work, and suspension is usually considered justified. Provided the correct procedures are carried out an Industrial Tribunal is likely to uphold the dismissal case. This means that the new employee protection laws only formalise and delay an employer's traditional manipulative freedom of choice in dismissal.

Another area where private disciplinary procedures arc criticised is the invasion of privacy. Many employers consider spot searches by security officers necessary in order to cut down pilfering, even though this is a blatant breach of privacy. Companies have taken to including 'right to search' provisions in contracts of employment and collective agreements.

Finally, compared with the amount of evidence required to secure a conviction in the formal courts, private justice can operate with minimal evidence. As Martin (1962, p.75) has pointed out, this form of justice creates the possibility that employees may suffer sanctions or even be sacked for offences which in law would only lead to their being treated as suspects. In other words, the abuse to which the traditional private system of control is vulnerable is in direct contrast to the principles of formal justice.

If legal control may be characterised as having a moral basis, guilt orientation, formally bureaucratic style, technical judicial decision making and public hearings; then in contrast, commercial social control has a calculative basis, a profit orientation, an ecletic ad hocness in the procedures by which it comes to decisions, a 'rough' sense of justice, with mock 'trials' held in private. Not to put too fine a point on it, commercial social control is everything legal social control should *not* be. Ditton, 1977c, p.8

Towards democratic private justice

Although critics of the existing formal system of justice have undoubtedly got a strong case, the vigour of their argument is a considerably wasted effort. While the formal system is deficient, its deficiency is not as important as that of the system of informal private justice that lies beneath it and upon which it depends to handle the large majority of offences. The idea that some form of community justice would be a key element in a decentralised system of formal justice is, I believe, missing the point. The idea of community justice would, however, seem most appropriate for the existing system of private justice in order to introduce some measure of democratic justice to an area which for years has remained wide open to abuse.

Community courts

As Nils Christie has argued, 'The ideal is clear, (the community court) ought to be a court of equals representing themselves, when they are able to find a solution between themselves no judges are needed. When they are not, the judges ought also to be their equals' (Christie, 1976, p.20). A community court is defined by Fisher as 'a lay body dealing with a population that has objective features in common, with jurisdiction over offences otherwise criminal and with power to impose meaningful sanctions' (Fisher, 1975, p.1253). 'Community' is taken to mean a group of people living or working in the same locality, supporting common goals and subject to the same laws or regulations.

Under a community court, offenders are brought before their collegues who hear the evidence, pronounce a verdict and pass sentence. The system closely resembles the medieval form of jury trial in which only the offender's equals could judge him. In this way strong moral pressure is brought to bear on the offender and much use is made of his sense of shame in the eyes of those who know him.

The evidence which is drawn on to support this view is of variable quality. Studies of the system of justice of early colonial America, for example, have been used to show that the family, community and church maintained a firm grip on its members through the exercise of a Durkheimian 'community sentiment', which was a more powerful determinant of who was arrested than written law. Although open to abuse, there was little crime, and most offenders were dealt with through informal proceedings (Ferdinand, 1977, p.3).

In the context of total institutions a similar form of community control has been termed the 'just community'. Where this has been applied in prisons, for example, its advocates, such as Peter Scharf, have claimed some success. Inmates, guards and administrators adopt a democratic framework in which they collectively control, discipline and define objectives and activities. In the six years such a system has operated at one American prison, it is said to have cut escapes and recidivism rates by half (Scharf, 1977, p.104).

A form of community court has been used to a limited degree in the special arbitration programmes involving citizen participation which have been set up for juveniles in the United States (Statsky, 1974) and for special groups such as Eskimos and Indians (Conn and Hippler, 1974). More systematic use of the community court concept is found in exclusive membership organisations, institutions and societies.

Most universities, trade unions and prisons have recognised procedures for deciding disciplinary problems within their respective communities. The same is true of a number of professional practitioner bodies such as lawyers, doctors, dentists, pharmacists and social workers. The disciplinary boards of these organisations are composed of members of the profession and have the power to adjudicate cases arising in their communities and to impose sanctions and ultimately withdraw the membership rights of the individual.

However, it is believed that these forms of community court, although having written procedures, are not usually democratic because they rarely allow for the accused to participate and the members of the council are not usually drawn from the offender's immediate social context. As Fisher says, when talking about prison tribunals, they 'rarely allow for prisoner participation, thereby raising doubts as to whether the "judges" are really "community" members' (Fisher, 1975, p.1271). But equal representation by members of the community is a crucial element of the community court model, since without it, the courts' activity may not be taken seriously by those involved. Indeed, to some extent this is just what has happened in the planned more formalised use of community courts which have been such a significant, though little documented, component of the system of administering criminal justice in socialist countries.

Socialist community courts

Virtually the same form of community court has been used under different names in a variety of socialist societies. These courts have been called *comrades' courts* in the Soviet Union, *people's courts* in the Republic of China, *popular tribunals* in Cuba, *social courts* in Hungary, *disputes commissions* in the German Democratic Republic and *workers' courts* in Poland. The origin of the socialist use of community courts is generally put around 1919 and stems from Lenin's philosophy that workers should participate in the management of all state and communal affairs, including the administration of justice (Ramundo, 1965). However, in most socialist countries, with the possible exception of China (Garbus, 1977), the courts did not flourish until their reintroduction between 1959 and 1962. A good illustration of how they operate can be got by looking at comrades' courts of the USSR.

Soviet comrades' courts are established at enterprises, institutions and organisations, schools, collective farms, apartments and rural settlements (Berman and Spindler, 1963). Their members are elected by secret ballot for periods of two years by general meetings of the collective. The courts deal with a range of offences that include breaches of discipline at work, minor civil cases, some criminal offences such as embezzlement, theft of state or social property, and all minor infractions when it is evident that the offender can be rehabilitated by means of applying *social pressure,* rather than punishment. Comrades' courts are entitled to impose various sanctions such as: apology to the victim, a reprimand, a warning, a small fine or a short spell of manual labour (Lapenna, 1968). Although they are independent of the more formal peoples' courts, their elected members are encouraged to attend regional Councils of Comrades' Courts at which are present the best qualified members of comrades' courts and the lawyers and workers of judicial bodies (Ramundo, 1965, p.710).

The not unreasonable philosophy behind the comrades' courts is that offences are not simply the fault of the individual, but of the whole collective, who must take responsibility for them. Their purpose is 'to treat minor crimes as *moral* offences rather than to treat moral offences as crimes, and thereby to prevent moral offenders becoming criminals' (Berman and Spindler, 1963, p.844).

The courts have a two-fold aim: to educate the public to the rules of the socialist society by arousing public interest in social order through mass participation and to act as a vehicle through which the individual is re-educated and returned to society as a useful member (Rogovin, 1961, p.305). Thus in the comrades' courts the community is the mentor and the individual the student. The socialist vision is that as a result of comradely censure and criticism a new social morality will develop, become instinctive and cause crime to decline or disappear (Ramundo, 1965, p.699).

An important idea behind the comrades' courts is that only those people who are an offender's immediate community members can know his specific situation, conditions of life, relationships, and similar facts which, it is argued, have a significant bearing on the correct resolution of the dispute. In this sense the court is very personal and is encouraged to consider fully the mitigating circumstances of the background of the offender and the context of his offence. Unlike formal Western courts, not only the sentence, but the verdict itself, is based upon the defendant's character. Under the Chinese version of the community courts this leads to a situation where trials take place as mere ritual the day after judgment has been made, and after the opinion of co-workers has been canvassed as to whether a person is guilty and if so what the punishment should be (Garbus, 1977).

An important issue is the extent to which the courts are subject to restrictive pressures and to political controls by local party officials and press propaganda. It has been suggested that party or union control over the community court can result in the fabrication of an issue for the purpose of 'educating the public'. It is further argued that the function of the court is merely a means of giving the state greater penetrative power via the collective, to encroach on the sphere of the individual and inhibit any deviation which may be thought 'dangerously individualistic' (Rogovin, 1961, p.306). Controls and pressures such as these tend to distort the beneficial functions of community courts. As Fisher says, 'A true community court must remain independent of any political organisation and influence if it is to operate effectively as an instrument of justice . . . and its procedures should be overseen by the formal courts only to the extent necessary to insure that the constitutional freedoms and protections are not 'infringed' (Fisher, 1975, p.1278, p.1282).

There are clearly a number of dangers inherent in introducing the community court idea into the context of private justice, and some further questions have been raised by a special study carried out during the introduction of the workers' courts in Poland in 1962. People interviewed in the study felt that unless workers' courts were introduced on a universal basis, they would mean two kinds of justice – one for the workers who happened to be in factories that adopted the system and another for the population as a whole (Podgorecki, 1969). They also pointed out that because the system did not replace formal legal proceedings there was a possibility of a double trial, one in the workers' court and a second in the magistrate's court.

Several of the workers interviewed in the study expressed the view that the courts only examined cases of manual workers and did not look at the same offences that were committed by managerial or executive personnel. In other words they felt that 'workers' courts were courts for workers' (Podgorecki, 1969, p.148). There were also those who expressed fears about possible victimisation, incompetence and the relative *harshness* of disgrace before one's colleagues for such minor offences. Finally, people doubted whether the system would actually cut down the number of offences committed.

But the principal objection to community courts in socialist countries is that unions and party officials can, like managers and owners of private industry in a capitalist society, manipulate the system. The same kind of interested selectivity in discovering, reporting, judging and sentencing apply to community courts, and the same political use can be made of the system to control dissident party members. Any advantages that community courts have in terms of self-government and understanding are lost when the system is controlled by interested parties.

Perhaps a compromise between the socialist and capitalist forms of industrial discipline would be more appropriate for our present purposes. Indeed a few British companies adopt a system known as a Joint Disciplinary Tribunal. This system has existed in the sweet manufacturing industry since the 1920s and involves members of management and trades unions as well as the accused worker and his representative. The Joint Disciplinary Tribunal was designed to deal primarily with the hidden economy crime of pilfering, but it has been extended to deal with a range of other disciplinary matters. Because of the structure of the tribunal, any disciplinary measures are agreed jointly. The union has always had the opportunity to ensure fair play, and consistency and has on many occasions been able to prevent more serious incidents developing. It also allows those guilty of comparatively minor offences not to be branded as thieves and has created opportunities for them to recover from minor misdemeanours.

The major difficulty with this form of compromise is a problem affecting informality as a whole: it does not exist in isolation but is part of the wider political system. The major question to be asked in the case of community courts is how far do workers disciplining themselves serve to maintain the interests of the management, the company, the shareholders and ultimately the capitalist system of production and its property laws? Similarly we might ask how far self-help in housing, health and employment serves to deflect energy, attention and criticism away from the failures of formal systems. In doing so they provide a means of 'getting by' which patches over the cracks of a system which would otherwise be forced not only to change but to accept responsibility for its failures. While informal, locally based effort is containing the problems of a society within darkened corners of the community, formal dominance will be strengthened and effective radical critique diluted.

CONCLUSION: THE REVIVAL OF SELF-HELP

James Cornford

There is an old Chicago adage about sociologists and whorehouses to be kept in mind whenever a new trend is discovered. The essays in this book have explored and begun to chart areas of our society which fall outside conventional administrative categories and thus escape the formal record. But much of what is discovered is not new, and what is significant is the motive for undertaking the research and the attitudes taken to the findings. Twenty years ago social scientists (and social democrats) would have been inclined to dismiss these informal and irregular arrangements as peripheral, transitional or marginal to the development of an orderly, planned society. Today informal institutions are interpreted as evidence of a latent capacity to make good the inevitable deficiencies of the planned society; or even for an odd coalition of neo-classical Liberals and anarchists as the basis for replacing it altogether.

Take, for instance, the irregular economy. To anyone acquainted with the works of Mayhew (1851), Booth (1902) or Thomas Wright (1868, 1873) the shifts and strategems of the casual worker will be familiar (see also Stedman Jones, 1971). What we see here is the survival of patterns of 'making out', which have been rendered at once illicit and more attractive by the comprehensive embrace of modern regimes of taxation and welfare. Public administration requires neat distinctions between employment and unemployment, rather than the shifting and uncertain world in which some work is done for others, some for oneself, some for cash, some for kind, and where some is regular, some casual and some occasional. The suggestion in Ferman's

192

work (chapter 1) that taking casual employment enables the recipient of relief not only to make out better but also to find his way back into regular employment, demonstrates the conflict between the needs of welfare clients and those of administration, behind which there lurk the Victorian bogies of less eligibility and the undeserving poor. Self-help is nothing new, but as Lowenthal points out (chapter 5) it depends essentially on kin, neighbourhood, locality and personal knowledge, and there is a fundamental contradiction between the ways in which working-class people make out and what is looked upon as rational economic behaviour for 'labour' in the formal economy. If it is assumed that wages from formal employment are the whole income, it makes sense to migrate in order to get a job or to earn higher wages. If however wages are only part of the life-support system, moving to a job may jeopardise the local kin and neighbourhood parts of the system, and leave the mobile wholly dependent on formal employment and on official agencies in times of trouble. And those agencies, however complex and sophisticated their administrative procedures may have become, act on the crude old utilitarian assumptions of the Victorian Poor Law.

There is of course another Victorian legacy – the astonishing range and variety of the institutions of self-help – from the clubs and schools of the upper classes, through the Building and Friendly Societies, to the co-ops, trade unions and chapels of the industrial working classes. This great effort to make private provision for education, housing, health, work and play was a success but only a partial success. To the ruling classes it became increasingly clear that neither the market nor self-help would cater for the numerous and dangerous poor. Both on prudential and on charitable grounds, state intervention became increasingly attractive, and the Poor Law, public health and compulsory education became the forerunners and models for public provision in one field after another. The organised working class resisted because they did not want their own institutions bypassed or incorporated (Pelling, 1968; Bunbury, 1957). The resistance failed not only because their membership was limited, but because they were unable to protect their own members against the worst economic vicissitudes. The institutions of self-help were found wanting because they neither included everyone nor protected from major catastrophes those who belonged. As the tide of fashion turns, it is as well to remember that the welfare state, though of mixed and uncertain parentage, was created and is sustained for excellent reasons. However much one may want to stress the importance of self-help and of informal institutions, the formal economy remains the dominant influence in the distribution of opportunity and welfare, and its shortcomings need formal as well as informal correction.

There is a straightforward and important political debate about the welfare state and its failure to maintain or achieve adequate standards, or alternatively its wastefulness and extravagance. What particularly concerns the advocate of self-help is that public services are so often experienced by the recipients as something imposed to standards defined by professionals and experts, and administered according to rules they cannot understand and without regard to their feelings. Moreover the most recent phase in the expansion of government responsibility has seen an increasing tendency to co-opt what are formally private institutions as the instruments of public policy; and in any case self-governing institutions like the co-operative and building societies have largely lost their original character. This process of co-optation threatens to create a system of indirect rule in which voluntary bodies trade their advantages of independence and responsiveness for public money and privileges. The result is that private initiatives, the organized and self-conscious expression of self-help, move into the public sphere and lose their autonomy.

The first wave of reaction to the shortcomings of the welfare state, national and local, took the form of adversary groups demanding better treatment for particular minorities, more responsive and open administration and greater respect for the preferences of the administered. These groups are now being caught between their role as critics and the need to defend 'their' services against public expenditure cuts, in alliance with the public sector unions. A second wave of reaction involves the much more fundamental rejection of bureaucratic welfare state capitalism, associated with the attack on economic growth, the large organisation, advanced technology, and the commitment to material progress. In this reaction there is a more or less explicit, if not always coherent, alternative view of the good society which revives the defeated Utopias of the 19th century, peasant, communitarian and co-operative. It is also seized by the nightmare anxiety that mankind is poised on the brink of unimaginable disasters of his own devising. While these ideas, and the experiments to which they give rise, are adopted by a small minority and are treated with confident contempt by those in authority, they express indirectly a wider sense of unease and dissatisfaction. It remains to be seen whether this discontent will result in anything more constructive than a withdrawal of support for public institutions and a growing tolerance for 'private' solutions through tax evasion, pilfering and moonlighting, as well as respectable forms of self-help.

The plain fact is that for the great majority of people in Britain life is more comfortable, decent and secure than it has been for any previous generation, and their wrath will be reserved for the politicians who fail to deliver more of the same. There is a dawning awareness that the promise of unlimited affluence may be impossible to fulfil. But for the time being practical men of the world see present economic troubles as a temporary interruption in the upward spiral; and though there is some evidence of reduced expectations on the part of the electorate (Alt, 1979), politicians are understandably reluctant to advocate sacrifices except as a means to future prosperity — *'se reculer pour mieux sauter'*. This nevertheless does not prevent people from supplying for themselves the deficiencies of the system, those things they do not expect it to deliver, or indeed from influencing public provision in decisive ways by their own example, as Platt suggests is being done in the field of housing (chapter 6). Hence the persistence of informal institutions and the significance of their 'discovery': traditional forms of mutual aid and getting round the system become matters for discussion, dissemination and self-conscious adoption. They become the germ of an alternative policy. Thus we have seen a vigorous growth of new co-operatives in housing, wholefoods, and even in manufacturing; attempts to replace neighbourhood networks of mutual aid by baby-sitting groups, local amenity associations, garden sharing schemes, bulk buying groups; and the development of barter and consumer protection against retail monopolies, alternatives to the prepacked abundance of the supermarket, which are the product of greater income, sophistication and leisure from formal work, and new experiments in mutual assistance in mental illness and addiction.

The important point is the change of consciousness: political learning is contagious and fungible. One experiment leads to another, co-operation for one purpose becomes a general resource, and the experience in itself engenders confidence. Alternatives to state or commercial provision become increasingly recognised and attractive. Yet it is hard to tell if they have the capacity to be more than marginal additions to formal institutions, or whether those informal institutions which have always been substantial will become more important.

The answer will depend partly on political choice and partly on what happens to the relations between the various economies identified in the introduction. Here we enter the realm of speculation, but on the basis of evidence and the arguments of other contributors to this book, it is certainly reasonable to expect a continued decline of employment in the *regular economy,* as a result both of the increased productivity of capital-intensive technology and of the cuts in labour-intensive public services, which were made in order to release resources for capital investment. At the same time we may expect an increase in self-employment due to technical changes, especially in communications, which will make possible more flexible and less hierarchial patterns of organisation, especially in the provision of technical and professional services. An increase in self-employment may also be encouraged by changes in public policy, such as the switch from major housebuilding schemes to conservation and repair. The effect of these changes will be to transfer some activities to the *social economy,* through an increase in do-it-yourself activities and the informal replacement of social services, and some to the *black economy* via illicit self-employment. In the *hidden economy* we may·expect to see a continuity of informal and invisible wages, since those are built into the structure of rewards for many occupations, and the possibility of an increase if there are further attempts at an incomes policy or minimum wages legislation. The *social economy* can certainly be expected to grow because of shorter working hours and increased unemployment in the regular economy, increased need for self-help and mutual aid in the face of public expenditure cuts, the choice of non-monetary rewards and preference for DIY. These tendencies, as Gershuny and Pahl have argued (chapter 4), will be strengthened by the availability of a growing range of small powered equipment, from electric drills and sewing machines to mini-computers and rotavators. For similar reasons there will be a growth in the *black economy.* How far this will go depends upon the severity of the decline of employment in the regular economy, on the introduction of shorter working hours, and on the persistence of high levels of taxation and extensive regulation of employment, which provide an incentive to illicit economic activity. It will depend also on the availability of an easily exploited workforce, through the disproportionate decline of female employment in the regular economy as a result of automation and public service cuts.

It is readily apparent that not all of these predictions are benign: in particular the decline of employment in the official economy may have the consequence of forcing women back into an unwanted domestic servitude or, worse, their exploitation through a full-scale revival of the sweated trades in the black economy. It is possible to imagine more desirable outcomes, but they will all depend on general access to employment and income in the official economy and therefore on the creation of opportunities for small-scale production and domestic industry, which are both legitimate and independent of capitalist middlemen. Gershuny and Pahl's work (chapter 4) suggests the possibility of a tripartite economy with the infrastructure (social insurance, energy, transport etc.) provided by the state, a capital-intensive, high technology sector mass-producing machines, which in turn are employed in the self-service and low-technology sector, which consists in part of domestic production for the market and in part of the social economy of home consumption and exchange. Those employed in the state or manufacturing sector would work a relatively short week (25 hours?) and devote the rest of their time to other forms of work or not as they choose. State provision of services might vary from the comprehensive (health?) to the minimal (education, housing?) with the balance supplied by independent co-operative enterprises and self-help. This Utopia is equally compatible with an expanding economy, unconstrained by shortages of natural resources, or one approaching stasis; what it requires is a dispersion of political influence and wealth, which there is no reason to anticipate. Self-help requires means, and it will be a bitter mockery if it becomes the excuse for a prosperous, secure and well paid majority to turn its back on the sick, disabled, poor and unemployed.

BIBLIOGRAPHY

ABRAMS, M. (1978) *Beyond Three-Score and Ten: a just report on a survey of the elderly,* Age Concern Publications, London

ABRAMS, P. *et al* (1979) *Neighbourhood Care: some preliminary research findings,* Association for Researchers in Voluntary and Community Involvement, Berkhamstead

ACAS (ADVISORY, CONCILIATION AND ARBITRATION SERVICE) (1977) *Disciplinary Practice and Procedures in Employment,* HMSO, London

ALDEN, J.D. (1977) 'The Extent and Nature of Double-Jobholding in Britain', *Industrial Relations Journal,* vol. 8, pp.1-33

ALDEN, J.D. AND SAHA, S.K. (1978) 'An Analysis of Second Jobs in the EEC' *Regional Studies,* vol. 12, pp.639-650

ALT, J.E. (1979) *The Politics of Economic Decline,* Cambridge University Press, Cambridge

AMOS, M. (1926) 'A Day in Court at Home and Abroad' *Cambridge Law Journal,* vol. 20, pp.340-349

APPLEBY, G. (1978) *Small Claims in England and Wales,* Institute of Judicial Administration, Birmingham

ARENSBERG, C. AND KIMBALL, S. (1968) *Family and Community in Ireland,* Havard University Press, Cambridge

AVES, G. (1969) *The Voluntary Worker in the Social Services,* Allen and Unwin, London

BAKUNIN, M. (1872) *God and the State* (English translation by B. R. Tucker) Mother Earth Publishing Company 1916, New York

BALDWIN, J. AND McCONVILLE, M. (1977) *Negotiated Justice: Pressures on Defendants to Plead Guilty*, Martin Robertson, London

BARKER, D. (1978) 'A Proper Wedding' in M. Corbin (ed) *The Couple*, Penguin, Harmondsworth, pp.56-77

BAYLISS, F.J. (1962) *British Wages Councils*, Basil Blackwell, Oxford

BEDNARZIK, R.W.B. (1978) 'How many hours of work do the unemployed want? *United States Monthly Labour Review*, December issue, pp.70-71

BELL, D. (1974) *The Coming of Post-Industrial Society*, Heineman, London

BERGER, M.E. (1971) 'Trial Marriage: Harnessing the Trend Constructively', *The Family Coordinator vol. 20, pp.38-43*

BERMAN, H.J. AND SPINDLER, J.W. (1963) 'Soviet Comrades' Courts', *Washington Law Review*, vol. 38, pp.842-910

BIGUS, O.E. (1972) 'The Milkman and his Customer', *Urban Life and Culture*, vol. 1, pp.131-65

BOHANNON, P. (1955) 'Some Principles of Exchange and Investment Among the Tiv' *American Anthropologist*, pp.60-70

BOHANNON, P. AND DALTON, G. (eds) (1962) *Markets in Africa*, Northwestern University Press, Evanston

BOOTH, C. (1902) *Life and Labour of the People in London*, Macmillan, London

BOWER, D.W. AND CHRISTOPHER, V.A. (1977 'University Student Cohabitation: A Regional Comparison of Selected Attitudes and Behaviour' *Journal of Marriage and the Family*, vol. 39, p.447-453

BOWMAN, H.A. AND SPANIER, G.B. (1978) *Modern Marriage*, McGraw-Hill Book Company, New York

BOWEY, A.M. (1976) *Sociology of Organisations*, Hodder and Stoughton, London

BUNBURY, H.N. (1957) *Lloyd George's Ambulance Wagon, being the memoirs of W.J. Braithwaite,* 1911-1912, Methuen, London

BURNS, S. (1977) *The Household Economy,* Beacon Press, New York

BUSINESS WEEK (1978) 'The Fast Growth of the Underground Economy', March 13, pp.73, 74, 77

CAPPELLETTI, M. (ed) (1978) *Access to Justice* 4 vols., Sijthoff Giuffre, Milan

CAPPELLETTI, M. AND GARTH, B. (eds) (1978) *Access to Justice: A World Survey* Sijthoff Giuffre, Milan

CARDIFF HOUSING ACTION (1976) *Before you open your big mouth . . . Cardiff Housing Action, Cardiff*

CARTWRIGHT, A. *et al* (1973) *Life Before Death* Routledge and Kegan Paul, London

CHRISTIE, N. (1976) *Conflicts as Property* University of Sheffield, Centre for Criminology, Sheffield

CLARK, J.A. (1979) 'An Examination of the Historical Basis for some Recent Projections of Employment and Unemployment in the U.K.', *Mimeo* paper presented to SSRC/IDS Conference on Employment Projections, 25 May

CLAYTON, R.R. AND VOSS, H.L. (1977) 'Shacking Up: Cohabitation in the 1970s' *Journal of Marriage and the Family* vol. 39, pp.273-283

CLOUT, H. (1972) *The Geography of Post-War France* Pergamon Press, Oxford

CLUTTERBUCK, D. (1979) 'Moonlighting comes out of the shadows' *International Management,* June pp.27-31

COLLINS, A.H. AND PANCOAST, D.L. (1976) *Natural Helping Networks: a strategy for prevention,* National Association of Social Workers, Washington D.C.

CONN, S. AND HIPPLER, A.E. (1974) 'Conciliation and Arbitration in the Native Village and the Urban Ghetto' *Judicature,* vol. 58, pp.228-235

CONSTANTINE, L.L. AND CONSTANTINE, J.M. (1977) *Group Marriage: A Study of Contemporary Multilateral Marriage*, Macmillan, New York

CONSUMER COUNCIL (1970 *Justice Out of Reach: A Case for Small Claims Courts*, HMSO, London

CO-OPERATIVE HOUSING AGENCY (1978) *A Directory of Housing Co-operatives*, The Housing Corporation, London

CORT, D. (1959) 'The Embezzler' *Nation*, April, 18, pp.339-342

DALE, J. (1979) 'Boom Goes the Black Economy' *The Observer*, June 24, pp.33-34

DALTON, G. (1971) *Economic Anthropology and Development*, Basic Books, New York

DALTON, M. (1964) *Men Who Manage*, John Wiley and Sons, New York

DANZIG, R. (1973) 'Towards the Creation of a Complementary Decentralised System of Criminal Justice' *Stanford Law Review*, vol. 26, pp.1-54

DAVIS, J. (1972) 'Gifts and the UK Economy' *Man*, vol. 7, pp.408-429

DHSS (DEPARTMENT OF HEALTH AND SOCIAL SECURITY) (1977) *The Way Forward*, HMSO, London

DEAN, D.G. AND SPANIER, G.B. (1974) 'Commitment: An Overlooked Variable in Marital Adjustment' *Sociological Focus*, vol. 7, pp.113-118

DEITER, J.C. (1966) 'Moonlighting and the Short Work Week' *South Western Social Science Quarterly*, vol. 47, pp.308-314

DEPARTMENT OF EMPLOYMENT (1972) 'Analysis of Secondary Occupations' *Department of Employment Gazette*, June

DEPARTMENT OF EMPLOYMENT (1975a) 'The Changing Structure of the Labour Force' *Department of Employment Gazette*, October

DEPARTMENT OF EMPLOYMENT (1975b) 'The Changing Patterns of Working Hours', *Manpower Research Paper no. 13*

DINHAM, B. AND NORTON, M. (1977) *The Directory of Social Change: Education and Play*, Wildwood House, London

DITTON, J. (1977a) *Part-Time Crime: An Ethnography of Fiddling and Pilferage*, Macmillan, London

DITTON, J. (1977b) 'Perks, Pilferage and the Fiddle: The Historical Structure of Invisible Wages' *Theory and Society*, vol. 4, pp.39-71

DITTON, J. (1977c) 'A note on commercial social control' *mimeo*, The Outer Circle Policy Unit, London

DOE (DEPARTMENT OF THE ENVIRONMENT) (1975) *Consultation Paper on Squatting*, Department of the Environment, London

DOE (DEPARTMENT OF THE ENVIRONMENT) (1977) 'Use of Vacant and Underoccupied Dwellings' *Circular 76/77*, Department of the Environment, London

DORE, R.P.C. (1976) *The Diploma Disease: Education, Qualification and Development*, London

DOUGLAS, M. (1964) 'Marriage' in Gould and Kolb eds. *A Dictionary of the Social Sciences*, Tavistock, London, pp.409-10

DOW, L.M. (1977) 'High Weeds in Detroit' *Urban Anthropology*, vol. 6, pp.111-128

DRAKE, M. AND BIEBUYCH, T. (1977) *Policy and Provision for the Single Homeless: A Positive Paper*, Personal Social Services Council, London

DWYER, D.J. (1975) *People and Housing in Third World Cities*, Longman, London

ECKHOFF, T. (1966) 'The Mediator, the Judge and the Administrator in Conflict Resolution' *Acta Sociologica*, vol. 10, pp.148-166

THE ECONOMIST (1979) 'Exploring the Underground Economy' September 22, pp.106-107

ELKAN, W. (1978) The Informal Sector in Low Income Countries, *Mimeo*, Brunel University

ENGELS. F. (1942) *The Origin of the Family, Private Property and the State*, International, New York

ENGLAND. K.A.D. (1973) 'A Consideration of the Alienated Conditions of Shopworkers in the Retail Trade', *mimeo*, University of Swansea

ENGLAND, K.A.D. (1976) 'Fiddles in the Distributive Trades' *mimeo*, University of Swansea

EPSTEIN, S. (1962) *Economic Development and Social Change in South India*, Manchester University Press, Manchester

EVANS-PRITCHARD, E.E. (1951) *Kinship and Marriage among the Nuer*, Oxford University Press, London, pp.116-17

EVERSHED COMMITTEE (1954) *Final Report of the Committee on Supreme Court Practice and Procedure*, Cmnd 8878, London, HMSO

FABERMAN, H.A. AND WEINSTEIN, E.A. (1970) 'Personalisation in Lower Class Consumer Interaction', *Social Problems*, vol. 17, pp.449-457

FABIAN SOCIETY (1968) *Justice for All*, Fabian Society, London

FAIRFIELD. R. (1971) *Communes USA: A Personal Tour*, Penguin Books Inc, Baltimore

FAIR PLAY FOR CHILDREN (1979) *Why Lock Up Our Schools?*, 248 Kentish Town Road, NW5, London

FEIGE, E.L. (1979) 'The Irregular Economy: Its Size and Macroeconomic Implications' *mimeo* Social Systems Research Institute, University of Wisconsin, Madison

FERDINAND. T.N. (1977) 'Criminal Justice in America: From Colonial Intimacy to Bureaucratic Formality' *mimeo*, Northern Illinois University

FERMAN, L.A., BERNDT, L. AND SELO, E. 'Analysis of the Irregular Economy: Cash Flow in the Informal Sector' *mimeo*. A report to the Bureau of Employment and Training, Michigan, Department of Labor and Industrial Relations, The University of Michigan-Wayne State University, Ann Arbor, Michigan

FERMAN, P. AND FERMAN, L. (1973) 'The Structural Underpinnings of the Irregular Economy', *Poverty and Human Resources Abstracts*, vol. 8, pp.3-17

FINER COMMISSION (1974) *Report of the Committee on One-Parent Families*, HMSO, London

FIRST INTERNATIONAL CONGRESS ON THE LAW OF PROCEDURE (1978) *Towards a Justice with a Human Face*, Kluwer, Antwerp

FIRTH, R. (1965) *Primitive Polynesian Economy*, Routledge and Kegan Paul, London

FISHER, E.A. (1975) 'Community Courts an Alternative to Conventional Criminal Adjudication' *American University Law Review*, vol. 24, pp.1253-1291

FORDHAM, P., POULTON, G. AND RANDLE, L. (1979) *Learning Networks in Adult Education: Non-formal Education on a Housing Estate*, Routledge and Kegan Paul, London

FOSTER, H. (1966) 'Conciliation and Counselling in the Courts in Family Cases' *New York University Law Review*, vol. 41, pp.353-381

FRANKLIN, A.P. (1975) 'Internal Theft in a Retail Organisation: A Case Study' *PhD Thesis*, Ohio State University

FRANKS REPORT (1957) *Report of the Committee on Administrative Tribunals and Inquiries*, Cmnd 218, HMSO, London

FRIEDSON, E. (1978) 'The Official Construction of Occupations' *Mimeo*, New York University

FREUD, D. (1979) 'A Guide to Underground Economics' *Financial Times*, April, 9, p.16

FRIED, M. (1965) 'Transitional Functions of Working-Class Communities' in M. Kantor (ed) *Mobility and Mental Health*, Springfield, Charles Thomas, Illinois

GARBUS, M. (1977) 'Justice Without Court: A Report on China Today' *Judicature*, vol. 60, pp.395-402

GEIGER, J. (1976) Cited as 'Geiger's Law' in S.F. Jencks 'Problems in Participatory Health Care' in *Self-Help and Health: A Report*, New Human Services Institute, New York, 1976, pp.86-98

GERSHUNY, J.I. (1977a) 'Post-industrial Society: The myth of the service economy' *Futures*, April issue, pp.103-114

GERSHUNY, J.I. (1977b) 'The Self-service Economy' *New Universities Quarterly*, Winter issue, pp.50-66

GERSHUNY, J.I. (1978) *After Industrial Society?* Macmillan, London

GERSHUNY, J.I. (1979) 'The Informal Economy: Its Role in Post Industrial Society', *Futures* February issue, pp.3-15

GERSHUNY, J.I. AND PAHL, R.E. (1979) 'The Future of the Informal Economy' *New Society*

GIMSON, M. *et al* (1976) 'Squatting – The Fourth Arm of Housing? *Architectural Design*, April

GLC (GREATER LONDON COUNCIL), (9177) *Annual Abstract of Statistics*, London GLC

GLICK, P.S. (1975) 'A Demographer Looks at American Families' *Journal of Marriage and the Family*, vol. 37, pp.15-26

GODWIN, W. (1793) *An Enquiry Concerning Political Justice*, W. Johnson, London (reprinted Penguin Harmondsworth, 1975)

GODWIN, W. (1799) *The Enquirer*, W. Johnson, London

GOFFMAN, E.C. (1961) *Asylums: Essays on the social situation of mental patients and other inmates*, Penguin, Harmondsworth

GORER, G. (1970) *Sex and Marriage in England Today*, Nelson, London

GROVES CONFERENCE (1974) 'Groves Conference on Marriage and the Family' *mimeo*, Myrtle Beach, S.C., USA

GUTMANN, P. (1977) 'The Subterranean Economy' *Financial Analysts Journal*, November/December, 1977, pp.26, 27, 34

HALL, J. (1952) *Theft, Law and Society*, Bobbs-Merrill, Indianapolis

HALLER. W. (1976) 'Statt Arbeitgeberjahr Mehr Urlaub' *Wirtschaftswoche*, Dec. 17, p.58

HATCH. S. (1978) *Voluntary Work: a report of a survey* The Volunteer Centre, Berkhampstead

HATCH. S. (1980) *Outside the State: Voluntary Organisations in Three English Towns*, Croom Helm, London

HAYGHE. H.V. AND MICHELOTTI. K. (1971) 'Multiple Jobholding in 1970 and 1971' *Monthly Labour Review*, October

HEDGES. J.P. (1975) 'How Many Days Make a Work Week? *Monthly Labour Review*, April

HENRY. S. (1978) *The Hidden Economy: The Context and Control of Borderline Crime*, Martin Robertson, Oxford

HENRY. S. AND MARS. G. (1978) 'Crime at Work: The Social Construction of amateur property theft', *Sociology*, vol. 12, pp.245-263

HENRY. S. AND ROBINSON. D. (1978) 'Understanding Alcoholics Anonymous: Results from a Survey in England and Wales', *The Lancet*, February 18, pp.372-75

HENZE L.F. AND HUDSON. J.W. (1974) 'Personal and Family Characteristics of Cohabiting and Non-cohabiting College Students', *Journal of Marriage and the Family*, vol. 36, pp.344-354

HOME OFFICE. (1977) *Judicial Statistics Annual Report*, HMSO, London

HORNING. D.M. (1970) 'Blue Collar Theft: Conceptions of Property and Attitudes Toward Pilfering and Work Group Norms in a Modern Plant' in E. Smigel and H. L. Ross (eds) *Crimes against Bureaucracy*, New York, Van Nostrand Reinhold, pp.46-64

ILLICH. I. (1971) *Deschooling Society*, Calder and Boyars, London

ILLICH. I. (1973) 'The Deschooled Society' in P. Buckman (ed) *Education Without Schools*, Souvenir Press, London

ILLICH. I. (1976) *Disabling Professions*, Marion Boyars, London

IRWIN. J. (1972) 'Participant Observation of Criminals' in J. Douglas (ed) *Research on Deviance*, Random House, New York, pp.117-164

ISHWARAN. K. (1966) *Tradition and Economy in Village India*, Routledge and Kegan Paul, London

JACOB. I.H. (1978) 'Access to Justice in England' in M. Cappelletti and B. Garth (eds) *Access to Justice; A World Survey*, Sijthoff Giuffre, Italy, pp.417-478

JUNOR. R. (1979) 'Britain's Black Economy' *The Daily Telegraph*, June 25, pp.14-15

KATZ, A.H. AND BENDER, E.I. (1976) *The Strength in Us: Self-Help Groups in the Modern World*, Franklin Watts, New York

KINGHAN. M. (1978) *Squatters in London*, Shelter, London

KOMAROVSKY. M. (1967) *Blue-Collar Marriage*, Random House, New York

KROPOTKIN. P. (1888) *Mutual Aid: A Factor in Evolution*, Extending Horizon Books, Boston, 1955

LAIRD. D.A. (1950) 'Psychology and the Crooked Employee' *Management Review*, vol. 39, pp.210-215

LAKE. T. AND HILLS. A. (1979) *Affairs − The Anatomy of Extra-Marital Relationships*, Open Books, London

LAMBETH BOROUGH COUNCIL (1974) *Unauthorised Squatting in Council Dwellings, Lambeth Borough Council*, London

LAPENNA, I. (1968) *Soviet Penal Policy*, The Bodley Head, London

LAPPING. A. (1970) 'Community Careless' *New Society*, April 9, pp.589-591

LEWIS, R.A. AND SPANIER, G.B. (1975) 'Sydiasmos: Married and Unmarried Cohabitation' *mimeo*, Pennsylvania State University, University Park, Pennsylvania

LEWIS, R.A., SPANIER, G.B., STORM, V. AND LEHECKA, C. (1975) 'Commitment in Married and Unmarried Cohabitation' *mimeo* American Sociological Association, San Fransisco

LOWENTHAL, M. (1975) 'The Social Economy in Urban Working-Class Communities' in G. Gappert and H. Ross (eds) *The Social Economy of Cities,* Sage Publications, Beverly Hills, pp.447-469

LOWIE, R.H. (1933) 'Marriage' in E.R.A. Seligman (ed) *Encyclopedia of the Social Sciences,* Macmillan, London

LOW PAY UNIT (1975) 'Low Pay in Hotels and Catering' Low Pay Pamphlet, no. 2, LPU, London

MACKLIN, E.D. (1974) 'Unmarried Heterosexual Cohabitation on the University Campus' *mimeo,* Cornell University, Ithaca, N.Y.

MACKLIN, E.D. (1976) *Cohabitation Research Newsletter Issue 5,* State University College, Oswego, New York

MALINOWSKI, B. (1922) *Argonauts of the Western Pacific,* Routledge, London

MANCHESTER, A.H. AND WHETTON, J.M. (1974) 'Marital Conciliation in England and Wales' *International and Comparative Law Quarterly,* vol. 23, pp.339-382

MARRIS, P. (1958) *Widows and their Families,* Routledge and Kegan Paul, London

MARS, G. (1973) 'Hotel Pilferage: A Case Study of Occupational Theft' in M. Warner (ed) *The Sociology of the Workplace,* George Allen and Unwin, London, pp.200-210

MARS, G. (1974) 'Dock Pilferage' in P. Rock and M. McIntosh (eds) *Deviance and Social Control,* Tavistock, London, pp.209-228

MARS, G., BRYANT, D. AND MITCHELL, P. (1979) *Manpower Problems in Hotels and Restaurants,* Saxon House, London

MARS, G. AND MITCHELL, P. (1976) *Room for Reform?: A Case Study of Industrial Relations in the Hotel Industry,* Unit 6, Industrial Relations Course, P881, The Open University Press, Milton Keynes

MARS. G. AND MITCHELL. P. (1977) 'Catering for the Low Paid: Invisible Earnings' *Low Pay Unit Bulletin No. 15*, LPU, London

MARS. G. AND NICOD. M. (1981) *The Worlds of Waiters: The Anatomy of an Occupation* (forthcoming)

MARTIN. J.P. (1962) *Offenders as Employees*, Macmillan, London

MARX. K. (1867) *Critique of Political Economy*, International, New York

MAUSS. M. (1954) *The Gift: Forms and functions of exchange in archaic societies*, Cohen and West, London

MAYHEW. H. (1851) *London Labour and the London Poor*, George Woodfall and Son, London

McINTOSH. M. (1975) *The Organisation of Crime*, Macmillan, London

MILLER, G.W. (1972) *Multiple Jobholding in Wichita*, Western State University, Wichita, Kansas

MITCHELL, J.C. (1966) *Social Networks in Urban Situations*, Manchester University Press, Manchester

MITCHELL. P. AND ASHTON. R.K. (1974) 'Wages Councils: Do They Matter?', *Hotel and Catering Institute Management Association Review*, Vol. 1, pp.20-28

MORONEY. R.M. (1976) *The Family and the State*, Longmans, London

NAILON. P. (1978) 'Tipping: A behavioural review', *HCIMA Review*, vol. 2, pp.231-243

NATIONAL EMPTY HOMES CAMPAIGN (1977) *Empty Property Surveys*, NEHC, London

NEDO (NATIONAL ECONOMIC DEVELOPMENT OFFICE) (1969) *Manpower Policy in the Hotels and Restaurants Industry*, HMSO, London

NEDO (NATIONAL ECONOMIC DEVELOPMENT OFFICE) (1975) *Staff Turnover*, HMSO, London

NEWCOMBER, M. (1961) 'The Little Businessman: A Study of Business Proprietors in Poughkeepsie, New York' *Business History Review,* Winter issue, pp.477-531

NEWELL, P. (1975) 'A Free School Now', *New Society,* pp.400-403

NEWMAN, M. (1979) *The Poor Cousin: a study of Adult Education,* Allen and Unwin, London

NICOD, M. (1981) 'An Anthropological Study of Hotel Waiters in Six Locations' *Unpublished PhD Thesis,* Middlesex Polytechnic (CNAA) Enfield, Middlesex

OCPU (OUTER CIRCLE POLICY UNIT) (1978) *Policing the Hidden Economy: The Significance and Control of Fiddles,* The Outer Circle Policy Unit, London

OCPS (OFFICE OF POPULATION, CENSUSES AND SURVEYS) (1979) *Changing Patterns of Family Formation and Dissolution in England and Wales,* Studies in Medical and Population Subjects, no. 39, HMSO, London

OSBORNE, T. (1980) 'Squatting-Outpost of a New Culture' in N. Wates (ed) *Squatting,* forthcoming

PELLING, H.M. (1968) *Popular Politics and Society in Late Victorian Britain,* Macmillan, London

PETERMAN, D., RIDLEY, C.A., AND ANDERSON, S.M. (1974) 'A Comparison of Cohabiting and Non-cohabiting College Students', *Journal of Marriage and the Family,* vol. 36, pp.344-54

PLATT, S. (1977) *Squatters in Haringey,* Self-Help Housing Resources Library, London

PLATT, S. (1978) *Self-Help, Squatting and Public Policy,* Self-Help Housing Resources Library, London

PODGORECKI, A. (1969) 'Attitudes to the Workers' Courts' in V. Aubert (ed) *Sociology of Law,* Penguin, Harmondsworth, pp.142-149

POLANYI, K. (1957) *The Great Transformation,* Beacon Press, Boston

POLANYI, K. (1968) *Primitive, Archaic and Modern Economics: Essays of Karl Polanyi*, G. Dalton (ed), Beacon Press, Boston

POOR, R. (1970) *4 days, 40 hours*, Bursk and Poor Publishing, Cambridge, Massachusetts

PUCCI, E. (1976) 'Deceptive air of calm hides tensions' in *The Times Europa Supplement*, February 3

RADCLIFFE-BROWN, A.R. AND FORDE, D. (eds) (1958) *African Systems of Kinship and Marriage*, Oxford University Press, London

RADZINOWICZ, L. (1964) 'The Criminal in Society' *Journal of the Royal Society of Arts*, vol. 112, pp.916-929

RAMUNDO, B.A. (1965) 'The Comrades' Court: Molder and Keeper of Socialist Morality' *George Washington Law Review*, vol. 33, pp.692-727

RÉE, H. (1972) reported in *The Teacher*, 8 April, p.8

REIMER, E. (1971) *School is Dead*, Penguin, Harmondsworth

REISS, A.J. (1974) 'Citizen Access to Criminal Justice' *British Journal of Law and Society*, vol. 1, pp.50-74

RICHARDS, A. (1932) *Hunger and Work in a Savage Tribe*, Meriden, New York

RIESSMAN, F. (1965) 'The "helper" therapy principle' *Social Work*, vol. 10, pp.27-32

ROBIN, G.D. (1965) 'Employees as Offenders: A Sociological Analysis of Occupational Crime', *PhD Thesis*, University of Pensylvania

ROBIN, G.D. (1970) 'The Corporate and Judicial Disposition of Employee Thieves' in E. Smigel and H.L. Ross (eds) *Crime Against Bureaucracy*, Van Nostrand Reinhold, New York, pp.124-146

ROBINSON, D. (1979) *Talking Out of Alcoholism: the self-help process of Alcoholics Anonymous*, Croom Helm, London

ROBINSON, D. AND HENRY, S. (1977) *Self-help and Health: Mutual Aid for*

Modern Problems, Martin Robertson, London

ROGOVIN, E.B. (1961) 'Social Conformity and the Comradely Courts in the Soviet Union' *Crime and Delinquency*, vol. 7, pp.303-311

ROSS, I. (1978) 'Why the Underground Economy is Booming' *Fortune*, October 9, pp.92-98

ROYAL COMMISSION ON MARRIAGE AND DIVORCE (1956) *Report 1951-1953* Cmnd 9678, HMSO, London

SALISBURY, R.F. (1962) *From Stone to Steel: Economic consequences of technological change in New Guinea*, University Press, Melbourne

SCARMAN, L. (1974) *English Law – The New Dimension*, Stevens, London

SCHARF, P (1977) 'The Just Community' *New Society*, April 21, pp.104-105

SECURITY GAZETTE (1975) 'Britain's record £100 million theft loss in 1974' November, pp.378-79

SHANKLAND, G. (1977) 'Towards duel economy' *The Guardian*, December 23

SHHRL (SELF HELP HOUSING RESOURCE LIBRARY) (1978) *Self-Help Housing: News and Information Bulletin of the Self-Help Housing Resource Library*, London

SIMKINS, T. (1976) *Non-Formal Education and Development*, Manchester University Dept. of Adult and Higher Education, Manchester

SMELSER, N.J. (1963) *The Sociology of Economic Life*, Englewood Chills, Prentice-Hall, New Jersey

SMITH, R. (1975) 'Squatting' *mimeo*, University of Bristol, School for Advanced Urban Studies, Bristol

SPANIER, G.B. (1976) 'Measuring Dyadic Adjustment: New Scales for Assessing the Quality of Marriage and Similar Dyads', *Journal of Marriage and the Family*, vol. 38, pp.15-28

SPECK, R.V. *et al* (1972) *The New Families*, Basic Books Inc, New York

SPIRO, M.E. (1970) *Kibbutz: Venture in Utopia*, Shocken, New York

SPRADLEY, J.D. AND MANN, B.J. (1975) *The Cocktail Waitress: Women's Work in a Man's World*, John Wiley & Sons, New York

SQUATTING ADVISORY SERVICE (1979) *The Squatters Handbook*, Advisory Service for Squatters, London

STACK, C.B. (1974) *All Our Kin: Strategies for Survival in a Black Community*, Harper and Row, New York

STAFFORD, R., BACKMAN, E. AND DIBONA, P. (1977) The Division of Labor Among Cohabiting and Married Couples', *Journal of Marriage and the Family*, vol. 39, pp.41-57

STATSKY, W.P. (1974) 'Community Courts: Decentralising Juvenile Jurisprudence' *Capital University Law Review*, vol. 3, pp.1-26

STEDMAN JONES, G. (1971) *Outcast London*, Oxford University Press, Oxford

TAYLOR, J. (1979) 'Hidden Labour and the National Health Service' in P. Atkinson (ed) *Prospects for the National Health*, Croom Helm, London, pp.130-144

TIRIET, B. (1977) 'Flexiyear Schedules – only a matter of time?' *Monthly Labour Review*, December

TOWNSEND, P. (1957) *Family Life of Old People*, Routledge and Kegan Paul, London

TROST, J. (1978) 'Married and Unmarried Cohabitation in Sweden' in M. Corbin (ed) *The Couple*, Penguin, Harmondsworth, pp.158-168

TURNER, J.F.C. (1972) 'Uncontrolled Urban Settlement: Problems and Policies' in G. Breese (ed) *The City in Newly Developing Countries*, Prentice-Hall, New Jersey

UNGER, R.M. (1976) *Law in Modern Society*, FreePress, New York

VAN TIJEN, *et al* (1978) *Kraken: Squatting in Amsterdam*, Self-Help

Housing Resource Library, London

VERSELE, S.C. (1969) 'Public Participation in the Administration of Criminal Justice' *International Review of Criminal Policy*, vol. 27, pp.9-17

WARD, B. (1976) *The Home of Man*, Penguin, Harmondsworth

WARD, C. (1974) *Tenants Take over*, Architectural Press, London

WARD, C. (1976) *Housing – An Anarchist Approach*, Feedom Press, London

WATES, N. (1976) *The Battle for Tolmers Square*, Routledge and Kegan Paul, London

WATES, N. (ed) (1981) *Squatting*, London (forthcoming)

WATSON, W. (1958) *Tribal Cohesion in a Money Economy*, Manchester University Press, Manchester

WEEKS, J. (1975) 'Politics for Expanding Employment in the Informal Urban Sector of Developing Countries' *International Labour Review*, January, 1975, pp.1-13

WELLMAN, B. (1979) 'The Community Question: The Intimate Networks of East Yonkers' *American Journal of Sociology*, vol. 84, No. 5

WHYTE, W.F. (1948) *Human Relations in the Restaurant Industry*, McGraw-Hill, New York

WILLMOTT, P. AND YOUNG, M. (1960) *Family and Class in a London Suburb*, Routledge and Kegan Paul, London

WILSON, G. AND NIAS, D. (1976) *Love's Mysteries*, Open Books, London

WOLF, E.R. (1966) 'Kinship, Friendship and Patron-Client Relations in Complex Societies' in M. Barton (ed) *The Social Anthropology of Complex Societies*, A.S.A. Monographs 4, Tavistock Publications, London, pp.1-22

WOLFENDEN COMMITTEE (1977) *The Future of Voluntary Organisations: Report of the Wolfenden Committee*, Croom Helm, London

WRIGHT, T. (1868) *The Great Unwashed*, Tinsley Brothers, London

WRIGHT, T. (1873) *Our New Masters*, Strahan and Co., London

WRIGHT-MILLS. C. (1969) 'Situated Actions and Vocabularies of Motive in I. Horowitz (ed) *Power, Politics and People*, Oxford University Press. London, pp.439-452

YLLO. K.A. (1978) 'Non-marital Cohabitation: Beyond the College Campus', *Alternative Lifestyles*, vol. 1, pp.37-54

YOUNG. M. AND WILLMOTT. P. (1957) *Family and Kinship in East London*, Penguin, Harmondsworth

YOUNG. M. AND WILLMOTT. P. (1973) *The Symetrical Family*, Routledge and Kegan Paul, London

ZANDER. M. (1976) *Cases and Materials on the English Legal System*, Weidenfeld and Nicolson, London

ZEITLIN. L.R. (1971) 'Stimulus/Response: A little larceny can do a lot for employee morale' *Psychology Today*, vol. 5, pp.22, 24, 64

INDEX